A Clouded Leopard in the Middle of the Road

A Clouded Leopard in the Middle of the Road

*New Thinking about Roads,
People, and Wildlife*

Darryl Jones

Comstock Publishing Associates
an imprint of
Cornell University Press
Ithaca and London

First published 2022 by Cornell University Press

Printed in the United States of America

Library of Congress Cataloging-in-Publication Data

Names: Jones, Darryl N., author.
Title: A clouded leopard in the middle of the road : new thinking about roads, people, and wildlife / Darryl Jones.
Description: Ithaca [New York] : Comstock Publishing Associates, an imprint of Cornell University Press, 2022. | Includes bibliographical references and index.
Identifiers: LCCN 2021033348 (print) | LCCN 2021033349 (ebook) | ISBN 9781501763717 (paperback) | ISBN 9781501763731 (ebook) | ISBN 9781501763724 (pdf)
Subjects: LCSH: Roads—Environmental aspects. | Animals—Effect of roads on. | Wildlife crossings. | Habitat conservation.
Classification: LCC QH545.R62 J66 2022 (print) | LCC QH545.R62 (ebook) | DDC 333.95/4—dc23
LC record available at https://lccn.loc.gov/2021033348
LC ebook record available at https://lccn.loc.gov/2021033349

For those who were there when it all started:
Amy Blacker, Brendan Taylor, Cath Dexter, Mary O'Hare,
Rob Appleby, and Thomas Creevey

CONTENTS

Part III. Take Alternative Route

ILLUSTRATIONS

PREFACE

I am standing high on a ridge in a subtropical forest of eucalyptus and wattle trees. It is late in the day, but the setting sun is still sharply hot on my back. Last night's storm saturated the dense leaf litter at my feet and ensured that the humidity today is uncomfortably high. My shirt is sticky and I can feel tiny trickles of sweat running down my neck. But I dare not budge. I am holding my binoculars awkwardly, at chest height; I had been slowly raising them to investigate a rustle in the dense undergrowth just ahead when something moved . . . and I freeze. I can just make it out: gray, dark, maybe the size of a small dog—but more rounded. Stay still. No, it hasn't seen me; it's moving again, slow and ponderous, pushing the wet vegetation aside rather clumsily. Still too dark to see clearly. Wait, it's emerging into a patch of sunshine. It's a koala, an adult male, I think: solidly built, neckless, and powerfully compact. Very rarely seen on the ground, koalas spend virtually all of their time high in the tall trees. I realize that I am trembling slightly. I've seen plenty of koalas before, but this is different. It is not just unusual or unexpected—it is much more significant than that.

This forested hill near Brisbane in eastern Australia looks completely normal, boringly typical of any bit of bush (as natural forest or woodland is called in this country) found in the surrounding region. There are tall, scantly foliaged trees, spindly shrubs, and scattered clumps of grasses and sedges. Several smaller trees—wattles mainly—have died and toppled over, and now form complex tangles of dry branches and twigs. A couple of huge logs lie at awkward angles, bark and rotting pieces of jagged wood buckling under the heat of the relentless sun. If you are still and quiet, you can see skinks and legless lizards nervously peeking out from the logs and debris, snakes sunning themselves, occasionally a large monitor lizard striding arrogantly through the open patches. Small birds are everywhere, swallows swooping above, honeyeaters singing from the canopy, flycatchers darting through the midstory vegetation. At night, possums, gliders, marsupial carnivores, and bandicoots pass through. Just what you expect for a healthy, natural, fully functioning Australian ecosystem. Except it's not—"natural," that is.

The hill I am standing on is a completely artificial structure.[1] It was designed by people who sat around a table making notes and sketches using pencil and paper. Every plant and pole and piece of fencing has been discussed and costed. Vast amounts of concrete and soil were brought to the site and methodically positioned. Thousands of tube stock were selected and carefully planted. Now, more than a decade later, I can stand in what appears to be an entirely natural forest, identical to the vegetation that sweeps away in all directions. This forested ridge rises in a narrow plateau over multiple lanes of busy roads carrying relentless traffic, which barely pauses day or night. Directly beneath me, the endless procession of vehicles is evident only as a dull low-frequency hum. The forest that surrounds me declines steeply away toward the large conservation reserves that lie on each side of the road. If you walk in either direction, the transition into the original forest is virtually seamless.

A structure of this scale is obviously expensive to build. It involved a huge amount of time to design and required considerable effort to construct. What is really remarkable, however, is that this vegetated hill, which rises above a major multilane road, was built by a bunch of hard-nosed road engineers. And their objective was not focused on traffic management or urban planning or connecting human communities. Astonishingly, this massive structure was designed entirely for wildlife, to provide a way for animals to move safely across a major road. It is a huge, complicated, expensive, carefully designed, and *unusual* artifice, engineered with wild animals—not commuters or vehicles—in mind. These structures are known variously as fauna overpasses, ecoducts, or land bridges.

And that's not all. This particular structure, admittedly the largest and most conspicuous, is just one of a series of engineering features that have been installed along a relatively short section of roadway. There are also two large concrete box culverts ("underpasses") beneath the road, installed not for managing water flow but to enable a range of smaller species to traverse the road. Wildlife can travel along raised ledges attached to the internal walls or use the elevated logs that run the length of the culvert, allowing the more dexterous species to scamper through, above the ground. There are three rope ladders ("canopy bridges") looping high above the traffic, to cater for the various tree-dwelling mammals, as well as a series of tall poles arranged in a line over the length of the overpass. These were initially installed to encourage the movement of gliding marsupials, a function now redundant as the trees planted all over the overpass are now much higher than the "glider poles."

Almost fifteen years earlier I had stood in a similar spot—on top of what was, back then, basically a bare, exposed mound of dry soil and bark chips. The sun was intense and the hundreds of recently installed tube stock seemed appallingly vulnerable to desiccation. The artificial, human origins of the structure were all too obvious: the bright-blue plastic planting tubes, the starkly obvious glider poles, the brutally conspicuous fencing. It seemed pathetically contrived. Why would any animal venture onto this forbidding, exposed pile of dirt? It was impossible to conceive that this would "work," that the theoretical "safe passageway for fauna" described in the tendering submissions was indeed anything but a preposterous pipe dream. Standing there, sweating and skeptical, it was all too easy to agree with the multitude of naysayers: "It's a shocking waste of scarce public money, with little chance of success. The only animals actually likely to use the thing to cross the road are probably going to be feral cats, foxes, and invasive cane toads." That day, as I trudged uncomfortably down the slope, the increased roar of the traffic as I neared the roadway blanketed my thoughts and exacerbated my unease. Hadn't we just wasted a massive amount of money?

And yet, right now, those early misgivings seem almost blasphemous. Or at least, disrespectful. I had reasoned back then that it would take some time before we might see results. We had to take the long view and allow the theoretical to slowly become reality. We had to have faith in the ecological processes, to trust in the sound knowledge that had been applied, and to *believe*—even when the evidence was slow in coming, or apparently not there at all.

Because right now I am watching a plump, healthy koala wandering somewhat clumsily through the mature vegetation on this artificial hill, crossing from one area of natural forest to another. He is doing this without paying the slightest regard to the endless procession of vehicles thundering along the road beneath his padded feet. Without this structure, crossing the road would have been impossible, or at least extremely risky. In the year leading up to the construction of the overpass, local naturalists had compiled a shockingly long list of koalas (and wallabies, kangaroos, possums, and bandicoots) killed while attempting such a crossing. This ongoing carnage had been particularly devastating for koalas, who seem to have very little road sense. Sightings of these iconic Australian animals

Figure 1. The Compton Road fauna overpass in 2019, fourteen years after construction. Near Brisbane, Australia. Photographer Darryl Jones.

had been dwindling steadily in the surrounding area, and it looked as though they might be headed for local extinction within the next decade without serious intervention. And despite the fact that many other species had been detected using the overpass, this was not the case for koalas. Solitary animals were reported sporadically in the surrounding forests, but after more than a decade of intensive surveys, there was still no evidence of any koalas actually crossing the road via the overpass.

Until now—when I examined the images from a series of remote cameras set up on the overpass. These cameras had been installed to record everything that moved, day and night, over the entire structure, during the course of a couple of months. I had expected to see quite a few animals but was utterly overwhelmed by the result: hundreds of images of more than twenty species had been recorded, wild animals simply going about their daily (or nightly) business, which included crossing one of the busiest roads in the region as though it simply wasn't there at all. The seemingly endless number of animal images was extraordinary. But it was nothing compared to seeing nine individual koalas, of all sexes and sizes, wandering through the undergrowth. Nine! Barely able to believe it, I stole out to the site just to stand on the spot and somehow imagine that these animals had actually passed through. I did not expect to see anything. And yet, here he is.

This is an actual story of a real place. The overpass and the other fauna-crossing structures are located on Compton Road, in the suburb of Kuraby, in the southern part of Brisbane. Go to Google Maps and look it up—it's just to the east of a huge motorway. You will clearly see the strange hour-glass shape of the overpass, although the other structures are difficult to make out (and of course, the two underpasses are invisible beneath the road).

It is also a personal story, because I have been involved, directly and intimately, in this place and these structures for well over a decade. This involvement has entailed a wide range of professional, logistical, and scientific challenges, but also deeply personal and emotional engagement. There has been surprise, euphoria, despair, wonder, bewilderment, depression, astonishment, satisfaction, anger, and pride (sometimes all on the same day). Compton Road has been a central part of my life for so many years and for so many reasons that I would like to share some of the key parts of that story with you at various points throughout this book.

This place and what happened here is, however, just one example of something that is happening all over the world. Even in Australia, Compton Road is not that unusual; there will soon be eight dedicated fauna overpasses in this country. Canada, Sweden, and the United States have similar numbers. All of them are special and important; however, to provide a bit of perspective, several European countries have hundreds of crossing structures, some of which are enormous. But similar structures have also been built in other countries: Malaysia, India, Kenya, and Brazil, for instance, have all installed wildlife passageways in recent years. I have highlighted overpasses mainly because they are large, expensive, and conspicuous, but there are many other components to this story. These include other types of crossing structures that enable animals to safely traverse roads—underpasses, canopy ladders, fish passageways, bat flyovers, glider poles—as well as broader, landscape-level considerations. These include the planning of alternative routes for new roadways that have reduced impact on sensitive areas; raising roads above valleys and wetlands; and the installation of noise-barriers along roads through important conservation sites.

All of these ventures require significant time for planning, design, and implementation, and necessitate discussion between people with diverse expertise: landscape architects, ecologists, hydrologists, project managers, transportation engineers, and community groups. Bringing these projects to fruition required agreement and collaboration among a lot of specialists with very different perspectives, as well as the involvement of various levels of government and land, transport, and conservation agencies. And with every additional dimension and stakeholder, the costs and complexity keep rising.

Despite these difficulties and challenges, however, more and more remarkable projects are being planned and constructed every year. Proposals that seemed either fanciful or hopelessly optimistic only a few years ago have become standard or routine exercises.

And it's not just roads that are receiving attention. Railways, pipelines, electricity easements, geological survey transects—any form of linear infrastructure—also pose the same issues of forming barriers and increasing habitat fragmentation. Increasingly, the same radical rethinking is transforming the way these landscape-scale projects are being planned and designed.

This is the story of road ecology. It starts as a tale of human and animal tragedy, ecological catastrophe, and impossible challenges on a terrifying scale. But this is a field of knowledge and action that couldn't have emerged at a more urgent moment in history. As rumors of massive new global transportation networks continue to emerge, it is time to learn what road ecology has achieved and where it is going. At a time when much of the news about our environment is depressingly familiar, here at last is something genuinely positive.

ACKNOWLEDGMENTS

I visited a lot of roads in gathering the information and experiences that formed the roadbed and driving surface of this project. At every turn and parking bay along the way, remarkably generous people were there to make helpful suggestions, politely correct, or vehemently deny. They didn't just make the journey more enjoyable (and hopefully accurate)— their advice and encouragement actually made this book possible.

As should be obvious, the significance of Compton Road in this (my) story cannot be overestimated. My tentative and naive involvement in this somewhat revolutionary collaboration was an introduction to the challenges and possibilities of road ecology and became my springboard into the field. From the very beginning, Mary O'Hare and Tom McHugh from the Brisbane City Council, and their adversaries/partners Thomas Creevey, Bernice Volz, and Ted Fensom from the Karawatha Forest Protection Society, were inspirational in their unstinting dedication to getting this pioneering project right. I now realize that their willingness to work together to achieve a shared goal was crucial and unusual; naively perhaps, I thought this level of cooperation was normal. They were joined by Amelia Selles, Stacey McLean, and Kristy Johnson, who continued to be involved for many years.

Almost from the minute the bulldozers withdrew from the site, we have been trying to understand what was happening in, on, and around the Compton Road Fauna Array. I have been extremely fortunate to have had so many enthusiastic and dedicated students and research collaborators working there and at other locations, during these last fifteen years: Adam Abbott, Kat Aburrow, Rob Appleby, Lilia Bernede, Amy (Bond) Blacker, Bob Coutts, Cathryn Dexter, Jason Edgar, Chris Johnson, Ben Mackenzie, Kelly Matthews, Mel McGregor, Jackson Owens, Stuart Pell, Jonny Pickvance, Lee-Anne Veage, and Steve Wilson. I am immensely proud of what these extraordinary young (mostly) scientists have been able to discover and contribute to this still emerging field.

In 2010, more by blind good fortune than design, I had the opportunity to undertake a Road Ecology Grand Tour of many key locations in Europe. For no logical reason, a number of people openheartedly guided a total stranger around their countries, in the process utterly transforming my perspectives and becoming lifelong friends. I have remained in close contact with all of these people, mainly through the biannual Infra Eco Network Europe (IENE) conferences. I will forever be in debt to Éric Guinard, Edgar van der Grift, Juan Malo, Cristina Mata, and Carme Rosell for their hospitality and willingness to share their stories and knowledge. Edgar, in particular, should be mentioned for somehow managing to get me included in the 2010 IENE conference program (well after the closing date), which was held at Velence in Hungary. This full-emersion IENE experience was genuinely paradigm altering, and also enabled me to meet a number of influential people with whom I have remained in professional and personal contact ever since: Hans Bekker, J-O Helman, Marcel Huijser, Jochen Jaeger, Lars Nilsson, Fabrice Ottburg, Miklós Puky, Andreas Seiler, Anders Sjölund, and Paul Wagner. (I need to acknowledge the passing of Miklós in 2015, one of the brightest stars in road ecology, especially in terms of amphibian research. He was irrepressible, unstoppable, and generous; his enormous smile and outrageous sense of humor will be missed.)

A second, more ambitious, tour occurred in 2019 and took me literally around the world: Washington State in the United States (to visit the I-90 highway, thanks to Sharon Birks and Robert Reed); Banff National Park, Canada (where Tony Clevenger arranged for Trevor Kinley and Leah Pangelli to show me the famous crossing structures); the United Kingdom (to look at bat structures, thanks again to Dave and Carol Clark); the Netherlands (where Hans and Arien Bekker provided warm hospitality while recalling Hans's decades of work and influence); Sweden (where J-O Helman introduced me to the unexpected juxtaposition of Viking history and contemporary road ecology); and Singapore (to visit the wonderful Eco-Link@BKE with Bryan Lim). On an earlier visit to the UK, I was guided around the Isle of Wight with Steve Béga, Sophie Hughes, and Dean Swensson from Animex, who constructed the experimental dormouse bridge.

In Australia, the small but energetic road ecology community has had many spectacular wins (and some equally spectacular failures). Led by the irrepressible Rodney van der Ree, the Australasian Network for Ecology and Transportation has now held three conferences and is working across many states and projects. I am grateful and honored to have worked with all these inspirational colleagues: Amy (Bond) Blacker, Cathryn Dexter, David Francis, Ross Goldingay, Kylie Soames, and Brendan Taylor.

As this book has developed, I have had the unreserved assistance of a lot of friends and colleagues from around the world who have read and critiqued various sections and chapters: Dan Becker, Hans Bekker, Tony Clevenger, Lenore Fahrig, Ross Goldingay, Edgar van der Grift, Éric Guinard, J-O Helman, Sophie Hughes, Marcel Huijser, Jochen Jaeger, Mary O'Hare, Rodney van der Ree, Inga Roedenbeck, Carme Rosell, Kylie Soames, Josie Stokes, and Brendan Taylor. I am extremely grateful for their constructive and detailed comments, and sometimes strong opinions.

This book has been underway since 2016 and was written during rare gaps in my overfull academic life, but especially during prolonged periods such as sabbatical leave. At Griffith University, I am grateful to my successive heads of school, Chris Frid and George Mellick, for granting me those invaluable moments to be away and at the Environmental Futures Research Institute to the director, Zhihong Xu, and manager, Dian Riseley, for their unstinting support.

Significant sections of this book were written in Seattle, Washington; Braggs Creek, Alberta, Canada; Uppingham, England; Steenwijk in the Netherlands; Kumagaya, Japan; and—especially—in the State Library of Queensland, Brisbane. The book was completed in the strange

COVID-dominated world of 2020, where I was lucky to have been able to set up a pleasant working environment on my verandah overlooking Toohey Forest in suburban Brisbane.

The publishing world can be a disconcerting and sometimes mysterious landscape. I have been truly fortunate to have had a range of people to guide, prod, advise, and encourage me through this maze/meandering garden path/minefield. Kitty Liu at Cornell University Press has continued to be a steady hand and wise counselor, and her colleague, Allegra Martschenko, has provided a wealth of technical advice, especially on the challenging issue of selecting and managing the photographs.

Enormous praise is due to my editor, Diana Hill, who has been an exceptional and sensitive guide and critic. Her immense experience in the book realm and her almost supernatural gifts as a wordsmith and phrase conjuror have made important differences to many passages and whole sections. And as always, my agent, Margaret Gee, has continued to be a solid supporter and confidante; somehow, she makes each of her authors believe they are the favorite. That, too, is a gift.

I would also like to mention the less tangible but no less important support from two different sources. Avid Reader, in West End, Brisbane, is "my" bookshop: a wonderful, quirky, passionate place full of book nerds and writers, and staffed by a diversity of people who all really care about writing. They have always been unceasingly enthusiastic about local authors, and their in-house launches are legendary. I hope this one has a similar birth there. And I must publicly acknowledge the enormous strength and encouragement I have received from my friend and fellow nonfiction writer, Jennifer Ackerman. She has been a powerful ally in those Intruder Syndrome moments and has had a major impact on the way this book has evolved.

Finally, the extended period during which this book was produced has included the successful fledging of all three children, Dylan, Caelyn, and Manon. They probably didn't notice, but I thank them for their forbearance and patience with my preoccupations. And of course, Liz has remained a rock, feigning interest in whatever fascinating anecdote I just had to share about gibbons or turtles crossing roads, but always there and always completely supportive.

A Clouded Leopard in the Middle of the Road

INTRODUCTION

Waking the Sleeping Giant

I visit a lot of roads. Actually *visit*. Not just travel along them, oblivious to the surrounding landscape flying past in a blur, semi-hypnotized by the pulsing white lines disappearing into the distance. Everyday car travel induces a form of cognitive anesthesia; rather than framing the outside world, car windows may as well be flatscreens showing changing patterns that you don't really notice. Even when I am driving, I am only vaguely attentive; passengers are typically concentrating on a device or engaged in their own thoughts. We may be thinking about the destination, or maybe the departure, but the journey itself is just time spent in limbo. And certainly no one is actually thinking about the road.

Yes, the road. Any journey across town or across the country would simply not be possible without these long, linear surfaces that crisscross the landscape in every direction. They are among the most monumental of all human constructions, yet they are effectively invisible. No one seems to register them "consciously." And for most of my life, neither did I. But over the past decade or so, I have become much more aware of these omnipresent ribbons and networks of asphalt. I have started to see them as part of the landscape, and I have been trying to understand what they are for and what they mean. This has come about gradually, through a lot of visits to roads all over the world. I guess I'm a road tourist. These experiences are, however, almost the opposite of those associated with a regular car journey, in which you start at A and end up at B, with minimal awareness of how you got there. *Visiting* a road requires paying close attention to what lies between those two points, and being aware of the surrounding landscape—the overlap of the human and natural worlds. And it often means pulling over and getting out of the car. It's time to check what is going on beyond the vehicle.

This particular visit is not what I have been expecting.[1]

I have brought the car to a stop on the verge of an obviously new road. A few students and I are now deep within a large conservation reserve in the center of the great equatorial island of Borneo. On either side, the vast, solid, brooding presence of towering tropical rainforest stretches away to the distant horizon. There is absolutely no traffic, but there is a lot of noise, a multilayered, broad-frequency universe of sound—the calls of frogs, insects, and unseen birds of bewildering diversity; the low murmur of the wind; the swish of flowing water; the distant rumbling of a receding storm; and other improbable noises I can't even begin to identify. The heat of the sun is ferocious, the light blindingly direct, yet the road is still awash from the violent rain shower that has just, abruptly, ceased. The water flowing off the road into the massive concrete gutters along its edge is clear, but the sheets of runoff emerging from the wall of rainforest some distance away is rich red-brown, foaming like a chocolate milkshake. Far above us is a remarkable, incongruous sight: a male gibbon is standing conspicuously on the exposed limb of a dead tree, arms outstretched like Rio de Janeiro's *Christ the Redeemer*, drying his sodden fur after the recent downpour. A group of massive hornbills fly silently across the vast gap in the jungle above the road. The sight of these two magnificent species is always a pleasure, but today their silence seems to reinforce my bewilderment. Standing here at the edge of this brand-new road, I am deeply disturbed. Let me explain why.

Exactly a year ago, I stood with some student assistants on this very spot, early in the morning, preparing to count birds flying across the road. The dark rainforest was close, mysterious, and alive. The dense canopy

Figure 2. New road constructed through tropical rainforest near the Maliau Basin conservation area, Sabah, on the island of Borneo. Note the extensive areas cleared on either side of the road. Photographer Darryl Jones.

above cast deep shadows, making it difficult to see very far in the gloomy light. We had parked our vehicle some distance back and had walked quietly ahead to avoid disturbing any animals that might be nearby. It was still and quiet. A dense, low mist drifted up from the wet road. Gradually, we became aware of a shape—something large—standing silently, just ahead of us, in the middle of the road. We peered into the gloom, trying to make it out. The mist momentarily parted. A clouded leopard stared back at us, barely a stone's throw away, watching us intently, with confident calm, before crossing the road and instantly disappearing into the curtain of vegetation. We stood still and silent, astonished, barely believing what had just happened. Clouded leopards are among the rarest and most elusive animals in the world. It was some time before we spoke and reminded ourselves what we were supposed to be doing.

That encounter had occurred exactly a year ago. It was a euphoric, memorable moment. Today, however, I am bewildered and angrily confused. We have come back to this site to record any animals crossing (what had been) a relatively small gap in the forest, formed by the narrow, unpaved road. Studies in forests around the world have found that some animals—including quite a few birds—are often reluctant to move through even moderately open spaces in their forest habitat.[2] The knowledge that natural openings discourage certain species from moving across them has obvious implications for unnatural gaps such as roads. We are back in Borneo to see whether these observations applied to Bornean animals as well.

Those earnest conjectures now seem shatteringly redundant. What had been a small forest track—effectively a tunnel through the jungle, the flanking canopy of huge trees meeting far above the road—has been transformed into a gigantic, landscape-altering, fully paved "super highway." Although this new road is only two lanes wide, vast swaths of the rainforest on either side have been entirely removed, leaving a broad, bare, muddy hinterland extending far beyond the road surface. It is hard to imagine almost any species—let alone a clouded leopard—used to living in this rainforest ever moving across a gap this wide.

The fact I have lost a study site is not the only alarming aspect of the situation. Much more significant are the many possible consequences that could result from the establishment of this dramatic new incursion into the rainforest. The highway is only a few months old, but already we can see areas of extensive erosion along the newly cleared land on either side of it. In a place with this much rain, removing all of the vegetation cover has made massive erosion virtually inevitable. Already the culverts under the road look to be clogged with debris and silt, and the numerous small streams emerging from the forest seem to be flowing with liquid mud. All along the recently exposed forest edge, many small trees have been scorched by the sun, their leaves wilted or dry. Even some of the larger of these trees—now towering over an open expanse of bare ground—are looking stressed, their unnaturally brown foliage contrasting with the vivid greens around them.

Far more ominous are the possible threats that this new, improved road might bring.[3] Just to the south, similar new roads had quickly been followed by illegal logging. Timber smuggling is rife in this region, with secretive but well-equipped gangs despoiling and denuding what had been, until recently, extremely remote and untouched forests. On paper, the really valuable tree species are apparently protected by impressive-sounding international laws. As are the orangutans, sun bears, and other animals—including clouded leopards—that are being captured by poachers or opportunistic adventurers and traded throughout Asia and beyond. It's a familiar story: soon after these roads are completed, crude temporary camps spring up, soon to be abandoned once the valuable trees and animals have been cleared out. It is distressing to think about these possibilities, but we know that this is the reality in many tropical places, from Southeast Asia to the Amazon and West Africa. Is this to be the fate of this precious reserve as well? Who knows? Right now, however, it is a monumental catastrophe.

Connectors

I am describing this personal experience, admittedly extreme and dramatic, because it exemplifies something of the significance, scale, threat, complexity, and challenges associated with the interface between roads and nature. It's a big, convoluted picture, but because roads usually seem to be overlooked in our daily lives, I want to start by drawing attention to what can happen because of these ubiquitous constructions.

The global road system has been described in many different ways. These include "the single most conspicuous manifestation of human activity on the planet," with transportation stated to be "among the most influential forces modifying the earth." This form of linear infrastructure is an "artifact of culture," a requirement and precondition of human productivity, and "necessary for the promotion of progress."[4] Roads are planetwide and almost inconceivably complex systems of what are simply long, flat pathways, which facilitate the unimpeded movement of people and goods over vast areas. Modern roads have been imposed on the landscape; the more recent are often brutally direct and efficient, oblivious to natural contours. For humans, roads are essential connectors linking places and purpose, but almost always with negligible regard for the landscape in which they occur.

Yet, despite its extraordinary scale, this vast, inescapable, indispensable network is effectively invisible. As we hurtle through the landscape (at speeds unimaginable to our recent ancestors) between the places where we live, shop, learn, and play, the road on which we are traveling is unlikely to cross our minds. (The traffic with which we share the road is, of course, another matter.) We are even less likely to conceive of this road as one component of all the other roads it intersects with, or of the huge, sprawling web made up of all the roads spreading out throughout the region and the entire continent.

Because of roads, it is possible to drive a very long way indeed. Ignoring national borders and political impediments for the moment, you can travel for extraordinary distances. The world's longest driving routes are the 11,217 kilometers (6,969 miles) from Cape Town in South Africa to Fes in Morocco; the 11,394 kilometers (7,079 miles) from Calais in France to Vladivostok in Russia; and the 11,811 kilometers (7,339 miles) from Panama City, near where the two American continents join, to Deadhorse in Alaska. And if it were not for a mere 160 kilometers (99 miles) of impenetrable mountains between Turbo in Colombia and Yaviza in Panama—the Darién Gap—the Pan-American Highway, which theoretically stretches from the very top of North America to the bottom of South America, would be a continuous journey of almost 22,000 kilometers (13,670 miles).[5] These roads really do connect different worlds. And in the process, they also divide and sever.

Barriers and Filters

The cumulative distance of all roads globally totals about fifty million kilometers (thirty-one million miles), or 130 times the distance to the moon—and this figure is increasing rapidly. Yet, imagining such mind-boggling distances can be misleading when considering the reality of roads. Such an exercise might suggest a long and linear route from enthusiastic start to exhausting finish. Our conception of almost any road is typically simplified to that portrayed by our map app, the most direct route between two places. What is less easy to envisage, however, is the complex network of interconnected roads that covers virtually the entire planet. It is this gigantic net, or web, that we also need to imagine and understand; while enabling connections for people, it is also subdividing the landscape into pieces of land bounded by roads on all sides. This network can be seen at one extreme in the typical rectangles of streets in most downtown central business districts, and at its most diffuse in the most remote places. Unsurprisingly, there is a strong and obvious relationship between the density of human populations and the intensity of roads. This is most evident in small areas with large populations. The Netherlands, for instance, has a road density of 1.9 kilometers (1.2 miles) of road per square kilometer. Even in a country as apparently spacious as the continental United States, 97 percent of the land is less than 7 kilometers (4.3 miles) from a paved road.[6]

Now imagine a large animal—say, a deer or a kangaroo—that needs to travel for any typical but compelling reason: finding food, seeking a mate, avoiding a competitor, or as part of its regular migration. Sooner or later, it will meet a road. What happens next will depend on a lot of different factors. The animal may travel this route regularly and be quite familiar with this disruption to the landscape, or it may never have encountered a road before. It may even be attracted to the roadside: to feed on the dead animals or edible trash found there, or to nibble on the well-watered grass along the verge. On the other hand, the traffic noise or lights may be so disturbing that the animal retreats as far from the road as possible and never again ventures near. It may cross if there are no vehicles, or it may inexplicably wander straight into the traffic. It may learn to judge what are safe intervals between moving vehicles or it may delay crossing until the quietest parts of the night. All of these responses are happening, everywhere.

Figure 3. Bighorn sheep (*Ovis canadensis*) ruminating beside a road, Alberta, Canada. Photographer Marcel Huijser.

Crossing a road with traffic is clearly dangerous for wildlife, especially for the slower ground dwellers. Collision with a vehicle almost always leads to the death of the animal, and the numbers involved are almost unbelievable. Although reliable data on roadkill is often difficult to obtain, it is estimated that about a million individuals of all species are killed each and every day on the roads of the United States. For larger species in North America, the cumulative scale of all that roadkill has surpassed hunting as the main cause of death, and vehicle collision is now regarded as an "evolutionary novel threat."[7] And while certain larger, more conspicuous species—such as deer—dominate the statistics for roadkill, the numbers of smaller, less easily detected animals—such as birds and amphibians—are likely to be truly enormous. For most places and most species, we really have no idea of the scale of the slaughter.

Not every road is a threat, however. Some have very little traffic, or virtually none at night. Certain species appear to have learned how to avoid vehicles or to somehow safely cross between the cars. And even shockingly high numbers of animals being killed will not necessarily mean that the species or even the local population is imperiled. A lot of visible roadkill may simply be an indication of the general abundance of animals in the area. Certainly, the scale of mortality indicated by the enormous numbers of white-tailed deer (in North America) and roe deer (in Europe) found dead along the roadside appears to be having very little effect on the abundance of these common species. But there is also plenty of evidence that the populations of some animals in some locations have been seriously impacted by collisions with vehicles, in certain cases to the point of local extinction. Infamously, during the 1980s almost 10 percent of the entire population of the Florida panther was being killed on roads annually (a realization that led to a dramatic change in their fortune, as will be discussed later).[8]

Although the unavoidable evidence of dead animals along the roadside may be compelling and emotive, influences other than vehicles may be far more important but much harder to perceive. For many species, it is not the traffic that is the main issue; rather, it is the physical characteristics and dimensions of the road and the associated space that matters. These features may include the surface of the road (its composition, exposure, width, and temperature, for example); the altered conditions and habitat along the long, narrow roadside; or the various emissions associated with traffic (noise, fumes, vibrations, dust, and so on). Perhaps more unexpectedly, even the space occupied by the road—measured by the gap between the habitat on either side—can be the main problem for some animals. In some cases, entire communities of species—small forest-dwelling birds or rodents, for example—will simply never move across such a space, whether cars are present or not. Even small dirt roads are known to prevent voles and beetles from moving between otherwise suitable habitat. For these species, the main significance of the road is as a partial or complete barrier. This "barrier effect" is one the most profound and far-reaching discoveries made recently by scientists studying roads.[9]

These insights have added a new and alarming dimension to our understanding of the impact of habitat destruction on biodiversity. The relentless fragmentation of natural environments for any number of legitimate reasons—food production, housing, mining—typically and obviously has a devastating impact on the communities of animals and plants that originally occupied these areas. The cumulative effect is that, piece by piece, what was a more or less continuous natural landscape becomes steadily subdivided and separated into smaller, more isolated, patches. At its most pronounced, the resulting landscape is made up of a series of discrete islands of original habitat, separated from one another by a surrounding "sea" of new and entirely different landscape. This is classic habitat fragmentation, a standard scenario affecting both recent and ancient human-dominated landscapes. For many of the animals—and plants, of course—that are able to survive in these patches, movement across the surrounding matrix can be irrelevant, inconvenient, potentially dangerous, unlikely, or impossible, depending on the species we are considering. As with any community of species confined to an island, isolation and restricted movements often mean diminished opportunities and an increased risk to survival. A single drought, fire, storm, or disease can be catastrophic.

These well-established ecological principles underpin two important priorities in the conservation of biodiversity in areas of natural habitat or reserves: big is best, and close is vital. A conservation park with the largest possible area will provide the best chance of ensuring that the species within can withstand the normal threats to their survival, both natural and human in origin. But to further enhance the persistence of populations within these areas, it is critical that a least some individuals are able to travel across the space between without major impediment. This enables youngsters to disperse to seek their fortune elsewhere, and allows animals to find mates and access new foraging places. These movements are essential for almost all species. Anything that limits or prevents these opportunities is a threat to long-term survival. Which means that the discovery that even small roads can act as a significant barrier to many species is a serious issue. Suddenly, that minor road (or cleared pipeline route or exploration throughway) traversing a national park or local conservation reserve may not be so "minor."

Breaking Barriers

"If roads are barriers, they can be breached!"[10] Until relatively recently, such a statement might have been attributed to militant activists opposed to development, or environmental campaigners protesting intrusions by miners or loggers. In reality, this declaration arises from the insights of ecologists applying their knowledge of natural processes to anthropogenic problems. While animals have always lived close to permanent natural barriers or along natural contours (think of rivers, rocky cliffs, or changes in the density of vegetation), the imposition of roads on the landscape has often been instantaneous and arrogant, ignoring the geological and ecological "grain." Despite the disturbance and physical interruption associated with the construction of a road, some species will attempt to continue their regular daily, seasonal, or migratory movements. For some—larger birds, for example—the road is likely to be of negligible consequence. For others, as we have already discussed, an attempt to traverse the road could be fatal. And that risk may also apply to the humans seemingly safe within their vehicles.

This is not simply a story about human impacts on nature. The tragedy includes us. While the numbers are horrific to contemplate, the reality we face is both sobering and consequential. The million mammals killed daily on the roads of North America are also implicated in around two hundred human deaths, thousands of serious injuries, and over a billion dollars of vehicle damage each year.[11] Clearly, it's best that cars and deer (or moose, or kangaroos) don't meet. Fencing would seem to be the obvious solution, and many major roads are thus protected. But fences, by design, enhance the barrier effect. Fences are also expensive and require maintenance, and they are almost never completely impenetrable. Species that really want to cross the road will try all means to do so, sometimes with predictable outcomes. And we actually *want* these animals to be able to move through the landscape—preferably not where they may encounter cars. We want them to breach the road barrier, but safely.

Our attempts to understand and overcome these sorts of complex problems constitute the motivation for the new field known as road ecology. This emerging way of thinking is a great example of the importance, effectiveness, and promise of bringing different disciplines together to address a major issue of the contemporary world. The nature and scale of this challenge requires collaboration between a diverse array of scientific fields (for example, landscape ecology, animal behavior, wildlife management, conservation biology) and seemingly disparate professional disciplines such as transport planning and policy, road design, engineering, and economics. The ambitious objective of this partnership is to develop

Figure 4. Fauna overpass in arid rural landscape near Madrid, Spain, constructed mainly for roe deer. Photographer Darryl Jones.

an effective system of designing transportation networks that enhance human movement while minimizing the impact on the natural environment. In fact, it could be said that this partnership aims to break down the road barrier. Well, that's the theory. How far we have come and what remains to be done will form the core of this book.

The Sleeping Giant

Roads are invisible yet monumental. Most of the time, we are simply oblivious to their colossal scale. Once we begin to perceive their impossible expanse, they become impossible to ignore. Their ubiquity and dominance breed endless metaphors. Roads are like some sort of elongated, ancient, virtually permanent, life form. If we were able to picture their progress and development throughout their "lifetime," they would appear to be disconcertingly alive. Roads—seemingly organically—expand and extend, change their shape and appearance. They often divide, branch, and alter their course. At the same time, they are reluctant to move from their original locations and very rarely expire. This long-term dynamism is somewhat similar to that of rivers, with their historic routes solidly determined by the physical terrain. Old roads trace ridges and gently skate along contours; they cross watercourses at the shallowest point and ascend hillsides along the easiest gradients. Their routes reflect the forms of the traffic that sculpted them: centuries of foot, hoof, and wooden wheel.

Many of the roads we drive along today closely follow routes taken by ancient travelers. They are like an elaborate and permanent tattoo on the body of a giant. But a tattoo that starts as fine lines on a modest scale, and then slowly and relentlessly subdivides, spreading outward into increasingly complex patterns. A living network that the giant is unable to control.

Almost all roads grow and expand over time, so the rare exceptions are worth considering. The oldest road in Britain is one such example.[12] Its name, the Ridgeway, offers an obvious explanation, as this ancient pathway runs along the high ridges of the chalk hills it follows for much of its length. About 140 kilometers (87 miles) of this five-thousand-year-old road have been identified, running in a broad arc to the west and north of London. These formed part of a much longer road—the Icknield

Way—which allowed journeys from the Salisbury Plains, in the southwest, to East Anglia. Although exuberant vegetation growth now obscures the view along many sections of the route, early travelers took advantage of its high, open position as a means of detecting possible threats from below.

Today, most of the Ridgeway is designated a National Trail, allowing people to wander its length in much the same manner as they have for millennia: as pedestrians, or on horseback. At various times in the distant past, larger groups of people and animals—invaders, and drovers with their flocks—began to make use of this route. But the Ridgeway's defining geographical feature was also its limitation: there was not enough space for the road to expand. With the advent of horse-drawn carts and carriages, the narrowness of the ridges precluded the development of the road to accommodate them. When the vehicles became wider and the traffic busier (and the risk of banditry had eased), this track in the hills was abandoned in favor of flatter terrain in the valleys. Today, wanderers using the Ridgeway can pause at scenic lookouts and observe the cars and trucks below, congested along the much more recent road. (They can also view the astonishing Uffington White Horse, 110 meters [360 feet] in length, carved thousands of years ago into the chalk immediately adjacent to the Ridgeway.)

The literature discussing roads is replete with picturesque—and sometimes confounding—attempts at capturing their scale, shape, and constantly changing nature through terms such as *net, web, artery, mesh, maze, grid* . . . even *tapestry*. The metaphor of the giant is often evoked, and this has a prominent role in the written history of road ecology. One of the most influential players in this field, American landscape ecologist (and so much more) Richard Forman, employed the image to convey the immense potential of this unavoidably multidisciplinary endeavor. In one of the first major reviews of road ecology (published as recently as 1998), he ventured that "few environmental scientists . . . recognize the sleeping giant, road ecology," suggesting that his colleagues urgently needed to rouse themselves into action.[13]

Characteristically, Forman himself was well and truly awake and active, organizing an influential collaboration of fourteen international experts in an attempt to synthesize as much insight and information as possible into a single publication. The result, published a few years later in 2003, immediately became the primary text of the field: *Road Ecology:*

Science and Solutions.[14] In unexpectedly poetic—yet stark—prose, for what is otherwise a fairly formal academic book, Forman this time described two different giants:

> The land and the [road] net, lie intertwined in an uneasy embrace. The road system ties the land together for us yet slices nature into pieces.

"Humans have spread an enormous net over the land," explained Forman. "The largest human artifact on earth." But rather than the gentle compliance apparent in many ancient roads, contemporary roads "are superimposed on mountains, valleys, plains, and rivers teeming with natural flows." The result is indeed a most uneasy embrace: nature degrading roads and roads degrading nature. It is a fast-moving catastrophe, with immense financial, environmental, and social costs. The challenges are enormous and daunting and are almost impossibly complex. Effective solutions are simply beyond the usual players working alone and without the necessary insights beyond their specializations: the road engineers, urban planners, traffic modelers, and transportation experts. Yet, with an arresting level of vision and optimism, so characteristic of Forman himself, *Road Ecology* offers realistic hope:

> Perhaps just in time, a solution appears to lie before us. Its underlying foundations include knowledge in transportation, hydrology, wildlife biology, plant ecology, population ecology, soil science, water chemistry, aquatic biology, and fisheries. Fitting these fields together should lead to a science of road ecology, bulging with useful applications. However, landscape ecology has emerged as a key ingredient, or glue, elucidating spatial patterns, ecological flows, and landscape changes over large areas.[15]

In other words, the field of road ecology is an extraordinary attempt to meld the theories, principles, models, and concepts developed by a bewildering array of fields and professions, which have displayed scant regard for one another—with some barely on speaking terms. Will it be business as usual, with destructive motorways further fragmenting and degrading, or shall we see, as Forman and his colleagues modestly envision, "a gentle *roadprint* on the land"?[16]

The impact and influence of this strange new hybrid field of road ecology is profoundly changing one of the most destructive human activities around the world. It's an unexpectedly positive story. And there is a lot to see and think about.

Although I will be trying hard to avoid too much jargon and technical terminology, there are some common terms that are unavoidable. I could provide a typical glossary, but it would be much more fun to explain these important terms by seeing how they are applied out in the field. My friend and colleague Éric Guinard, a government road ecologist based in Bordeaux, France, has invited us along to visit some brand-new wildlife-crossing structures in the south of his beautiful country. I have warned him that some of you may not be entirely comfortable with road definitions, so he has promised to explain these as we go. The key terms are given in **bold** and the explanations are adapted from the formal definitions.[17]

"I am glad to show these new constructions," says Éric, as we speed off down the **motorway** toward Pau. The **pavement,** or **road surface,** is obviously new, still shiny and dark because of the recently applied layer of asphalt. The painted line markings contrast brightly with the black road. "The French transportation agency have just **duplicated** this road; you might call it '**twinning,**'" Éric explains.

> Because of the growth in traffic volume, they decided this region needed a much bigger road, so they more or less **doubled** what was here before. There are now two separate **carriageways** for vehicles traveling in each direction. It is a much faster road now, because the **alignment** of the road was made a lot straighter; several sharp corners were removed and the **grade**, the amount of steep or sudden changes in slope, were made flatter. But if you can drive quite fast [*as we are now doing, I think to myself!*], you still need to feel safe. So, to make sure that cars cannot collide, the road engineers have separated the **dual roadway** with a fairly wide **median**, an area of grass and small shrubs. And where there are features close to the road that it would not be good to hit—such as large rocks, or trees, or steep gullies—they have installed.

These guardrails are mainly of a kind made of metal rope woven along short flexible poles. A car running into these, even at speed, gets caught by these ropes and does not travel far.

> On the side of the road there is a broad grassy **verge**. Quite a few small mammals and insects live happily in the thick layers of vegetation, despite

the noisy cars going past very slowly. But as you can see, looking ahead, these verges, the two carriageways, and the wide median between—the **roadbed**, the surface where the cars drive—are just a proportion of the overall **road corridor**, which stretches all the way from the farms on one side of the road to the forests on the other side. The area beside the road, but not on the road itself, is the **road reserve**. The amount of space that roads use—we call it the **land-take**—is a major concern; especially for me, when I am thinking about the impact on the environment. But mostly, those designing roads are concerned with the safety of the motorists.

We suddenly leave the large road and head down an exit onto a smaller—but still significant—road, running parallel to the motorway, which is now well above us. This is an arterial road, which connects two local townships; however, at the bottom of this valley we turn off onto a local road. These smaller roads are usually the responsibility of town or district councils. Éric pulls the car onto the road shoulder, a flat section of the verge, and we park at a **rest stop**, a paved section where it is safe to stop. Unlike the rest of the verge, this area for temporary parking has a concrete **curb** along the far side. This channels water running off the road surface into a large gutter, which directs stormwater into a nearby creek.

We leave the car and Éric directs us down the sloping side of the road onto a small path that leads toward a river. "We are proud of what we have constructed for the wildlife here . . ." says Éric, but I interrupt him to point out that we don't actually get to visit these structures until chapter 3.

Part I

Warning

Dangerous Road Ahead

DEATH, DUST, AND DIN

How Vehicles Harm

The scene was profoundly tragic. A warm, dark night, punctuated by ominous red-and-blue flashes reflecting off the car windows and wet pavement. Numerous police officers stood in clusters at the side of this small road in southern Texas, talking quietly among themselves, taking notes, some speaking on their phones. Two others, reflective clothing glowing brightly as the lights of the slowly passing cars swept over them, waved the vehicles on, their illuminated batons sweeping through the mist. A detective walked along the side of the road with deliberation, gazing intently at the road surface. Two long, parallel arcs of black skid marks were clearly visible in the torchlight, dark lines tracing straight along the lane, then veering abruptly left and disappearing off the side of the road. The car was still there—grotesquely misshapen, having slammed into the base of a large tree at considerable speed. The driver-side door and much of the roof had been removed to allow the paramedics access. Their skills were not needed. The ambulance had just departed, with resignation rather than urgency.

Back on the road, where the tire marks silently denoted a sudden, desperate change in angle, something that looked like a solidly built dog lay unmoving on the road. An expanding pool of blood spread blackly around the body. A closer look by the light of several flashlights drew hushed exclamations: it was a large male ocelot, a distinctive and exceptionally rare animal. The police would later learn that the young woman driver had been heading home along this quiet rural road from her ecology studies at the University of Texas in Brownsville. She almost certainly knew the animal was an ocelot when it suddenly appeared in her headlights. The front-page article in the local newspaper the following day quoted a police spokesperson: "The deceased appeared to have been attempting to avoid hitting the animal. This was unsuccessful and has resulted in two tragic deaths."

This undeniably poignant story is disturbing and enormously sad. But it does encapsulate a number of the themes that this book will explore. One is that roads can be deadly, not only for wildlife but also for people. A shocking number of humans are killed daily throughout the world because of collisions with animals, although a much larger number are injured or remain deeply affected by the event. Even if a person is left unscathed emotionally, their vehicle may be damaged or even written off. In the case of the animals involved, however, the vast majority will die, either at the time of the collision or sometime later. One estimate is that less than 2 percent of all animals involved in any sort of vehicle strike will survive.[1]

Roads Kill

The epitaph "roadkill" is brutally appropriate for an appalling, and global, phenomenon: wildlife slaughter by vehicle. If that sounds overly dramatic, consider some of stark numbers right now. Just a sample taken from some reliable sources giving the annual number of animals killed on roads: 5 million frogs in Australia; 7 million birds in Bulgaria; 14 million birds in Canada; 365 million mammals in the United States.[2] These figures are usually based on imaginative extrapolations from smaller-scale studies, but most authorities regard roadkill estimations as significantly underestimating what is really happening. Running your eyes over these bald figures can be numbing, and even counterproductive; who wants to think about all that death? Nonetheless, this carnage is central to this story, and we must be willing to consider what these numbers mean. Not individually, but collectively. (Having said that, the death of a single ocelot or any other animal belonging to a seriously endangered species can obviously be significant; quite literally, extinction by a thousand accidents.) But do these numbers actually matter?

The traditional perception of roadkill in general has been that the succession of dead animals along the roadside is simply an indication of the relative abundance of wildlife in the area. The wildlife–vehicle strikes that caused the carnage are regarded as a sample of local abundance, with lots of decomposing carcasses clearly demonstrating that there must be plenty of animals in the vicinity. This is one of those commonsense, straightforward, logical ideas that barely raises an eyebrow. No one was particularly surprised when recent studies found that the numbers of dead white-tailed deer (North America), roe deer (northern Europe), and gray kangaroos (Australia) strewn along roads and highways correlated closely with their abundance.[3] Lots of roadkill means lots of animals, right?

Although these generalizations are still with us, they have proven to be far too simplistic and often extremely misleading. A more nuanced consideration of all this death began to emerge when ecologists started to pay closer attention to the victims. As far as we know, the first systematic roadkill survey was conducted by Dayton Stoner in 1925 as he drove along 632 miles (1,017 kilometers) of country roads in Iowa.[4] As has been the standard practice ever since, Stoner simply noted all of the carcasses he saw while driving, dictating the details to his wife as they traveled along. Most of the time he was able identify the species without pulling over—they rarely exceeded twenty-five miles (forty kilometers) per hour—although he does state: "Stops were made for some of the less common and unusual finds." Stoner's tally was 225 animals, or about one animal killed every three miles (or every five kilometers). This tally of casualties was shocking at the time, yet it undoubtedly represents just a fraction of what would be found on those roads today, especially when considering the differences in the number of vehicles and their speed.

What is also astonishing is the variety of species Stoner did, and did not, detect. Remarkably, there were no deer, but he does list six reptile, nine mammal, and thirteen bird species (including, intriguingly, seventy-six individual woodpeckers of four species). Although little more than a somewhat mundane list of dead animals, Stoner's article was sufficiently noteworthy for it to be published in the prestigious journal *Science*, under the title "The Toll of the Automobile," with Stoner concluding that the automobile "demands recognition as one of the important checks upon the natural increase of many forms of life."[5] This was an admonition many decades ahead of its time. Nothing similar (or at least published) seems to have been attempted until well into the 1980s.

Most surveys of roadkill conducted over the past decade have typically followed Stoner's approach of recording all the roadside carcasses observed from a vehicle moving at the local speed limit. Generally, the researchers do not stop to examine the bodies detected, primarily because of legitimate concerns about safety. When some brave (and presumably insured) researchers took the logical approach of walking carefully along the roadside (suitably clad in hi-vis protective clothing and with companions watching the traffic), actively searching for dead animals, they quickly realized what was being missed from the moving cars: almost all of the smaller species. These included rodents, rabbits, reptiles, and birds; but road-killed amphibians were especially common. Experimental investigations—involving deliberately placing artificial "roadkill" along the road verge and then comparing the levels of detection made by observers either driving or on foot—have found that fewer than 5 percent of the carcasses of smaller animals are detected from cars, and that foot surveys typically miss more than half.[6] This is sobering news when you appreciate that even those appallingly large numbers are probably grossly underestimated.

Of course, certain times and places are worse than others. Roads located near wetlands or bodies of water are particularly bad, as are periods when large numbers of animals are on the move (large-scale mass migrations, for example, as well as occasions when animals of a certain age disperse away from their natal location).

In many parts of the Northern Hemisphere, the early weeks of spring are associated with localized migrations of many species of amphibians. Typically, these movements are from hibernation sites in the hills down to breeding locations in rivers, ponds, and wetlands in the valleys below. Extraordinary numbers of animals are involved, and if the route taken involves crossing a road, the results can be catastrophic; in fact, the roads

Figure 5. Western painted turtle (*Chrysemys picta bellii*) laying eggs along a gravel road in Kootenai National Wildlife Refuge, northern Idaho. Photographer Marcel Huijser.

in such areas can be among the very worst sites for roadkill *anywhere*. For example, at a single site in the United States, more than 10,000 migrating amphibians were killed over a seventeen-month period.[7] Even in the absence of migration, the numbers can be extraordinary. On one wet, warm night in Australia, researchers recorded 419 frog carcasses along three kilometers (1.9 miles) of a small country road.[8] Obtaining accurate numbers of road-killed frogs, toads, and salamanders is, of course, extremely difficult. Their small size means that many are almost certainly missed by even well-trained observers. Their tiny bodies are often completely obliterated by vehicles, and plenty are removed by scavengers or washed away by heavy rain. Nonetheless, it is generally accepted that amphibian mortality on roads probably accounts for about 70 percent of all roadkill.[9]

The sheer scale of this carnage can be astonishing, but the key issue is whether this loss of life is of significance to the local populations. Again, this depends on the species involved. Where this question has been directly investigated, the answers have been reassuring. For example, an enormous roadkill toll seems to have had no discernable impact on populations of song birds in the United Kingdom, rodents in Texas, or small mammals in the Mojave Desert of California.[10] In most cases, if the animals are small, fast, abundant, and widespread, even relatively high rates of road mortality appear to have little impact on local populations. In these instances, the generalization that roadkill reflects abundance appears to be about right. For other species, however, especially those that are slow, terrestrial, or have restricted ranges or declining populations, the effect of even moderate levels of roadkill can be very significant. To illustrate, let's visit two beautiful but very different places.

The state of Florida features prominently in this story, for some unfortunate reasons. The Florida panther is a very good example of a very bad situation. This animal is an isolated subspecies of the North American cougar (or mountain lion), now present only in a tiny fraction of its original distribution. The Florida animals are the only remaining cougars found anywhere in the eastern United States, and they are now seriously endangered. Habitat destruction and fragmentation has had a devastating impact on this large predator, which requires a substantial home range. Although its numbers have risen from a terrifying low of 20 or so in the 1970s to around 230 in 2017, today its biggest threat is from roads: half the annual mortality of Florida panthers is now directly due to vehicle strikes.[11]

And it's not just panthers. Vehicle strikes on Florida's roads are now the principal cause of death for key deer (a subspecies of the white-tailed deer), now numbering fewer than three hundred animals, which live only in the Florida Keys, as well as for the American crocodile, black bear, and bald eagle. (It is tragically ironic that another endangered Florida species, the Florida manatee, is also subject to vehicle strikes, with about eighty being killed each year in collisions with boats.)[12] We know about these cases because a lot of attention is paid to these animals—and to the state of Florida in general. It is almost certain that similar things are happening in lots of places that are more remote and less populous, where there are fewer people to notice or care. One alarming exception to this general pattern comes from Tasmania, Australia's island state (a place literally down under Down Under), a terrible story we know about because one person did notice and care.

Tasmania Bedeviled

Tasmania has the dubious honor of having one of the world's highest rates of roadkill.[13] The visibility of dead animals—many of them well-known and well-loved native species such as wallabies, echidnas, and wombats—is inescapable on almost every road in the state. Despite the relatively small human population of the island (only about half a million people live there) and apparently low traffic levels, roadside carcasses seem to be everywhere. This is not a reputation Tasmanians are proud of, and it has led to high-level government initiatives seeking to address the problem. "It's not a good look," a senior tourism spokesperson was quoted as saying. "We're supposed to be clean and green, but the first thing that visitors see is dead and stinks!"[14] They tend to be straight-talkers in Tassie.

These dead and stinking bodies strewn along Tasmanian highways are almost all widespread and abundant species. The official concern is primarily about perceptions and tourism marketing, and is focused on the main highways and visitor destinations. In the meantime, something far more serious has been occurring deep within the remote terrain of a large national park and centered on a road with very low traffic. What follows is a story of shocking serendipity, which forces you to wonder how often similar catastrophes occur without anyone noticing.

In the center of the island is a large conservation reserve, Cradle Mountain–Lake St Clair National Park, part of the much larger Tasmanian Wilderness World Heritage Area. This remote, ruggedly beautiful landscape is home to two iconic marsupial carnivores, the Tasmanian devil (an actual animal and nothing like the cartoon version) and the eastern quoll, which is much smaller but equally as ferocious. Both predators are strictly nocturnal and are usually elusive. In this area they make use of the roads for ease of movement (avoiding the dense and tangled ground-level vegetation) and as the site for some opportunistic scavenging of road-killed animals.

Zoologist Menna Jones is an internationally recognized specialist on Tasmania's marsupial carnivores, a reputation earned the hard way during countless freezing, wet nights in Tasmania's inhospitable forests. It goes without saying that she is also tough; she has to be. In 1990, Menna started a major investigation of devils and quolls at Cradle Mountain.[15] In this part of Tasmania it rains—hard and heavy—two days out of three, but that's what you have to endure if you want to study these animals in what seems to be ideal habitat for them. At the time of the study, this location supported the state's densest populations of both species, even though Cradle Mountain is in the middle of one of Tasmania's favorite tourist spots. Visitors traveling to the picturesque chalets at Dove Lake, at the northern end of the national park, drove along a single unpaved road, which was so rutted, narrow, and muddy that speeding was impossible. People sometimes reported driving slowly along the road at night with a devil trotting along beside them, apparently taking no notice of the noisy vehicle. This benign relationship between driver and devil, however, was about to change completely.

If you want to study nocturnal predators that live in the depths of dense, dark forests, you can't simply go out and watch them. Indeed, about the only way to learn anything is to catch them so they can be tagged with radio transmitters. Which is all very well—but these are dangerous animals, equipped with jaws full of huge and effective teeth; in fact, a recent study has determined that Tasmanian devils have the most powerful bite of any animal, hyenas and crocodiles included.[16] Nonetheless, Menna was able to capture a large number (without losing any fingers), which were measured, weighed, and fitted with transmitters to enable their movements to be tracked. In addition to trapping, she undertook spotlighting surveys along the road at night and checked for roadkill during the day. This punishing schedule allowed her to determine with quite a bit of confidence that the area supported about forty devils and twenty quolls. That is a remarkable density of meat-eaters for an area only about 20 square kilometers (7.7 square miles) in area. It would have been hard to find a better place for marsupial carnivores.

In the expressionless language of the scientific article Menna subsequently produced, she states: "In 1991, part-way through a field study . . . half of the access road . . . was widened and paved to carry an increasing volume of heavy traffic such as tourist coaches."[17] At the time, she felt a lot less neutral. Horrified at the disturbance caused by the roadwork, but determined to press on with her demanding studies, Menna continued her schedule of trapping and surveys as best she could. But it didn't take long before the impact of the new road was starkly revealed. Over the next two years, the numbers of both species declined dramatically, with half the number of devils and only a single quoll being detected. Manna subsequently abandoned trapping—a laborious and dangerous task at the best of times—as there was now little point to it; spotlighting and roadkill surveys became the main way of tracking the animals. Over the next few years, both species were rarely detected.

It would be tempting, perhaps even reassuring, to think that all of those animals had simply been frightened away by the noise and disturbance. If only. Within three months of the road being paved, Manna's roadkill surveys found almost half of all of the quolls that had been captured and marked in the area dead beside the road. Others almost certainly died from their injuries away from the road, as is always the case. Even more shocking was the fact that the paved section of road was only 2 kilometers (just over a mile) in length. Yet that was enough to wipe out a huge proportion of the local populations. The obvious question is, why? Why did the simple addition of an asphalt surface to the unpaved road have such a catastrophic impact on these two species?

Without question, the main answer was speed: paving the road allowed vehicles to travel about 20 kilometers (12 miles) per hour faster than had been possible on the dirt road. The new, smooth surface—so different from the muddy, rutted conditions of the original—seemed to encourage faster driving. It was still a narrow two-lane passageway, enclosed on both sides by dense vegetation, yet many cars were recording speeds of 80 to 120 kilometers per hour (50 to 75 miles per hour).[18] Even slowing for the corners would have been of little consequence for any animal crossing on the other side of the bend. And to make matters worse, the dark color of the asphalt, in the heavily shaded forest landscape, made the animals even more difficult to detect. These features combined to provide a setting that almost resulted in local extinction.

Stricken

Collisions between vehicles and animals are extremely common, resulting in enormous amounts of roadkill throughout the world. But these events—known in the trade as wildlife–vehicle collisions, or wildlife–vehicle strikes—are not only a danger to wildlife. The resulting damage to vehicles exceeds a billion dollars annually in the United States alone. These collisions lead to thousands of serious injuries and many hundreds of human deaths. Such traumatic accidents are a major impetus for trying to prevent animals from being on the roads in the first place. Understanding the many ways that are being developed to address these critical concerns forms the heart of this book. Here, we will explore what is known about the implications of wildlife–vehicle collisions for people.

It's an obvious generalization, but the bigger the animal, the worse the outcome for the people involved. High-speed collisions with, for instance, a deer, kangaroo, or bear are all likely to be catastrophic, although the details of the interaction between the machine and the animal can be quite different. Let's think about why.

Picture if you can—in ultra-slow motion—a collision involving a typical suburban car and a typical suburban deer on a typical suburban street. The deer is constructed so that almost all of its bulk is well above the ground, atop four rather thin and lightly structured legs. When a car hits the animal, the front of the car usually collides with the legs first, causing the deer's body to roll onto the bonnet and potentially into the windscreen. This is a familiar scenario for family-style vehicles (although the front of the increasingly common SUVs or pickups is higher

Figure 6. Bison cow and calf (*Bison bison*) crossing road, Yellowstone National Park, Wyoming. Photographer Marcel Huijser.

above the ground and therefore more likely to slam directly into the animal's body).

The severity of the consequences increases dramatically with greater speeds and larger animals. In Canada and Sweden, for example, potential collisions with moose on remote roads is certainly one of the greatest risks for anyone undertaking an overland driving trip: slamming into something almost three meters (ten feet) tall and weighing up to about 800 kilograms (1,700 pounds) is almost always going to end badly. When the animal has a huge body and a particularly high center of gravity—as well as a massive head with antlers—the interactions between animal parts and rapidly moving vehicle can be horrifying. The aftermath of something along these lines was described to me by a heavy-vehicle driver (still noticeably shaken) who had encountered the results of a collision between a large truck and a wild camel in Central Australia. The camel's head had swung around into the driver's window, while its hind legs were entangled in the door on the other side of the cabin. Its body was firmly embedded in the entire space where the windscreen had once been. No one survived.

Throughout most of the Northern Hemisphere, deer (roe, white-tailed, and red) and moose are the primary concern for motorists. In Australia, kangaroos are just Deer Down Under. Both are superabundant large grazing mammals that have proliferated in the absence of their main natural predators (wolves, dingoes), especially in rural and outer suburban areas where hunting is severely restricted or nonexistent. All of these species congregate along the road verge to graze. White-tailed deer, roe deer, eastern gray kangaroos, red-necked wallabies—same deal and similar risk on the roads. Collisions with kangaroos (and other large macropods) are the major concern on almost any drive in Australia, including the outer suburbs of even the largest cities. The risk is especially high during the poor-visibility times of dawn and dusk. Everyone seems to have had a 'roo incident or near miss story, and the insurance agencies put a figure of billions of dollars on the accumulated costs of this issue.[19]

One important difference between kangaroos and deer, however, is their method of locomotion. The kangaroo's quintessential bounding gait is superbly energy efficient and enables them to reach speeds of up to 40 kilometers per hour (25 miles per hour). The key feature of this mode of motion is the regular alternation between being fully airborne and crouching low, an undulating movement that can result in very different outcomes in a collision. In the close-to-the-ground phase, the impact of hitting 40 kilograms (90 pounds) of solid flesh can result in major damage to the front of the vehicle. When airborne, on the other hand, the kangaroo may literally sail over the bonnet or smash through the windscreen without making contact with the rest of the car.

Extreme unpredictability is another well-known characteristic of these animals. Compared with the often closely coordinated movements of a herd of deer, the way a group of kangaroos grazing by the roadside is likely to react to an oncoming vehicle is impossible to determine. An individual kangaroo may panic and bound in any direction, while other group members remain immobile, seemingly unaffected. Sometimes you can drive safely past a grazing mob (the collective name for macropods). The next time, some or all might careen straight into your path. Careful drivers are sensibly attentive in 'roo country.

Finally, there are the slow-moving, solid-bodied mammals that may as well be a furry boulder in the middle of the road. Wild boars and bears are obvious examples; a collision with one of these is almost certainly going to cause considerable damage, especially if the vehicle is moving at speed.

Badgers, beavers, and wombats are a subcategory of this type of living obstacle, similarly solid in build but much smaller in size; nonetheless, a collision can still be significant. These smaller mammals are responsible for a large number of serious accidents in which vehicles are "bumped" off course and into other traffic—or off the road entirely. Fatalities are somewhat less likely in collisions with these species, but the resulting damage to the vehicle can be extreme.

So far we have only looked at the larger species, those that can cause a lot of damage to vehicles and people should they collide. And while the number of these accidents is enormous, they are but a minute fraction of the overall carnage caused by interactions with a huge variety of much smaller animals. These species are more likely to be slow and inconspicuous, and the collisions often remain completely undetected by the humans sealed inside their vehicles. In every country, reptiles—especially turtles and snakes—rodents, birds, and unknowably large numbers of insects, are all mown down by cars and trucks. But unquestionably the greatest toll of road victims is found among the amphibians, as mentioned early in this chapter. On warm, wet nights around the world, the number of frogs, toads, and salamanders killed on roads is simply unfathomable.

There is one other species we need to consider here: us. Humans are killed and injured in appalling numbers as a result of wildlife–vehicle strikes, although these are a tiny fraction of the overall road toll.

The Human Toll

We have already been forced to look at some disconcertingly large numbers of individual animals killed on roads. These are almost impossible to comprehend in their scale. But then, if we are honest, so are the bald statistics concerning the numbers of people killed in road accidents. Let's pause and consider these figures for a moment. According to the latest data (2020) from the Association for Safe International Road Travel:[20]

- Worldwide, about 1.25 million people are killed in car accidents every year. That's 3,290 every day. Around 20 to 50 million others are injured or disabled.
- Road accidents are the leading cause of death in people aged fifteen to twenty-nine, with an average of about one thousand fatalities occurring daily around the world.
- More than 90 percent of all road-related deaths occur in low- to middle-income countries (and is the primary cause of death for Americans traveling overseas).
- Globally, these accidents cost US$518 billion every year.

These numbers are not presented for macabre fascination. Every death is a profound tragedy. What is needed, quite obviously, is some way to prevent such an appalling loss of life. Collisions between vehicles and stationary objects are overwhelmingly due to driver behavior, and government agencies and transportation authorities are trying to reduce human mistakes. For example, most countries identify so-called black spots where unusually high numbers of accidents occur. Sometimes, that's all that happens. In other cases, these locations become prioritized for road improvements or signage. Virtually every country is committed to improving the preparation, training, and advice provided to learner drivers. Theoretically, at least, it is possible to equip drivers with the skills needed to use their vehicle safely: to react appropriately to changes associated with traffic, road-surface conditions, and weather. Theoretically, it is possible to influence the behavior of drivers. Unfortunately, drivers tend—for the present—to be human.

Accidents involving animals are almost completely unpredictable. No one can anticipate a deer or bear appearing around the next corner or a kangaroo or baboon suddenly sprinting across the road directly in front of your vehicle. There is little that even a well-trained driver can do in such circumstances.

The contribution of collisions with wildlife to these appalling figures has not been estimated at the global level. Most countries appear not to record whether animals were involved in car accidents—and when they do, the statistics are not particularly reliable. Even in the United States, the data are poorly synthesized. One estimate suggests that between one and two million collisions with animals occur each year in the United States, with approximately two hundred human deaths resulting, but this is at best an approximation.[21] There is an understandable tendency to focus on the human component of wildlife–vehicle collisions, rather than dwell on the animals involved, possibly out of imagined respect for the people who have been affected. This is unfortunate; such details may be essential for planning how to mitigate these terrible accidents.

The interaction of vehicles with the environment does not always present itself in the shockingly tangible form of wrecked cars and dead bodies. Vehicles also have impacts well away from the road itself, though these are often less substantial or invisible.

Emissions

It might be appropriate to discuss here the colossal contribution of the world's vehicles to global greenhouse gas emissions. That is a critically important topic, obviously (and has been thorough discussed in several recent books), but I am going to ignore it in favor of the more immediate and local impacts of vehicles.[22] The emissions referred to here are the various particles or energy waves that emanate from the traffic as it moves along the road. These include dust, fumes, vibrations, and noise, all of which can affect the plants and animals (and of course, people) living beside the road, sometimes in unexpected ways.

An informative place to start this exploration is beside a simple un-paved country road, a possible progenitor of many of the multilane mo-torways that now crisscross the countryside. In this particular case, the site we are visiting is on the fringes of Brisbane, in Queensland, Australia. It's classified as a "minor road,"[23] but that can be dangerously mislead-ing, as the combined length of these dirt or gravel—or unpaved—roads is far greater than that of paved roads.[24] "Minor" roads are a major part of road ecology. If its lanes were actually marked, it would be called a two-lane road. But what it definitely *is* called is "The Worst Road in the Region"—by some of the local residents, and by their political represen-tatives, who see votes in a campaign to have the road paved as a sign of "delivering for the community." Currently, it is a winding, heavily rutted, and poorly maintained path through a forest reserve, linking two small townships and used mainly by tradespeople and locals who are willing to put up with the choking dust and rivet-loosening corrugations. Most sen-sible drivers avoid what could be something of a shortcut in favor of the longer route around the forest on much smoother and safer paved roads.

It is the dust that has brought me and several students to stand just inside the forest edge, a few yards from the roadside. Incongruous large plastic boxes on robust tripods have been installed at increasing distances into the forest, in rows perpendicular to the road. These boxes contain layers of glass marbles, which entrap the dust particles that settle into the open-topped boxes. These will be collected and replaced monthly over the coming year, providing a detailed measurable picture of dust levels within the forest. A single, much more high-tech-looking device has also been set up, which will operate only on the days we are in the field. This machine records the dust levels immediately beside the road in very fine detail. This is a new gadget, and I am here to ensure that it is working properly.

A shout from one of our team positioned further down the road warns us that a vehicle is approaching. It's a veteran pickup, and it doesn't sound too healthy. It labors past at only moderate speed, visibly and audibly shaking as it bounces over the corrugations. In its wake, a thick, smoke-like cloud of dust rises high into the air and spreads slowly into the forest on either side. As the dust reaches us, everyone instinctively covers their faces with hats or scarves; we have all seen cars on this road stir up bil-lowing particles innumerable times before, but it is still alarming just how much dust is produced by a single vehicle. Literally every leaf within about five meters (fifteen feet) of the road is coated in a thick layer of chalky white powder. It seems obvious that this covering of dust will make it very difficult for the trees and shrubs to "breathe" or photosynthesize. Simply walking along the forest floor raises a continuous white fog. Could anything actually survive under these conditions?

The students and I are attempting to answer this question: the second of two scientific reasons that we are here.[25] Throughout the year, a variety of devices designed to capture small to moderately sized mammals (alive and unharmed) have been placed in two lines parallel to the road, one immediately nearby and the other about eighty meters (ninety yards) away, deeper within the forest. We hope that these activities (monitoring the dust levels and trapping ground mammals) will provide answers to the two main objectives of this study: to ascertain how much dust spreads into the forest, and how far; and how many animals—if any—live in the roadside vegetation. But there is a much larger question hanging in the dust-laden air: how might all this change when the road is finally paved? This is a question of considerable interest to a range of people with direct and rather more peripheral connections to this otherwise insignificant

Figure 7. Coal trucks and their dust, between Tsagaan Khad (White Rock) and Gashuun-Sukhait, Gobi, Mongolia. Photographer Marcel Huijser.

road. Local community groups are either desperate for an improved road that will save time and be much safer than the existing "goat track," or they are fundamentally opposed because of fears that traffic levels—and speed—could increase markedly, with all too predictable impacts on the local wildlife and their (the people's) "quality of life." In the road's unimproved state, it would be virtually impossible for an animal to be run over by a vehicle rumbling noisily along this road, unless it was temporarily blinded by the dust or resting peacefully in a rut. As it is, most of the ground-dwelling animals (in common with almost all Australian mammals) are nocturnal and could safely cross the road at night, when traffic is almost nonexistent. Paving the road would almost certainly change this state of affairs completely. Animals attempting to cross would be at much greater risk, at all times of the day. For motorists, on the other hand, the shorter, smoother, safer passageway would be of undeniable benefit.

Let me pause briefly to give a context update. The conflicting concerns and aspirations described here would be thoroughly familiar to almost everyone, anywhere, who has experience in the dramas associated with plans for upgrading or building new roads. The dilemmas and debates surrounding even this small-scale, very local situation exemplify those of almost all transportation projects. The answers to questions such as who benefits, and at what cost, can never simply be a matter of facts and figures. Naively, my colleagues and I had thought—admittedly only briefly—that simply presenting our graphs and statistical findings would resolve any apparent conflicts. I wonder whether that has ever been true. But the point of this small detour is to draw attention to the complexity of all infrastructure projects and the need to recognize that people must be considered from the very first steps in the process of planning. We shall see these so-called human dimensions emerge in virtually all of the examples and stories presented in this book. Once you expect them, you can at least try to be prepared. Now, back to the dust . . .

It is almost two years later. As was always going to be the case, the road has been paved. However, following impassioned submissions from local environmental groups, a series of "traffic-calming" features were added to the road design. These made it difficult for cars to reach high speeds, before then being forced to navigate some tight bends. Whether these features "work" in terms of slowing traffic, and thereby reducing roadkill, will be evaluated once volunteer citizen-scientists complete their daily surveys of the entire length of the road over the course of a year.

After our fair share of dramas in the field (including a once-in-a-decade storm, which flooded the dust-deposition boxes and brought down dozens of trees throughout the site, all of which miraculously missed our sixteen devices), my fellow researchers and I have finally washed all of the dusty marbles, identified the trapped animals, run the analyses, and contemplated the findings. Some things were anticipated, while others took us completely by surprise; this is why science can be so exciting (as well as perplexing and frustrating). First, those clouds of dust.

We had certainly expected that the devices would gather plenty of dust, and that this would penetrate quite a long way into the forest. What the data showed, however, was extreme: close to the road, about 550 grams per square meter (just over 20 ounces per square yard) of dust was being deposited annually. Almost all of this settled within thirty-five meters (forty yards) of the road, although some reached very much further into the forest.

Much of Australia is dry and barren, and major dust storms are a familiar though irregular phenomenon in large parts of the mostly open landscape. These fairly typical dust storms redistribute dust particles at a rate of around 200 grams per square meter (7 ounces per square yard) over a year. The gritty tumult enveloping the vegetation beside this road was, however, much greater than the levels occurring during these major but infrequent natural events. One of the soil specialists to whom we showed these data exclaimed that it was the equivalent of a major once-in-twenty-years dust storm occurring every day![26]

There was indeed a lot of dust emanating from the unpaved road and settling all over the roadside vegetation. This was one of the really conspicuous impacts of the perpetual dust wafting through the trees: every leaf was powdery white in color. Quite obviously, this was going to substantially impair the ability of the plants to photosynthesize (the process that converts sunlight into the energy that plants need to function). If we regard leaves as tiny solar panels, the effect of the coating of dust is similar to a home's rooftop panels being covered by an inch of snow. But snow on solar panels is usually only a temporary condition; when the sun comes out and the day warms up, the covering disappears and the panel can do its job again. In the subtropical environment of southern

Queensland, rain falls frequently and often heavily. The rain washes the leaves and transfers the dust to the ground below, where this fine-grained layer of minerals rapidly becomes part of the nutrient cycle that keeps the trees and shrubs growing. (Of course, in areas where the rainfall is less frequent, the dust covering can be a serious problem.)

So, unexpectedly, we learn that all of this nasty dust is actually an important resource for plants, provided it reaches the humus layer on the forest floor below. And one more surprise: this "powder-coating" is also a very effective protective covering for the leaves, deterring lots of herbivores, from caterpillars to koalas.

After those unexpected revelations, let's turn to the impact of all that dust on the ground-dwelling animals. It was surprising to learn that the dust can actually be beneficial for the plants, but we were fairly confident that the small mammals living on the forest floor would be far less impressed. Indeed, we predicted that few animals would be able to cope with the super-dusty zones next to the road and that most would be found in the relatively dust-free areas far away from the edge of the road. This was hardly a provocative conjecture; simply walking around in these forests stirred up clouds of choking dust. The small species that lived entirely at ground level—rodents, bandicoots, and marsupial carnivores—would surely be unable to cope. Astonishingly—though happily—we were again completely wrong! The number of species of small ground-dwelling mammals for all sites was remarkably high, with eight being captured in our traps. Two of these species, house mice and black (or ship) rats, were ubiquitous invasives found almost everywhere, and were most common near the road; part of their global success has been an ability to live in extremely disturbed environments. The roadsides here were certainly that. That result we *did* expect.

What we most certainly did not anticipate was the high numbers of antechinus and dunnarts (both diminutive but ferocious marsupial carnivores) and native bush rats found in the dustiest zone immediately beside the road. We could imagine the invasive rats and mice somehow coping with the noisy and ultradusty conditions near the road, but the natives are supposed to be more sensitive, preferring undisturbed habitats. Yet, here they were, living in relative abundance alongside lots of introduced rodents. Just how these dusty places enabled all these small species to thrive is something we have never really figured out.

But if this apparently vibrant and productive, yet profoundly disturbed, habitat was somehow functioning because of the dust (don't ask me how), what would happen when the daily dust deliveries cease? Because that is what happened. We gathered up our dust collectors and mammal traps and disappeared just before the bulldozers, graders, asphalt spreaders, and all of the other equipment transformed the original road into something altogether different. When we were eventually able to return and begin our post-upgrade surveys, almost a full year had passed. What we found was a very different place.

The first thing we noticed as we walked through our old sites was the enhanced colors—rather than the dark, dull, muted green of the dust era—and the clarity of the light. It had rained overnight and the forest was gleaming, sunshine glinting from a million droplets of water suspended on clear, clean leaves. The entire forest seemed brighter, the air clearer, devoid of the foggy soft-focus effect caused by the suspended dust. It was also a much more pleasant place for human-sized mammals to work. We replaced all of our traps and devices and began the post-upgrade surveys: how would the small residents respond to these dramatically altered conditions?

Well, if the native small mammals had been able to cope with the dust, they appeared to like the clean forest floor even more. The numbers of both antechinus and bush rats had more than doubled, while another species of native rodent, the swamp rat, joined them next to the road. In contrast, the numbers of house mice, previously the most abundant small mammal, declined to less than a fifth of levels detected before the upgrade. These were all positive and promising results, but it also meant that there were more animals living immediately adjacent to the road.

And that was a problem, because the new road had a lot more cars driving at much higher speeds. The predictions of the city council—clearly designed to placate the concerned locals—had forecast a modest but gradual increase in vehicle numbers, with the likely improved speeds being adequately controlled by the traffic-calming structures. The reality was vastly different. Traffic volumes exceeded all predictions very quickly, and the average speed was much higher than the recommended speed limit. Clearly, the motorists were utilizing the improved road with enthusiasm. Much more alarming was the massive increase in the number of animals killed by these cars. Prior to the upgrade, fewer than twenty animals per one hundred surveys were detected as roadkill. This increased by a factor of about five following the upgrade and was especially evident for reptiles, which comprised more than half of all casualties. The most plausible explanation seems to be that these so-called cold-blooded animals found the strange, new, flat, and dark surface ideal for basking.

This early investigation was invaluable for developing my appreciation of the complexities of roads and traffic. My team's confident predictions were challenged, and in some cases reversed. There is still a lot we do not know. For example, traffic produces a range of emissions other than dust, including fumes, vibrations, oil, and light. All of these can and do have lasting impacts on the surrounding plants and animals. But there is another by-product of traffic, which may be the most significant of them all. It is completely invisible and has no physical presence, yet its influence can be detected far from the road. This emission has changed the structure of entire animal communities and even dramatically altered the behavior of animals living close to roads. It was one of the most noticeable changes following the paving of the dusty road. Noise.

Din

Roads are invisible until you see them. Roads are also silent until you hear them, and then you realize just how pervasive the sound of traffic is. One of the genuine privileges of my job is to spend a couple of weeks each year in an extremely remote location in the middle of Borneo (as mentioned already), a huge conservation reserve that exists mainly to preserve the Maliau Basin, one of the least disturbed places on the planet. Up until the 1990s, humans had never lived in the area permanently and roads were almost nonexistent. The wildlife there has never been hunted and most species are either mildly curious about people or completely indifferent. This is a place where it is still possible to catch a glimpse of extremely rare animals such as pangolins or clouded leopards. And while these occasional sightings are wonderful, it is the sound of the reserve that makes the biggest impression, at least on a city dweller. The place is quiet but never silent. All day and all night, the aural landscape is an intricate tapestry of endless bird, frog, and insect sounds, punctuated now and then by the whooping of gibbons, the pterodactyl-like scream of hornbills, or the dentist drill of cicadas. There is just so much to hear that you *can't*; it's as though the air itself is a multidimensional sea of sounds washing over you, infinite in variety and texture, mostly gentle, both endlessly repetitive and always changing. Entirely natural in origin.

And that's my point: for several weeks each year, I experience life completely without traffic noise. Typically, however, I don't actually notice this until I am back in town. Surrounded by the all-too-familiar roar of cars and trucks, I realize, too late, that this is what I have not been hearing. For most of us, throughout our waking lives, the sound of traffic—that low, pulsating, growling hum, interrupted by sudden abrasive bursts, roars, and squeals from horns and alarms and sirens—is a permanent and unavoidable soundtrack to our existence. Most of the time this is muffled and filtered by distance, walls, windows, and vegetation into a dull murmur that our senses sensibly ignore. It only becomes pervasive or noticeable if we are trying to communicate in an environment where the noise is too loud. Usually, we don't try to talk in such places, moving somewhere else quieter if possible.

Just as the dust cloud drifted into the forest on either side of the unpaved road described above, so an invisible plume of noise permeates roadsides, penetrating nearby habitat and persisting at considerable distances from the road. Unlike dust or chemicals, however, these emissions don't alter the physical landscape. But they do completely change the soundscape beside the road. And if we try to envision the total area affected by traffic noise, those parallel strips of land running along both sides of all the larger roads amount to an enormous area of otherwise apparently suitable habitat. These are places where a large number of animals can live.

But does this really matter? Isn't it likely that the animals living in these noise-affected but otherwise appropriate zones have simply habituated to the continuous sound, just as we have done; eventually not even noticing, and simply carrying on with their busy lives? These are important questions, which have received quite a bit of attention.

First, in a very general sense, there is strong evidence that many fewer individual animals and a lot fewer species live close to roads rather than further away.[27] This effect applies to a zone within about ten meters (thirty feet) of the passing traffic and is especially clear for busier and therefore noisier roads, compared to roads carrying less traffic. These findings have come from research undertaken all over the world, in all sorts of landscapes, forest types, climates, and latitudes. Although most of these studies were conducted for birds (the most conspicuous, detectable, and arguably more attention-grabbing type of animal), there were similar results for frogs and some mammals. Quite clearly, many species don't like living near roads if they can avoid it. The obvious question is: why?

The obvious answer would have to be noise, wouldn't it? So obvious in fact that this explanation has been erected as the Traffic Noise Hypothesis. When something acquires that label, it might seem that it is effectively "true," and that no further discussion is required. But from a serious science perspective, a hypothesis is really just a carefully developed possible explanation, potentially only one way of looking at a phenomenon. However, in terms of the noise idea, the above hypothesis makes good sense, for numerous reasons. It is likely, for example, that traffic noise may interfere with an animal's ability to communicate. This is particularly relevant for species whose normal vocalizations are in the same frequency range as the traffic noise, which is usually below about three kilohertz; this is the low rumble we are all familiar with. Of course, it also matters how loud the noise is. The noise volume will be greatest immediately next to the road, diminishing ("attenuating") with increasing distance from the source. Noise travels much further in open habitat and when the air temperature is low; as a generalization, traffic noise will attenuate rapidly in a dense rainforest but continue for a much greater distance in grassland.

Vocal communication is extremely important for almost all smaller bird species; they are collectively known as "songbirds" for a reason. If a species' calls are in the lower frequencies, the sound of the traffic can obscure them or make it hard for other birds to hear the sound clearly or at all, a process known as "signal masking." Birds can have several behavioral responses to this problem. A bird may sing higher, sing louder, or sing at a different time of the day. Vocalizing at higher frequencies is the most common response and has been found in a range of birds that normally sing at a fairly low pitch (including gray shrike-thrushes, house finches, and song sparrows).[28] This requires much more energy but may do the trick; great tits and great crested flycatchers, for example, are among the species that appear to be able to live successfully in noisy roadside habitats by altering the way they sing. Remarkably, this effect has also been found in some amphibians (such as the American green tree frog and the brown tree frog), but it may inadvertently alter the "message" being conveyed by the singer. Generally, female frogs prefer their males to have lower-frequency calls, so this clever adaptation may not be a good long-term strategy.

A handful of bird species have developed ways of successfully living close to noisy roads (and are possibly enjoying the fact that many potential competitors have moved to quieter spots). But they are very much in a minority—most birds do not like the noise. In contrast, plenty of mammal species seem to live happily very close to the traffic, possibly because they communicate more with scent than with sound. In fact, the disturbed, noisy, polluted road verges—often full of discarded trash, cigarette butts, and weeds—support some of the densest and most successful populations of small mammals (for example, meadow voles in North America) found anywhere.[29] This seems to be related to the absence of certain predators and competitors that are much less tolerant of the prevailing conditions. So it seems that some species, at least, really don't mind the almost constant roar of the traffic—usually those that don't have an auditory signal that could be masked by the road noise.

Bad Vibes

There is, however, one very different group of small mammals living along road verges that *does* communicate using "sound." Kangaroo rats (confusingly, not marsupials—they live in North America rather than Australia) are odd and extremely cute desert-dwelling rodents that employ their massive kangaroo-type feet to drum the ground in order to communicate seismically with other kangaroo rats.[30] They literally "listen" with their enormous feet, communicating presence, territoriality, and courtship messages by foot-drumming, as well as keeping a close "foot" out for the vibrations of approaching predators. Kangaroo rats live their largely solitary lives in the arid and relatively quiet landscapes of western North America, and for most of their very long evolutionary history this distinctive form of communication has worked very well. The arrival of people and vehicles has brought massive changes to their formerly stable and generally vibration-limited world—some beneficial and others dangerously disruptive.

The construction of roads through their sensitive and fragile habitats has led to some serious problems for the kangaroo rats, including the risk of being run over and an increase in the number of predators, such as coyotes, which use the roads when searching for prey. At the same time, the grading and management of the road verges (also known as berms) has inadvertently greatly expanded the amount of land available for digging burrows: bizarrely, the greatest densities of the highly endangered Stephens's kangaroo rat in southern California are often found within a few yards of the roads.[31] That might be regarded as an unexpectedly positive outcome of human disturbance of the environment, but there is a significant downside. The vibrations caused by traffic are so persistent and pervasive that they virtually eliminate the animals' ability to detect the foot-drumming of other kangaroo rats. This is industrial-strength signal masking. At least as important, the continual rumble of low-frequency traffic noise makes detection of predators almost impossible. Indeed, researchers have shown experimentally that the kangaroo rats initially react to every passing car as though it is a potentially dangerous threat.[32] But, just as people habituate to a regular stimulus, the animals soon give up responding completely, a "boy who cried '*Wolf*'" scenario with possibly deadly consequences.

Repellent

As already mentioned, for many bird species the immediate roadside is *not* a nice place to live—and most *don't* live there. But is this well-recognized effect simply a matter of birds avoiding the noise? Is that all there is to this story? Might there be other reasons for the lower numbers of birds? These are just the sorts of questions that Lenore Fahrig from Carleton University in Canada and her students have been tackling for years.[33] With their characteristically clear and critical approach to a problem that most of the rest of us had considered already solved, this group decided to put the Traffic Noise Hypothesis to the test. Detailed counts of birds and recordings of traffic noise were made at increasing distances from busy (more than ten thousand vehicles per day) four-lane highways in a forested part of Ontario. That seems like a fairly simple way to collect data, but it was conducted in such a way that any relationships between the number of birds and the noise level could be carefully examined with respect to distance from the highway, the source of the noise.

Not surprisingly, these researchers found that as they moved further from the road the number of bird species increased and the traffic noise decreased. So?

Examination of the data showed that the relationship between species count and noise level was not a simple one. The number of bird species detected peaked at 350 meters (380 yards), while traffic noise continued to decline in loudness beyond that distance, with its lowest point at 450 meters (490 yards) from the road; that's a remarkable 100-meter (110-yard) difference. The bird community was certainly being influenced by proximity to the road, but noise—while very likely an important factor—was only part of the story. So, if it is not simply about noise, why are there few species of birds living near roads?

This takes us from "din and bad vibes" back to "dust and death": in other words, to the emissions produced by vehicles, and the risks associated with encountering traffic. As well as raising dust, vehicles produce a range of toxic and unpleasant substances that can drift into the surrounding habitat. The influence of these substances on wildlife has not been investigated to the same extent as the effect of noise. An important exception is the research underpinning our growing realization that chemical emissions from vehicles (especially the fumes from unleaded gasoline) are having serious impacts on insects.[34] These by-products of the combustion process in vehicle engines are extremely toxic to invertebrates and have been implicated in the decline of insects at a global scale.[35] The consequences of having a lot fewer insects are truly terrifying, given the fundamental role these tiny but critical animals play in so many food webs. The scale of these changes to insect populations has already been blamed on the reduction of many smaller bird species in urban areas around the world. This is not only affecting insectivorous bird species; regardless of what the adults may consume—including those that only eat fruit, seeds, or fish, for example—all birds feed their nestlings insects. A lack of caterpillars (the universal bird baby food) has already been blamed for the catastrophic drop in numbers of the house sparrow, a species famous for being thoroughly granivorous as adults.[36]

Back at the roadside, we could envisage an invisible cloud of fumes drifting sideways into the nearby forest, continuously eliminating recently hatched midges and flies, and settling onto fresh leaves about to be consumed by moth larvae. It is hardly a surprise that birds that seek insects will avoid such areas. And it is not just birds. This scenario also accounts for the almost complete absence of insectivorous bats in the night sky above, or even near, almost any road anywhere in the world.

The dust, noise, and chemical pollution—and even vibrations and light—produced by vehicles or their movement all play a part in reducing the quality of the habitat close to roads. There is, however, one additional factor that is fatally significant. This is the greatly increased risk of vehicle strike associated with living beside a busy road. While some species, most notably certain small mammals, have successfully colonized the roadside—including grassy or bare verges within touching distance of passing vehicles—many others suffer severely because of their choice of real estate; or more likely, because they have colonized the only real estate available.

Species with a poor sense of the danger posed by traffic are particularly susceptible to vehicle strike. The males of many mammal species, for example, typically disperse as soon as they hit independence, sometimes wandering straight into oncoming traffic, oblivious to the noise. Likewise, huge numbers of birds are killed on roads everywhere, seemingly unable to judge the speed of approaching cars; many appear to have been foraging for items such as seeds, discarded human food, or carrion in the form of roadkill. Ironically, some inadvertently become roadside carrion themselves. Owls are notable examples—they are often hit while hawking for moths attracted to the lights of passing vehicles.

There is a grim irony associated with these roadside "killing fields," where, every day, appalling numbers of animals collide with speeding vehicles and are lost from local populations. In ecological terms, these roadside habitats are "population sinks," places that attract a regular influx of individuals because of the constant availability of new living spaces—spaces vacated as a result of seemingly endless unfortunate accidents. The animals that settle in these risky districts are often the young, inexperienced, or desperate, those with few other options. The noise, it seems, is just one of the problems facing newly arrived residents.

No-Go Zones

This rather disheartening chapter has attempted to paint a picture of the complex and multidimensional influences associated with the steady and growing stream of vehicles coursing through the landscape. The impacts and effects of the rapidly moving (or even, in a traffic jam, immobile) metal machines described here relate entirely to the vehicles themselves, the products they emit, and the indirect influences of their passage. None of these things is associated with the roads themselves, the physical structures that the vehicles move along; their impacts represent an entirely different story. What I hope you can now envision, if not smell and feel, is a perceptible plume of invisible or shadowy influences flowing slowly outward from the line of cars and trucks. This could be rendered into colors, perhaps rancid yellow for the toxic chemicals, or lurid purple for the pulsating noise, brightest nearest to the roadside and growing paler with distance, yet still visible hundreds of meters into the surrounding landscape. And along the edges of the road, a jagged, interrupted line of blood-red— thick and dark in places, smeared thinly in others. This represents the death that is unfortunately an undeniable part of this story.

The disturbing, pulsing cloud of chemicals, noise, and other vehicle by-products, spreading and branching away from the rigid straight lines of the road itself, represents the "road effect zone," one of the foundational concepts to emerge from the new field known as road ecology.[37] This concept is crucial because it forces us to think well beyond the road and the vehicles, to become aware that the influence of traffic extends outward and has many consequences. That's why we started here. Now, however, it is time to look at the roads themselves.

2

THE LAND FRAGMENTED

Why Roadways Matter

I usually try to sit in an aisle seat on flights, because I enjoy standing up to allow other people to get to the toilets, on the hour every hour, throughout seemingly endless, sleepless journeys (when you live in Australia, all international trips are horribly long). On this flight, however, I have found myself in a window seat, having swapped my aisle seat so that a mother could sit with her daughter (though by the look on the teenager's face when I made the offer to switch, the separation may well have been planned). My new seat is in the very back of the plane, but it does provide a great view. This unexpected vantage spot reminds me that observing the landscape from above can be fascinating: from a plane, you can see the geographical big picture, which inevitably leads to some big-picture ruminations.

This particular trip is from Seattle in the United States to Calgary in Canada. I'm on my way to meet some knowledgeable people and, I hope, see some significant places. This is one of many journeys made in search of insights and ideas about roads and to discover what people have been

doing to address some of the serious issues involved. As the plane levels
out at thirty thousand feet, the view beneath me takes in a sizable sample
of the expansive landscapes of Washington state and Alberta province.
For an observer on any flight, virtually anywhere in the world, similar
physical landscape patterns (and associated questions about them) will
arise. Next time you have a window seat, take a really good look out and
think about what you can see.

Almost every flight departs from an airport on the outskirts of a city
and then heads out over the surrounding landscape, typically moving
from the tightly packed, rigid geometry of commercial estates and suburbs into the less spatially defined countryside. The general purposes for
which the land is being used can usually be discerned: the chessboard
conformity of residential housing lots and warehouses; the larger rectangles of industrial zones; the broad, simplified patterns of agricultural or
grazing fields; symmetrical parks. These units of land are almost always
bounded by small roads, their layout defining each area's shape and size,
as well as its purpose. Major motorways, on the other hand, typically cut
across the landscape with complete disregard for the surroundings, their
objective being to provide the most direct route between A and B. This
is particularly evident with the most recently constructed major roads;
these massive, multilane symbols of human development carve through
the landscape in a way that is not so much a matter of "going against the
grain" as willful arrogance.

As the plane gradually rises, the finer details of the land below—vehicles
on the long, straight ribbons of road, the tiny blocks that are buildings,
the glinting rivers and farm dams—slowly disappear and fade into larger
patches of different tones and patterns. Settlements look like tightly clus-
tered mosaics; the farms, contrasting blocks of light brown, vivid green, or
bright yellow (depending on what is growing there); the forests and wood-
lands, uneven patches of lumpy dark green. At this height, the roads themselves are difficult to see, although the road reserves—the linear corridors
of space that run along either side of the roadway—are evident because of
the road's contrasting colors and their starkly direct alignment. Even from
cruising altitude, the road network is remarkably conspicuous. Roads are
everywhere, crisscrossing and slashing through the landscape spread out
below me, although the tightness or density—known as the *mesh*—of the
overall *net*work of roads certainly varies enormously.

And it is not only roads that are carving up the place. Railways, pipelines, electricity easements—and in more remote regions, resource exploration routes—all sweep across the countryside, thrusting over or through the landscape in a relentless quest to connect places with one another. (I will make this point numerous times. Although this book is focused on roads, all types of linear infrastructure bring up many of the same issues and challenges.)

Taking in the view from far above, the predominance of all these lines of connection becomes very clear. What was constructed as a means of joining locations across the land, drawing together spatially separated places in the human world, has also divided, subdivided, and fragmented. Connective intent has resulted in a network of long, thin, intersecting, and bisecting scars. Even somewhere as spacious and expansive as the continental United States (which, as I can see from the air, still retains some vast areas of wild country with very few people), it is impossible to be more than a few miles from a road. In parts of India, China, and Western Europe, where people have lived continuously for thousands of years, the density of roads is even greater. Everywhere, roads fragment as they connect. Jochen Jaeger, one of the leading authorities on this phenomenon, tells me that the Germans even have a word for this: *Landschaftszerschneidung*, literally "landscape fragmentation." (Jochen's extensive work was the inspiration for this section.)

One distressingly effective method used to quantify the extent of this fragmentation is to measure how many meshes occur in a given area, a parameter known as the "mesh density" (an entirely apt term to use, as it conjures up Forman's "fishing net cast over the land" analogy).[1] This technique determines the number of meshes created by roads (or by any of the other forms of linear infrastructure) and the probability of an animal having to cross one or more of these infrastructure barriers as it tries to move between two random points within an area of 1,000 square kilometers, the standard unit for these analyses (the equivalent of about 386 square miles). To simplify the concept: imagine an animal, say a deer, trying to walk between two fairly distant places in a particular landscape; next, count how many roads it would theoretically have to cross on its journey, for the purpose of this exercise ignoring fences and traffic as it travels. The average area available to the animal without having to cross any roads is known as the "effective mesh size." The number of these meshes per 1,000 square kilometers—let's call this the "standard mesh area"—tells us the density of the meshes.

One study applying this technique looked at all the transportation routes from twenty-eight European countries, with sophisticated computer programs utilizing a massive amount of geographical information. The findings, while not exactly unexpected, are shocking to contemplate.[2]

To illustrate the problem faced by traveling animals, let's start somewhere incongruous like the middle of London. Our imaginary (and extremely adventurous) deer would face 33,740 meshes in the standard mesh area of 1,000 square kilometers. In other words, in the course of an average journey of about 30 kilometers (just under 20 miles)—the distance across a standard mesh unit—the deer would be confronted by an average of 184 meshes. Given those figures, the real 600 or so red and fallow deer currently living in Richmond Park in London (a remnant of the hunting herd introduced by the royal family in the 1600s) are unlikely to leave the open spaces and relative peace of their home.

Huge cities are not particularly meaningful for this exercise, however. Measurements gathered from beyond the urban centers are much more informative. Over in continental Europe, one of the many roe deer that currently reside in the tiny country of Luxembourg would encounter about 135 meshes per standard mesh area, or 12 meshes when attempting a 30-kilometer journey. This is the densest road mesh for a country anywhere in the world. The next-highest mesh densities are found in the nearby countries of Belgium and the Netherlands (with national mesh densities of 105 and 61 meshes per standard mesh area, respectively); both are relatively small countries with large human populations. Elsewhere in Europe, the majority of countries (including Denmark, Portugal, and Italy) have a moderate mesh density of between 5 and 20 meshes per standard mesh area. The lowest mesh levels in this part of the world are found in a trio of northern countries, Norway, Sweden, and Finland, which each have a mesh density of about 0.5 to 1 meshes per standard area for the country as a whole. What is rather sobering is that studies of the thresholds within which larger mammals can persist found that local extinction is almost inevitable in landscapes with mesh densities above 20.[3] That is most of Western Europe.

This rather technical exercise may seem a bit tedious, but it describes a reliable way to compare the pattern of road networks in different places.

Over time, these measurements can also be used to assess the rate at which roads multiply and the meshes shrink. This allows us to see just how quickly the grid is intensifying, how the mesh of the net is becoming finer and tighter. And like a real fishing net, this seems to be catching more and more animals, confining them to smaller and smaller areas. For a lot of species, this situation is not simply a theoretical exercise involving imaginary boundaries. Wildlife populations are becoming increasingly enmeshed. In the real world, those thin straight lines on maps, or the geometric patterns we can see from a plane, are actually undeniable, inescapable features of many animals' daily lives—and I'm not just talking about the hard, flat, linear surfaces that vehicles travel along (and the associated risks from traffic and vehicle-related disruptions). Roads also include spaces with conditions and characteristics utterly different from the rest of the landscape. Animals usually perceive the broad area including and surrounding the carriageways (the road corridor) as being endless in length; experiencing it—and this is of fundamental importance—as an elongated, open space that offers no cover. The spatial dimensions of a road (the width of the pavement and the verge; the distance from the habitat on one side to that on the other side; the cumulative area the road occupies) have lots of important consequences for the animals living nearby.

To Cross or Not?

Let's make this more meaningful and turn our theoretical animal into the real thing: a living deer (of any species you may be familiar with) in a relatively quiet rural landscape. It stands nervously alone in the darkening forest at dusk, tentatively considering whether to continue walking toward the gap in the vegetation a short distance ahead. Beyond the edge of the forest is a broad open area, a wide space without any vegetation, which the deer knows from experience takes just a dozen quick paces to traverse. At the moment, it is quiet and dark—yet a few minutes previously, something huge and horribly noisy had rushed past at a rapid pace, its passage preceded by shockingly bright lights. The deer probably cannot project what a close encounter with one of these fast-moving objects might mean (unless it has already had a close but nonfatal call), and it has seen plenty of these disturbing things before, so it is not simply the presence of these fast-moving objects that is of concern. Much more important to the deer is the possibility that predators such as wolves or wild dogs could be waiting in ambush—and the open area ahead offers nowhere for the deer to conceal itself. Yet, there are excellent foraging pastures on the other side of the clearing. Maybe just run for it . . .

In the very top of a tall tree looming high above the open space beside the forest, a hawk (or crow or harrier) surveys the roadside for any casualties that did not make it across during the night. Already it has investigated one object, but found it to be an old, dry frog carcass; not worth consuming. It casts off, gliding effortlessly along above the road before veering off to fly low over the top of the forest on the other side.

Below the gliding bird, a young badger (or, elsewhere, a bandicoot or otter) moves cautiously across a similar open space, pausing at intervals to sniff the breeze, while continuing to move steadily forward. Like the deer, it is concerned about predators, but it has no experience with traffic. It stops momentarily at the edge of the blacktop to examine the strange hard substrate, and then defiantly sets off to cross the road, oblivious to the large object rapidly approaching.

A bewildered young lynx (or maybe a fisher or quoll) crouches silently within a dense thicket of brambles at the edge of the clearing. Only a few nights ago, it had taken the monumental decision, assisted by the violent behavior of its mother, to leave its childhood territory and head off in search of somewhere new to live. The journey so far had been frightening but uneventful. However, only a short time ago, something impossibly noisy and bewilderingly fast, accompanied by terrible smells and alarming brightness, had moved through the clearing just ahead. Nothing in the animal's short life had been so terrifying and unfathomable. As soon as it has recovered from the shock, it heads back into the forest, determined to avoid any such places again.

Early next morning, a snake (or chameleon or monitor) emerges from the forest and slowly advances into the sunlight of the open space. After several overcast days, the reptile is in need of the recuperative effects of a warm surface on which to bask. It can feel radiant heat emanating from the broad, flat surface just ahead, and this seems like an ideal place to soak up some warmth.

Nearby, tiny mammals (voles or dunnarts or mice) living in the dense sward of pasture grasses between forest and the road itself have never even tried to move onto that hot, rough, alien surface. One has just emerged from its compact burrow only a few meters from the asphalt. After a furtive glance skyward to scan for potential aerial threats, it immediately begins gleaning seed heads from the low grass, constantly alert for danger and ready to race back to its hole. These animals spend their entire precarious lives in this grassy, elongated strip near the road, ever vigilant and never far from the safety of their burrows. There is simply no reason to consider venturing onto that utterly exposed road surface.

Finally, a thrush (or creeper or fairy-wren), hidden within a thicket on the very edge of the clearing, sings lustily before diving into the dewy grass close to the forest edge. Worm caught, the bird is instantly gone, back safely within the shade and dense foliage. The broad open area beyond the forest is almost completely a no-go zone, regularly patrolled by several birds of prey. The thrush is happy to live next to the grassy area, as there are sometimes titbits to snack on. These birds never venture far into any wide-open space.

Space Risks

The above vignettes illustrate just some of the reactions that different types of animals may have to the road corridor. Their behaviors are not simply a response to moving traffic, although obviously the various features discussed in the previous chapter all play a role. The noise may be disturbing, distracting, and even frightening, and the fumes and smell may be distasteful or repellent. It might be the strange nature of the road surface that is the problem. Some species appear to be easily disturbed by even the slightest movements or activity, while others adapt quickly and may learn to coexist alongside the rushing traffic (crows, of many different species, seem especially adept at this). Others have learned how to avoid the heaviest traffic (by only crossing very late at night, for example) and, of course, many birds and bats are able to fly happily across without the least concern.

For many species, however, the space itself is the problem, mainly because it offers nowhere to hide, an issue well understood by small ground-dwelling mammals such as voles and rodents. This makes sense, as these little creatures are often a major food source for aerial predators, such as owls and hawks, and for terrestrial hunters of the canid (wolves, coyotes, dingoes) and felid (lynx, bobcat, wild cat) variety. These eternal predator-prey interactions have led to a well-founded wariness among most rodents and other small mammals that just can't run very fast. It's dangerous to move about out in the open, but if you do (and there are often great resources out there), be careful and make sure you are able to hide quickly.

Sure, but what about birds? Their situation is very different from that of slow, poor-sighted, ground-dwelling animals such as rodents. Birds usually have excellent vision; they can react very quickly should they detect movement; and, above all, they can fly. The vast majority will sail confidently above or across the space, as they do all the time—including those birds that live within heavily treed habitats. By contrast, the thicket-dwelling, forest-dependent species (such as the thrush, creeper, or fairy-wren mentioned in the example above) tend to be exceptionally wary of venturing out into open areas. Obviously, the open space we are talking about here is that associated with roads. But forested landscapes often contain plenty of naturally occurring open areas, such as grassy patches, treefall gaps, and storm-induced openings, as well as various water bodies. Indeed, although entirely natural, the space created by streams and rivers is remarkably similar to a road, being a long, wide, linear opening in the forest. Birds have had to deal with these features forever, so do they avoid crossing rivers and roads in the same way and for the same reasons? These are questions worth looking at in a little more detail.

Overexposed

Some of the most insightful studies looking at these "gap-crossing" issues were conducted deep in the Amazonian rainforest.[4] A number of species living in these forests are known as "forest-dependent," because they really cannot live anywhere else. Unlike many similar-sized birds from the temperate Northern Hemisphere, many of which undertake very long migrations, most tropical forest birds are strictly residential. Not only do they not migrate, most don't move very far at all after their initial dispersal from their natal territory. Once they settle in a suitable patch of rainforest, they have all the resources they need in very small area. There they remain for the rest of their often remarkably long lives (it is not unusual for a tropical bird weighing about ten grams (one-third of an ounce) to live for more than twenty years; an average chickadee or tit rarely lives for more than three years). As is the case everywhere in the world, the shape and location of their home range is usually determined by natural geographical features. These might be as subtle as different vegetation types, or physical realities like cliffs, lakes, and rivers—and, of course, roads. Studies showed that, in general, even the small birds living next to a river would be unlikely to fly across to the other side: many species were extremely reluctant to cross a distance of about forty-five meters (fifty yards) of open space.[5] As an even more extreme example, some very reclusive birds would not cross a gap of only six meters (seven yards) width.[6] These species would obviously be seriously affected by any road, let alone the massive swaths being cleared right now as dozens of new roads penetrate deep into this vast but rapidly fragmenting area.

Reluctant balls of feathers in the Amazon may seem a long way from the birds in your local conservation park, but these findings are turning out to be far from rare. In a recent Australian study, detailed observations of birds of all sizes and habitat preferences were made beside roadways varying in width from small local roads to vast multilane motorways.[7] The study found that the wider the road, the less likely birds were to cross, and that the small forest-dwelling species were the most reluctant to cross any road of any size. These are important findings, which expose a dangerous generalization. The simple fact that most birds fly—and often undertake large-scale migrations—has led to the assumption that birds in general are immune to the effects of roads. This is turning out to be far from the truth.

Experimental Motivation

You will recall that when this conversation started, I was on a flight en route to Calgary, on my way to visit the famous Banff National Park in the vast Canadian province of Alberta. As soon as I am through customs, I pick up my rental car and head west, being very careful to stay on the correct side of the road. Only a few minutes later I am on the main east–west motorway, the Trans-Canada Highway, one of the world's great roads. It runs through all ten of Canada's provinces, a total length of

7,820 kilometers (4,850 miles), making it one of the longest continuous roads in the world. But I am not here to traverse the North American continent. Rather, I want to visit one relatively small section of the highway, which starts at the entrance to Banff National Park and extends a little beyond the intersection leading to (the famously gorgeous and potentially loved-to-death) Lake Louise, a stretch of about sixty kilometers (thirty-seven miles). In terms of global road ecology research, this location may well be the single most significant site anywhere in the world; we will return to this spot numerous times. At the moment, however, we are here to consider some crucial early studies of direct relevance to this topic of crossing open spaces.

Personally, I find driving west through Banff National Park to be a rather dangerous exercise, not because of the traffic or the state of the road, but because it's almost impossible to concentrate on driving. In every direction, spectacular, arresting mountain ranges tower above, seeming to loom and glower menacingly as you pass. This stunning landscape is literally breathtaking in its utter wildness. It is also one of those places where you are thoroughly aware of your complete insignificance. The colossal walls of twisted, jagged, soaring rock are on a scale that the mind has trouble comprehending. The lower slopes of the broad Bow River Valley run between parallel ranges clothed in an extremely thick cover of pines. Within the forest of perfectly straight and utterly parallel pine trunks, it is dark, damp, and cold. Still, many species live here, including grizzly bears, elk, and a number of hardy birds.

The limpid glacier-blue waters of the sweeping Bow River rush impatiently down the valley. The river's organic curves and meanders contrast starkly with the dead-straight double-carriageways of the Trans-Canada Highway, which now occupy much of the limited flat land along the center of the valley. With an exceptionally broad grassy median and similarly expansive verges on either side, the entire road corridor is relatively wide, especially for what is mainly just four lanes of traffic. In places, the distance between the forest edges at either side of the road is up to ninety meters (one hundred yards) across; that's a very long way for any animal wanting to cross, let alone a tiny bird not used to flying any distance.

Colleen Cassady St. Clair, an ecologist from the University of Alberta, in Edmonton, has been returning to this place for almost thirty years. She has long been interested in the ways that animals negotiate the barriers and challenges they encounter during their daily or seasonal movements. These movements may involve simply wandering about in search of food or hiding from predators; larger-scale journeys, such as dispersal or migration, give rise to riskier issues. The Bow River Valley has provided her with an ideal place to assess some of the important questions around the way that animals negotiate open spaces.[8] All the animals living here have had to deal with the rapid and all-but-freezing waters of the Bow River for millennia; crossing the more recent Trans-Canada Highway, however, poses a very different challenge.

Colleen was interested in the extent to which the space occupied by the highway, which ranges from sixty to ninety meters (sixty-five to one hundred yards) in width, might represent a barrier to the movement of birds. The willingness to cross a relatively large area of open space varies, for all sorts of reasons. Some experiments testing these ideas had involved capturing the animals and releasing them on the far side of the road, giving them an extreme level of motivation to cross it: the need to return home. Colleen's approach was to try something a little less dramatic.[9] Birds almost anywhere respond to "mobbing" calls, the very conspicuous and specific vocalization that is produced when a predator is detected in an area. Certain species are particularly alert and observant, producing a specific call to which many other birds will rapidly respond—by rushing immediately to wherever the sound is coming from. The function of these calls is to draw attention to the presence of a predator and nullify any chance it has of a surprise attack. If you are a small bird, it is therefore a very good idea to respond rapidly, so that you can learn exactly what and where the danger is and contribute to the general chorus of vocal agitation.

In the forest of Canada, this "Neighborhood Watch" coordinator role is occupied mainly by black-capped chickadees and red-breasted nuthatches, among the most abundant species in many treed habitats. Colleen recorded the mobbing calls of these species and then watched what happened when they were broadcast from the far side of three different types of open space: a river, a treeless meadow, and the highway. As a comparison, she observed what happened when the calls were broadcast over the same distance, but from the birds' side of the gap.

The gap made a big difference, but not really in the way that was anticipated. Other studies had confirmed the extreme discomfort shown by these small forest birds at having to cross a similarly sized gap.[10] The studies had found that birds were more likely to fly all the way around the edge of the gap—a much greater distance—than go straight across. The Banff birds were much the same: although many did actually fly across the open space, they were far more reticent about crossing the river than (and this is the most surprising finding) the road. This was not the expected result, but it was a very convincing study, with more than a thousand birds of thirty-three different species responding to the recorded calls. Why would these birds be more wary of a river than a road?

This question was a source of considerable discussion among Colleen and her colleagues. Eventually they wondered whether the most likely explanation was evolutionary rather than anthropogenic. In other words, maybe the birds were still "getting used" to the road in a long-term sense, it being a relatively recent addition to the local landscape compared with the permanent presence of the river. Certainly, the clear reluctance of the birds to cross the river suggested that they perceived the risk to be greater. This risk would most likely be that of predation, mainly by birds of prey—perhaps the forest birds' finely attuned senses had been honed via millennia of evading hawk and falcon attacks. Such vital skills do not seem to apply to the risks associated with vehicles, however. The staggering numbers of birds being killed on roads may indicate that this type of risk has not yet entered into the fine-tuning of behaviors that might anticipate, detect, and avoid a collision with a car. The need to interact with this entirely new type of terrestrial hazard may still be too recent for car-appropriate responses to have evolved. Or perhaps there are simply too few close escapes for learning to occur or for natural selection to filter out the overly slow or the unobservant. This remains a topic requiring a lot more investigation and experimentation.

Back in the dark roadside forest of Alberta, these conjectures seem rather academic. Almost all of the species in question will soon throw caution to the wind as they set out on their long annual migration journeys away from the increasingly cold and bleak mountains. They will cross endless pastures, rivers, and yes, roads, as they head south. However, this form of movement is very different from flitting across a forest gap, and it is undertaken in a very different manner, often in large groups, high in the sky and during the night. These occasionally vast journeys involve an entirely different set of motivations and risks. Back in the not-so-dark roadside forests of the Amazon—or Australia, or Antigua—the small forest birds that do not migrate (including those hardy chickadees) will still view the nearby gap with familiar trepidation.

Taken

Once you become aware of the issues associated with the space occupied by roads, features such as the very generous separation between the dual carriageways of the Trans-Canada Highway may seem rather excessive. Yet these were included in the design of the road as a way to eliminate the possibility of interactions between vehicles traveling in opposite directions. Head-on collisions are the worst and most frequently fatal type of car accident and are a major concern for all road authorities. The designers of the Trans-Canada saw the "empty" expanses of the Bow River Valley as the chance to make a statement about road safety. And they certainly did: there is no conceivable way that any vehicle traveling westward could possibly run into someone heading east. The gap between the carriageways is up to 120 meters (130 yards) in places and is made up of either rough undulations of gravel in summer or huge piles of dirty snow in winter.

The gap in the middle of this road contributes significantly to the overall width of the highway's enormous footprint (but, again, such a gap is definitely not unique to the Trans-Canada). A rough estimation of the area occupied by the Trans-Canada Highway over the 88 kilometers (55 miles) of road that travel through Banff National Park is about 8 square kilometers (3 square miles). For its entire length, the Trans-Canada takes up an astounding 60,400 square kilometers (23,000 square miles) of land, entirely devoted to this single major roadway.

The main point of this discussion has been to draw attention to the significant area of land that roads occupy, space that was previously farmland, pasture, native or plantation forest, suburbs or natural areas. In engineering jargon, this is known as the "land-take," a term that is blatantly appropriate; roads "take" land from all other functions, permanently dedicating its use to that of serving the insatiable needs of human transportation. There can be some significant benefits: certain animals feed on spilled grain or scavenge on roadkill, while both wild and domesticated species may use road verges as breeding habitat or for grazing or lateral movement.[11] But for the most part, the land area occupied by the road reserve can be considered lost.

Unfortunately, that is only part of the story. While the scale of the land-take may be alarming, in many places in the world this is all too often the start of a much more serious process of destruction. Bill Laurance, from James Cook University in Queensland, Australia, is the leading authority on the way in which the expansion of roads is frequently accompanied by unplanned and often illegal activities.[12] Laurance and his associates have used satellite images and whatever mapping they can find to accurately determine where new roads are being constructed and to identify any sub-sidiary activities occurring in the land surrounding these constructions.

In the vast Amazon region, for instance, Laurance and his colleagues have shown that the proliferation of new roads penetrating into the rain-forest has led inexorably to a tsunami of illegal logging, poaching, mining, and even land speculation.[13] These completely unregulated activities have occurred entirely because of the construction of roads. Without roads, it is virtually impossible to access such forested areas. Once roads are in place, a remarkable array of well-organized and well-financed operations (both sanctioned and dubious) arrive in search of opportunities; the roads also bring small-scale subsistence farmers, who are simply looking for a way to eke out a living. Almost all of the habitat destruction (mainly through illegal clearing and burning) occurring in Brazil has happened in a zone within about five kilometers (three miles) of these new roads. The expansion of these activities and their effects can be viewed via online animations constructed using a series of satellite images taken over several consecutive years. The cancerous spread of this destruction is sickeningly graphic, the deep green of the rainforest steadily being replaced by the malignant yellow and brown of burned-out forest and dying trees—while the roads that enable this devastation are themselves just thin pale lines, barely visible in the context of the surrounding catastrophe.

These road-related activities are most certainly not confined to South America. Similar phenomena are spontaneously accompanying new roads throughout Africa and Southeast Asia. Recently Laurance and his col-leagues investigated the expansion of roads in the Congo Basin, the second largest area of tropical forest after Amazonia.[14] Although the region has always had a plethora of small, short, unpaved service roads, these often become impassable through erosion; once abandoned, they are quickly reclaimed by the jungle. The new roads being constructed and planned are far more durable, however. Governments and corporations (and, no doubt, criminal organizations) have long dreamed of a trans-African high-way connecting countries across the center of the continent. The major obstacle to this vision has always been the extremely remote and difficult terrain, especially the vast tropical forests and the extensive wetlands.

In 2004, however, the long-anticipated east–west connection was completed, and for the first time it became possible to drive from Brazzaville in the Republic of the Congo to Bangui in the Central African Republic. Since then, the pace of road building has ramped up enormously, with the overall length of new roads increasing by 61 percent (although formal details are difficult to verify, much of the funding for these new roads certainly comes from foreign sources, with China being the most prominent). Alarmingly, so have the associated impacts. These include sanctioned activities such as extensive logging leases (with the largest concession being awarded to Chinese corporations), but, again, around 90 percent of the clearing is "informal"—and almost certainly illegal. The timber harvesting has also been accompanied by a dramatic spike in poaching and bushmeat hunting. Conservationists are especially concerned about the future of the significant chimpanzee, gorilla, and forest elephant populations of the region.[15]

The large-scale, time-sensitive, visually engaging analyses being produced by Bill Laurance and others are entrancing but also convincing (check the link mentioned in the endnotes here).[16] The message is straightforward, unequivocal, and as objective as it is possible to be. As a result, these images are presenting the relevant authorities with the realities of what is happening in their backyards. Until very recently, this information was simply unavailable; today, a government official or park ranger can see with her or his own eyes the changes underway in their jurisdictions. In some places at least, there are signs this evidence is leading to acknowledgment that these opportunistic activities require more attention. In other places, of course, even the visual evidence is ignored and denied.

Between the Lines

So far, our discussion has mostly been focused on the roads themselves. We have considered the space they occupy and the way they cancel out and override previous uses or values. Our attention has been fixed on those lines on the maps and satellite images, and on the various human activities that may radiate out from them. We have talked about road density and the challenges animals face when encountering roads. It has all been about roadways, road networks, corridors, and reserves; the hard, flat surfaces that carry the vehicles and the area impacted by them.

Having tried to redress the apparent "invisibility" of roads, I now want to draw attention away from these networks and concentrate on what is—or was—beneath them, to understand what the land was like before the roads were imposed on the landscape and, especially, what happens after construction. The spaces between roads are often referred to as the "matrix," a label that conveys something of the foundational substrate within and on which things may be embedded, ideas developed, or structures arrayed. This perspective is not fixed or formulaic, however; many elements and influences remain in flux. This is very much the dynamic Forman had in mind when he described the "uneasy embrace" between roads and the land.

Once again, this is a perspective best achieved by viewing the landscape from far above. Try this: open the maps app on your laptop, position your location in the center, then expand out twice (say, two clicks up). This will provide an interesting spatial view of the place where you are right now and its geographical surroundings. Of course, as this visualization is in the form of a map, it is not actually a "view" but rather a greatly simplified pictorial representation: a "cartoon" version. All the distances and locations will be spatially correct, but many of the details are hidden. The program (usually) recognizes just a few basic categories, which are indicated in flat, featureless colors: business districts in dull orange, parks and open space in several shades of green, waterways in blue, and so on. Roads, however, are rendered with just a little more detail. Suburban roads are shown in two thicknesses of white, while the major roads have thicker lines in custard yellow (on my screen at least); the relative conspicuousness equates fairly simply to general traffic levels. This visualization shows us something of the road network that exists directly around where we live.

Now, depending on the human population size in your location, slowly scroll sideways until you arrive in a different type of land use—maybe moving into the countryside, or toward the inner city. As the density of the road grid or network or mesh increases, you will notice that the size of the areas between the lines diminishes. These patches may now be suburbs, pastures, industrial estates, farmland, or patches of the original vegetation. Before the roads arrived, however, it was almost certainly very different. What originally was a continuous, undisturbed environment has been subdivided. What was once whole has become fragmented. But what we are particularly interested in here are the patches of green: the parklands, conservation reserves, protected areas. These are critical, because most of the biodiversity of a region lives in these patches. Even in what appears to be leafy suburbs with a lot of wildlife, most of the species will stay put within these remnants—although some may temporarily visit the vast expanse of the suburbs. Relatively few species are able to live with us on a permanent basis in the strange urban ecosystems we have created.

These patches are critically important as reservoirs of nature, as places enabling animals to persist in an increasingly urbanized world. And the bigger the patch, the larger the number of species living within it. This idea—the theory of island biogeography—is one of the fundamental principles of ecology.[17] This theory predicted that a large island will be able to sustain many more species than a series of smaller islands, and remarkably strong support was found on real islands in the southwestern Pacific, around the huge equatorial landmass of New Guinea. These discoveries had a range of practical implications for nature conservation on reserves. Smaller islands were found to have fewer species compared with large islands, and the diversity of species decreased the further an island was from the large landmass that represented the main source of species in the area.

In addition, smaller islands had a greater turnover of species; that is, over extended periods of time (millennia), certain animals disappeared, while new ones turned up only rarely. Local extinction is an ever-present risk. A small island, far out in the ocean, is much more likely to be badly affected by a random event such as a major cyclone or earthquake, or an outbreak of disease, while colonization by new species becomes more difficult as distances between islands increase.

These ideas apply remarkably well to terrestrial "islands" as well, islands such as those patches of green on your screen (you might need to refresh, it's been a while). Some species—for example, certain birds and bats—are able to fly off in search of another patch, but many are not. While the surrounding land may not seem as utterly impassable as the ocean, for amphibians, small ground mammals, forest birds, and plenty of others, it probably is. And that's even without the roads. For many of these species, the fragmentation of the landscape means permanent isolation, remaining hemmed in behind the barrier of the roads, with the risks of traffic and the dangers of the hostile matrix beyond. Just as is the case with oceanic islands, animals confined to habitat remnants face a heightened risk of local extinction. All it would take is a wildfire, an influx of predators, or a catastrophic storm, for many populations to disappear.

Thinking of habitat patches as islands within an ocean of unsuitable land may be useful but is only partially effective. It may be more realistic to picture an island with a brick wall running along its beaches. For too many species, this is entirely appropriate—the road is just such an implacable barrier. The space, the exposure, the unfriendly materials, the sound, the emissions, and especially the traffic, all mean that even a moderately busy road can permanently separate members of the same species from contact, even over relatively small distances. When I followed my own earlier suggestion and brought up the map of my district, this was clearly evident. What appears to be a major green patch—and therefore a vital component of the region's conservation estate—on closer inspection has been split into three much smaller sections by two significant roads. One of these patches contains the university where I have been working for over three decades. During the relatively short time I have been studying the wildlife living within this forest, at least three species—a gliding marsupial and two small ground mammals—have become locally extinct. This was not because of the roads; the gliders were all consumed by native owls and the small mammals probably disappeared because of introduced predators. Nonetheless, the roads running through and around these habitat remnants contribute to their isolation from other nearby patches and have proven to be major barriers to natural recolonization.

Swedish Clarity

I am standing atop what appears to be a rocky hillock on the outskirts of Uppsala, Sweden, with Jan-Olof Helldin, universally known as J-O. J-O is a researcher at the Swedish University of Agricultural Sciences—although his work has long been focused on matters of roads and ecology. After starting to tell me about the structure on which we are standing, J-O soon ventures down more philosophical roads.

I have been directly involved in this field of study for over a decade now, and during this time I've noticed that a small group of Swedish researchers often seem to find the clearest route through difficult conceptual terrain and to ask the really uncomfortable questions. J-O is among the most notorious "repeat offenders." His insights and willingness to discuss issues all the way through to some eventual conclusion (or dead end) have been of enormous benefit. The field we now call "road ecology" has become significantly more critical and coherent—in terms of its triumphs, as well as its flaws and shortcomings—after being examined in the clear Nordic sunlight.

This visit is part of an ambitious and jet-lag-accumulating trip around the world. Over the course of a month, I regularly found myself walking over some sort of reconstructed landform, the noise of the traffic streaming beneath me filtered down to a dull rumble, in the company of a local expert who would explain the context and highlights. As expected, this time it is a bit different. "Yet another wildlife crossing structure, you probably

Figure 8. Female moose trying to cross a road in central Sweden. Photographer Mats Lindqvist.

assume?" J-O asks, with just a hint of mischief. "And you would be right, sort of," he continues, before I have time to respond. "Certainly, plenty of deer, foxes, and maybe a few moose do wander along this ecoduct. Yes, that's the word to use, because this is a genuine 'ecoduct,' functioning in the way it was originally intended, as a connection across the landscape. A much more holistic concept; not simply a way for animals to move across roads."

We will look at these ecoducts in more detail in the following chapter. Clearly, they are intended to assist animals in crossing the road. This term is used, primarily in Europe, to describe the relatively large overpasses, with smaller structures mainly referred to as "wildlife overpasses."

We walk along a little further, reaching an outlook that allows us to realize we are on an elongated, steep-sided ridge, which curves gradually off far into the distance. J-O explains that this huge physical feature is an esker, an accumulation of glacial debris—mainly large, rough rocks— which had fallen into deep, long crevices in the ice in the distant past. When the glaciers disappeared, they left behind a series of these elongated, roughly parallel eskers, which stretch across this part of the country. "If you have a good Nordic imagination, you can imagine these eskers at the base of deep cracks in the ice, which was at least a kilometer-thick right where we are standing." I'm afraid my limited, all too antipodean imagination finds that very difficult to achieve.

J-O points toward the north, his hand sweeping along the curve of the ridge to draw attention to several strange-looking features several kilometers away: three huge, grassy hillocks, bare and unnaturally symmetrical. Even from this distance, there is something powerful and unsettling about them. "The famous burial mounds of Gamla Uppsala, an ancient seat of Scandinavian kings." The earthly resting places of the Norse gods Odin, Thor, and Freyr; or, more pragmatically, the charred remains of warrior kings from the fifth or sixth centuries, violently interred through fire, following Odin's instructions, as the way to Valhalla. Whatever your preference, this is an enormously significant site for the people and history of Sweden. "Before any notion of 'Sweden' existed, actually," says J-O. "At the time these mounds, or barrows, were constructed, Gamla Uppsala would have been a well-known sea port. The mounds would have been by far the largest human constructions in this part of the world. Tangible evidence of power and a physical link to past glories. These connections across the landscape—the geographical relationship between the eskers and the mounds—are still important and greatly valued elements of the landscape around here."

The esker we are now walking along was severed, literally cut in two, back in the 1960s, to allow the passage of a new road. This would have been standard operating procedure for road building anywhere in that era. Big physical obstacle ahead? Blast a way through. Although it seems there wasn't much of a community reaction at the time, sensibilities were very different by the start of the twenty-first century, and the breach in the esker took on a new significance. Public concern over the environmental and cultural impacts of the roadway rose steadily. Physically and philosophically, this road had violated a vital connection, a cultural and historical link between the present and the past. This disquiet steadily permeated the corridors of power, so that when a large-scale transportation project involving construction of a major bypass around Uppsala was put into development, the design included an attempt to "reconnect" the esker. This was unexpected, because the new road was nowhere near the old one. Although the local Uppsala municipality, the Swedish Transport Agency, and the motorway operators were all involved, the cost was borne entirely by the government. The municipality argued that the earlier damage to the esker had been caused by the transport agency, and—despite having veto power over propositions from local governments—the agency agreed to pay for the costs. The construction of the ecoduct, which required challenging design features and considerable local disruption, was completed in 2009. There was no official opening event, no national news coverage, no public explanation. It almost seemed that no one wanted to draw attention to what had happened.

This remarkable story is unfolded by J-O as we work our way down the steep escarpment to the side of the motorway, in order to view the twin tunnels emerging from beneath what is now a large, elongated hill. The sheer volume of material required to reconstruct this massive feature was enormous, and the cost no doubt very significant. J-O has been trying to understand how decisions, such as the construction of this ecoduct, were made within the agency, and so far he has found out little in the way of a guiding process or procedure. You may ask why this matters, and that would be a very good question. From J-O's perspective, it is crucial that the motivation and drivers that lie behind these projects are explored.

"Otherwise, the process associated with the very large commitments of funding, resources, and time required to plan and construct any of these major structures remains mysterious and difficult to understand." J-O stops and turns to face me, looking particularly earnest. "When you meet the people involved in undertaking any big road project, always ask them 'Why?'" It is one more piece of advice I am happy to take on board.

Knowing What We Don't Know

"It's hard enough for me to 'get' all this stuff! All the different things that seem to be important but maybe aren't. How can we expect to explain how a project that is going to cut a conservation park, or farm, or community in half came about and why it is being done in a certain way? How, when even the people making the decisions are not that clear about what they are doing and why?" J-O is on his feet; animated but positive. We have paused at a café in a small town during our tour of southern Sweden, and knowing that I am keen to learn as much as possible about the state of affairs in his country, J-O is describing a major problem faced by road ecologists here—how to comprehend the sheer complexity of the apparently endless, often confounding, interactions that occur between transport infrastructure and the environment—and a possible way through it.

If you have been following the discussion so far, various disconnected concepts and unrelated images may be swirling around your mind: dead animals beside the road, crumpled cars, rodents living happily within centimeters of the traffic, dust and noise wafting through the forest, the grid of roads crisscrossing the landscape. All of this seems to combine into a bewildering and possibly debilitating mess; how on earth can we understand what is happening, let alone begin to do something about it?

"It's hard enough for the experienced people within road agencies who have to manage these concerns. As with almost all environmental issues, trying to fully understand the whole thing requires knowledge and abilities beyond those of the specialists." Having been directly involved in many such projects as an independent consultant working with the Swedish Transport Administration (Trafikverket, the overarching body responsible for all transportation planning in the country), J-O has observed these realities from within. "Even when people are open to learning from others, everyone comes with their assumptions and biases. Some push the road safety angle, others the engineering or maybe the conservation of rare species. It typically ends up as bit of a mess." It is not necessarily the lack of information—enormous amounts of highly relevant data are available these days—that is the obstacle to making sound decisions. Theoretically, today everyone appreciates that a multidisciplinary approach is essential, but that can be difficult to achieve. "Most agency people and consultants are committed to ensuring the best outcomes with the least impact but typically only have a vague idea about how to deal with what can seem like a lot of different types of impacts. Only certain of them will be well understood and then usually only by some. I've seen this so often: there is usually plenty of willingness to work together but uncertainty on what the priorities should be." What is needed is a strategy that enables all of the key impacts to be considered, in a way that all of the participants can work with.

This challenge had floated around Trafikverket for several years without really going anywhere. Finally, in 2015, J-O and several similarly frustrated colleagues decided it was time to tackle it.[18] Meetings were held, attended by representatives from throughout the country, who brought with them many years of experience and plenty of motivation. They wanted to find an approach that could, hopefully, work at both the national and local project level. Conceptual nuts and bolts were identified and placed on the table; discussion, debate, and coffee-fueled argument ensued. Eventually, a conceptual model emerged. This model has proved to be useful both in providing clarity for Trafikverket when considering all the competing elements of designing transportation projects and (at least as important) as an aid to communicating with the wider community. I think it could be valuable for anyone working in this field, so let's have a brief look at what the model's developers came up with. It is actually disconcertingly simple, at least to begin with.

The first step was to identify the main types of ecological impacts associated with roads and whether these could be classified into a few categories. This bit was fairly straightforward. The top three impacts are well known and obvious: (1) roads as barriers to wildlife movement, (2) wildlife collisions with vehicles, and (3) disturbances to roadside environments due to the noise and pollution of traffic. Remarkably, although there was quite a bit of refining and reconsidering, only three additional impact categories were eventually nominated. This meant that there were (just) six predominant environmental impacts associated with roads. The final selections were: (4) the loss of land and habitats, (5) the implications of creating new habitats, and (6) the potential for invasion by alien species. Impacts 5 and 6 are worth describing here in a little more detail.

Impact 5's "new habitats" refers primarily to the noisy, dusty, highly disturbed areas represented either by intentionally constructed parts of the road or simply by the bit of land along the edge of the carriageway: in most cases, animals will colonize the verge, although the median may also be a significant component of habitat. Not only do quite a few small mammals find these areas great places to live, but a wide range of other species regularly patrol the zones on the lookout for food; roadkill and unsuspecting rodents are popular snacks, as are spilled grain, dead insects, and edible human refuse.

Probably the least understood of these environmental impacts is Impact 6, the possibility that roads could enhance invasions of unwanted species; these include rodents, and predators such as feral cats and foxes, as well as introduced amphibians, invertebrates, and pest plants. Although we are well aware of the problems caused by these unwelcome animals and plants, when it comes to the ways in which roads may enhance their spread, there is still much we do not know.

This list of key impacts was not meant to be comprehensive, conclusive, and universally relevant, but it did seem to cover the main concerns in the Swedish context. Even coming up with this unexpectedly brief list was a significant outcome in the development of the model; it allowed the participants to realize that the range of major impacts was not endless but actually quite manageable. It was also clear that quite a lot was already known about most of the impacts.

For the next part of the exercise, the group attempted to consider what a long-term solution to each of these impacts might look like: an ideal, impossible, perfect scenario. This "dream big, entirely unrealistic, no-limits" exercise would have been fun (despite everyone being all too aware that brutal reality was never far away); nonetheless, it served a serious purpose in the process of thinking about how we might head toward this utopia. The resulting vision for each impact was as follows:

1. Infrastructure that is completely permeable, offering no barriers to movement.
2. Road mortality no longer occurs: animals are able to traverse the road without risk of being struck by a vehicle.

3. All habitats near roads are completely free of disturbance.
4. Although land-take is inevitable, impacted habitats should be protected.
5. Roadside verges are managed effectively to enhance biodiversity.
6. There are no species invasions.

Now, wouldn't that be nice! The reality, of course, even in a utopian, air-fueled, silent, no-waste, floating-solar-powered-car future, is that we are not going to get even close to achieving these visions. But a sensible and sensitive transportation agency will nonetheless begin with these ideals and work toward them.

With this list written on the whiteboard, the subsequent stages of the model-building process involved much more pragmatic discussions about three different elements of activity: the strategic goals that a committed and suitably funded transportation agency might seriously set; the relevant legal settings that either constrain or compel agency actions; and, finally, where the agency is currently sitting in relation to its commitment to environmentally sensitive road planning.

The latter stages of the process will clearly be different in every country and, indeed, at any given time. There is no point entering any further into what was, after all, primarily an internal bureaucratic government exercise undertaken by some overly motivated Swedish road people. What this does provide is a practical framework for anticipating, and then planning, what needs to be done. If those admittedly utopian visions listed above are to be seen as anything but a fantasy, there is plenty of serious thinking and planning to be done. Making genuine progress will be hard, but the Swedes have shown what is possible. Thankfully, they are not alone; hopeful signs are emerging all over the world. But with new roads being planned daily, we need to do something *now*.

Part II

Changed Road Conditions Ahead

3

BRIDGING THE GAP

Australia is very old, very dry, and very flat. There is a road all the way to the summit of the highest peak, Mount Kosciuszko, a dizzying height of 2,228 meters (7,310 feet) above sea level (only used in emergencies). Although it may not be particularly high, the surrounding area of mountainous ridges and deep valleys, known without irony as the Australian Alps, is rugged and cold, with extensive snow cover during winter. Any animal living permanently in this region would have to be tough and resilient, although even those characteristics may not be enough for long-term survival.

One such species is the diminutive mountain pygmy possum, a supercute marsupial whose entire distribution is limited to a combined total of only 12 square kilometers (about 4.6 square miles) spread over several widely dispersed mountaintops. Although it is often described as "cryptic," "invisible" might be a more appropriate word for this animal, which lives deep below the snowfields, hiding within the spaces of periglacial rock screes and boulder fields and very rarely coming to the surface. These jumbles of rocks, devoid of all vegetation other than moss and some stunted ferns, run up the slopes at erratic intervals throughout the mountains. Given that these harsh, patchy places are the preferred habitat of the pygmy possum, it is not entirely surprising that the animal was only discovered in 1966.

Studying this beast has been extremely challenging for obvious reasons, but through the strenuous efforts of a small number of researchers, some fascinating—and alarming—features of the possum have been (literally) unearthed.[1] This tiny mammal (it weighs only about 40 grams [1.4 ounces]) is Australia's only hibernating marsupial, sleeping away the cold months among the rocks deep below the snow. Strangely, for much of the year there appears to be almost complete spatial segregation of the sexes, with the females remaining in the highest parts of the mountains while the males spend most of their time in slightly milder conditions further down the slopes. With the coming of spring, the males make the arduous journey uphill in search of females, moving between the interconnected spaces between the rocks and boulders. The females prepare for the breeding season by feasting on the protein- and fat-rich bodies of bogong moths, which live within the same spaces among the rocks. Stupendous numbers of these moths emerge in early spring and undertake massive migrations down the mountains, sometimes causing blizzard-like conditions in nearby towns. At the completion of the breeding season, the young males—most of whom will die soon after the extreme exertions of mating—disperse downhill, via the same rocky subterranean passages used by their fathers. By late summer, the mountaintops have become virtually male-free again.

The complex interaction between critical timing, careful movements, specific nutrition, and constrained geography has always demanded a terrifyingly fine balance; virtually any alteration to these closely connected variables could have terrible consequences. Predictably, the warming of the climate has already been little short of catastrophic for these vulnerable animals. Less snow, more severe storms, higher temperatures, prolonged droughts, frequent fires, and especially the almost complete collapse of bogong moth numbers, are combining to pose very serious threats to the survival of this species. And as if all of that wasn't enough, these tiny, fragile, and sensitive creatures have found that their only habitat coincides exactly with places people love to visit. In a country where snow is a very limited resource, alpine tourism has long been a major threat to the possums. In such a fragile environment, any activity that disturbs the land surface can have serious impacts.

Ian Mansergh, a professional biologist with a passionate interest in the wildlife of Australia's so-called High Country, has been actively involved with mountain pygmy possums since the early 1980s. He was the first ecologist to investigate their strange, secretive lives beneath the boulders and has been directly engaged in their plight for decades. As well as being a thorough and careful scientist, Ian is also forthright, blunt, and direct when it comes to "his" possums.

> These poor buggers [the possums] spent millennia successfully hiding from people, only to have the misfortune of living where we like to play. Now they have to cope with the unholy reality that snow-covered mountains attract hordes of humans, and that means serious money for tourism operators. And state governments. If there is a buck to be made—or a few jobs—the rules that are supposed to minimize environmental impacts can be bent or ignored. The resorts have sometimes been a law unto themselves. If they wanted more roads or ski runs, the authorities were right behind them. There is often little anyone could do to stop them.[2]

Any road built along the slopes almost inevitably cuts through the boulder fields—including the original roads in the area, which were little more than dirt tracks. But it is the modern paved version, built to take masses of cars and tour coaches, that has had the biggest impact on these rocky sections. Road surfacing requires the substrate to be thoroughly compacted to provide a stable foundation for the blacktop, and the road construction process dramatically reduces or completely removes the interstitial gaps between the rocks. Soon after the first of these modern paved roads was installed, the normally invisible possums were detected on the surface, presumably because they were unable to find a way beneath the rocks. This exposed them to predators such as owls, foxes, and feral cats—and to (an increasing number of) cars. Instantly, the traditional way the males had always progressed uphill toward the females and downhill when dispersing was fundamentally changed. In the seasons that followed, the ratio of males to females in the upper areas was dangerously altered, with males, young and old, being unable to find a way through. Normally, this serious but very specific issue would not have been noticed or reacted to by the authorities. But mountain pygmy possums had become celebrities, supercute mascots whose images proliferated on mugs, bumper stickers, and merchandise. Word that they were in trouble quickly spread well beyond the resort coffee shops. As the situation became more widely known, pressure mounted. "These attractive and charismatic creatures attracted a lot of public attention and forced both the resorts and the state government to think seriously about doing something," says Ian. But just what was not at all clear.

Given his intimate knowledge of the species and the area, Ian was one of a small group of people who tried desperately to come up with some sort of solution. The characteristics of this particular problem were unique; simply copying an approach from elsewhere was unlikely to work (if some other rock-space dwelling mammal was having similar issues, they hadn't heard about them). It was an extremely specific and localized issue: how to allow the possums to travel up and down the mountain within the now-severed boulder fields. Obviously, the pinch point was the crushed rocks beneath the road; this was literally a roadblock. It was decided, therefore, to try to remove this obstacle by replicating as closely as possible the jumble of rocks that made up the boulder fields within which the animals lived. A long corridor of large rocks was constructed along the slope leading toward the females' habitat. Where this crossed the road itself, two concrete box culverts were installed, although unlike typical fauna underpasses, these were stuffed loosely with large rocks. At the entrances to the tunnels, metal grating allowed the possums access but prevented anything larger from entering. Well, that was the theory.

When word of these constructions got out, community interest in this unusual intervention was intense. The culverts were quickly and aptly dubbed "tunnels of love" by the media (some of whom were decidedly skeptical and critical of the approach), making Ian and his colleagues more than a little concerned. "We tried to explain that this was very much a one-off experiment and that we really couldn't predict what might happen. But no one listened to our typical scientific caution, of course, and expectations grew," Ian told me recently. To assess what was happening, traps that captured small mammals safely were set up throughout the area, while special cameras were set up in the tunnels. But would anything happen?

To quote directly from one of Ian's publications: "Within two weeks of the corridor being constructed, male mountain pygmy possums were using it. Within 90 minutes of the camera being installed [in the tunnel], the first possum was photographed."[3] Even this dry, scientific prose cannot hide the relief and excitement felt by the researchers. "We were ecstatic!" Ian told me. When they realized what the capture data and photographs were showing, their excitement only increased. "Following the very first breeding season, the sex ratio and survival rates returned to what we knew was normal in undisturbed populations. It was hard to believe! Somehow our clumsy, simplistic but ecological thinking had worked." However, he was also well aware that just because some possums seemed to be using the structures at the beginning, this did not necessarily mean they would continue to "work" in the longer term. Four years of patient and demanding fieldwork followed, and this confirmed their optimistic predictions: males routinely used the rocky corridors and tunnels to disperse, and survival rates were similar to those of populations in undisturbed areas.

When I spoke to Ian about those early days, he reminded me that the first tunnel was now more than thirty years old (a second was built soon after and another is currently being installed elsewhere, both following much the same design). A lot of research has been undertaken since and has established these Australian "tunnels of love" as one of the world's longest-lasting—and most enduringly successful—conservation interventions; those tiny marsupials are still squeezing their way through the boulders beneath busy roads as they search for mates. Whether they can withstand the effects of certain global changes is another matter.

Under and Over

I wanted to start with this story, because those "tunnels of love" represent the first example of something being constructed specifically to allow wildlife to safely cross a road that I can remember ever hearing about. And I wasn't the only one paying attention. For several reasons—the novelty of the approach ("A culvert filled with rocks!"); the fascination with mountains and snow in an otherwise flat, hot continent; and, undoubtedly, the attractiveness of the subject species ("Is this the cutest animal on the endangered list?")—interest in these animals and their tunnels has been enormous. This fascination continues today; as I write, massive fires are sweeping through the very locations where the pygmy possums live, again reminding us of the promise of these old tunnels ("Will they be 'tunnels of *life*' this time?" asks one headline).

The original tunnel was constructed in 1986, long before there was any coherent notion of "road ecology" as a concept or any general recognition of the threats posed by traffic and transportation infrastructure. The possum tunnels are fascinating—but mainly as a bespoke solution to a local problem, a practical way of addressing a specific issue: in this case, enabling a species with unusual habits to move about safely despite the impact of a particular road. This kind of response has been happening all around the world for decades. Just as one example, small culverts to protect migrating amphibians were being installed throughout Europe as early as the 1950s; these now number in the thousands. Much larger tunnels—initially, simply standard commercial culverts or pipes, originally designed for water—have also been installed, explicitly for larger animals. Among the first of these were the celebrated underpasses constructed in the 1970s to reduce the number of Florida panthers being killed on the roads of that American state.[4]

All of these underpasses provide a way for animals to cross roads safely in particular locations, and all are mainly direct or slightly adjusted copies of existing tunnel and culvert designs. The biggest change from the original has been in dimension: amphibians and small mammals prefer small tunnels—whereas elephant and cassowary underpasses, for example, are obviously much larger. The other significant modification has been the addition of ledges, hiding places, and other so-called furniture; some of these will be discussed later.

If crossing passages that go under the road have not evolved very far from the standard concrete box or pipe, the over-the-road variety has seen extraordinary innovations in terms of design, materials used, construction techniques, and the way in which the top of the overpass is handled. Enabling and encouraging a huge variety of animals to cross roads above the traffic has become the most creative and exciting element of contemporary road ecology. These fauna overpasses are now the largest and most complex (and expensive) crossing structures. When these structures are especially long and wide, and provide continuous habitat over the road, they are often known as ecoducts or landscape bridges.[5]

Fauna overpasses are undoubtedly the wildlife-crossing structures most people are aware of, being enormous, conspicuous, and—in Europe at

Figure 9. Wet culvert with fauna furniture allowing access for smaller species, and showing exclusion fencing above with metal strip to prevent climbing by arboreal mammals. Near Brisbane, Australia. Photographer Darryl Jones.

least—seemingly everywhere. France probably has the most (numbering in the hundreds), and that country also appears to have started the whole thing. As far as I have been able to determine, the first such structure was built in 1963, in the Forêt de Fontainebleau on the A6 motorway, not far from Paris.[6] Its function was not, however, related to road safety or conservation; it was a bridge for game (*passage à gibier*), installed explicitly so that roe deer could move freely throughout a hunting reserve without being hemmed in by the roads. It was a structure with a genuinely revolutionary purpose. Prior to the French Revolution, hunting was strictly reserved for the nobility. Since those tumultuous times, the symbolic importance of the citizenry—as opposed to the privileged elites—being able to hunt has been fiercely protected, with the hunting lobby retaining enormous political power in France. These early overpasses were modest in size (only about 5 meters/16 feet in width) and cheaply constructed of wood. They were only able to span fairly narrow roads. The rapid evolution of modern-day ecoducts, from these simple structures to the extraordinary and sometimes gigantic spans now crossing motorways and rail corridors throughout the world, is evidence of the creativity possible—even among transportation engineers.

Indeed, this ability to provide a design solution to a specific problem, often by adapting an existing design, is what the best engineers have always done. Every bend, river, hill, swamp, and cultural site requires its own local solution to what is almost always just a slight variation of what has been done a thousand times before. Engineers are masters of applying familiar concepts to a new challenge.

Increasingly, however, entirely new concepts and approaches have become necessary. Stricter regulations, societal expectations, and the necessity to cater for the needs of unfamiliar species have led to even more innovation and creativity. Later, we will visit strange suspended metal waves built to guide bats safely over a motorway in France, have a guided tour of a flexible dormouse ladder in England, and marvel at what has been done for langurs in India. These are all local—and very clever—solutions to the problem of assisting animals across the road in specific places. But what about doing this for entire sections of road?

Whether intended to assist possums, panthers, or peccaries, all crossing structures aim to eliminate some sort of impediment to the movement of the species. In the language of road ecology, these structures attempt to overcome the barrier effect of roads. In other words, they should enable the animals to cross the road without the risk of interacting with traffic. In many ways, this remains the primary focus of the field; a place where the engineers, designers, and even local community groups can concentrate their efforts and concerns. The often-remarkable constructions that result are rightly celebrated, admired, and even copied. They provide a tangible—indeed concrete—manifestation of all that effort and thought.

There is another component of the structure of a road that has provided an enormously useful way to enhance permeability, the fundamental concept of enabling animals to move "through"—permeate—the road. Virtually all roads cross watercourses, and finding ways to manage these extremely dynamic natural features has been a major challenge for road engineering since Roman times. In most cases, it is critical to allow the water to flow unimpeded. If this imperative is neglected or ignored, moving water has a way of getting its way in the end. There are endless examples of inappropriately designed sections of road being slowly undermined or suddenly swept away. Typically—depending on the size of the water body—pipes, culverts, bridges, or viaducts are installed, allowing the water to flow safely beneath the road. This space offers another opportunity for wildlife movement, provided the terrain and geological features allow it. A major new approach has been to greatly expand this space beneath the road, forming a viaduct. If properly designed, this a simple way for animals to wander under the road, almost completely unhindered by the physical features of most underpasses.[7]

But it's not just about managing the occasional storm. River systems, and the complex riparian habitats along their banks, support an extraordinary diversity of aquatic animals and plants, all of which may be impacted by any roadworks that occur in these water bodies. The management of issues associated with roads in riverine environments is one of the most important areas of road ecology, and considerable effort is being put into understanding how to replicate natural features such as riffles and

Figure 10. Recently constructed viaduct crossing showing planted vegetation and refuge poles, Brisbane, Australia. Photographer Darryl Jones.

reedbeds, which are essential for the continuing existence of many species living in these areas.[8] One key challenge is how to enable the seasonal migrations of species up and down watercourses, as has happened for millennia. Such ecological restoration activity is currently one of the most creative areas of this field. It is also fair to say, however, that this crucial issue receives much less attention than it deserves, possibly because it appears to be only indirectly associated with the road above. There has been a tendency to think that "the hydrologists will take care of that stuff," in much the same way that we used to think that "the road engineers will take care of the wildlife stuff." Roads need aquatic ecologists as well.

Roads and Creatures, Great and Small

Animals have been encountering and crossing roads since the very first tracks, paths, or trails were formed by our very, very distant ancestors. Actually, this may be the wrong way around: humans were probably using trails originally formed by animals over the course of millennia, long before there would have been anything resembling a human-produced passageway. Eventually, however, the number of people using these paths and the increasing size of their modes of transport would have required wider passages. As these paths became busier, the animals would have been less likely to continue using them, as least during the day. Sleds, sledges, wheeled carts, carriages drawn by donkey or horse (or ox or elephant or camel), bicycles, automobiles, trucks, and eventually giant road trains; the bigger the vehicle, the bigger the required passageway. And with an increase in the size of vehicle came an increase in weight and the need for carriageways with a solid surface. In the blink of an eye, we have gone from avoiding a bear in our horse-drawn carriage to worrying about moose while careening down a twelve-lane autobahn in an airtight metal box. For the animals living nearby, the dangers have also increased enormously.

By the time we had progressed to a tarmac road a couple of lanes wide with a steady stream of traffic, the risks and concerns for local animals considering crossing to the other side had become serious. As well as the width of the space that needs to be traversed, the abundance of vehicles represents a very significant issue. For the many nocturnal species, the simplest approach is to wait until there are fewer passing vehicles; humans tend to travel about much less frequently late at night. This can be misleading, however, as the most dangerous roads to cross are those with moderate and unpredictable traffic levels: many more animals are killed when road traffic is intermittent. Very low levels of traffic tend to be relatively safe, while most species do not even try to cross when there is a continuous flow of vehicles. There are some important exceptions to this generalization, of course, with migratory amphibians being an obvious example.

As should be clear by now, a vast and extremely diverse array of species face immense problems when confronted by roads and traffic. This is a global issue posing enormous challenges. Prosperous and poor nations alike face similar difficulties. Yet, unlike so many other huge environmental problems, this multidimensional, technically difficult, ecologically complex suite of concerns has somehow resulted in an unprecedented level of international cooperation and collaboration. Innovative technical solutions and unexpectedly courageous engineering approaches have become almost normal in this very new but rapidly maturing hybrid field. The resulting remarkable structures, and the tangible hope and sense of achievement they bring, and—most importantly—the animals that use them every day, are the beating heart of this book. This is a story that needs to be told.

I have already alluded to some of the innovative crossing structures being designed and installed around the world. We will get to more of those a little later. But before we do, I want to explore just how we got there. How is it that I am currently standing on a gigantic artificial hill, constructed over a large freeway in Europe, built primarily for snakes? Or that we are now able to watch video of rare pangolins using a rainforest-covered overpass in Singapore? Such structures would have been complicated, potentially risky, and undoubtedly costly to build. Why didn't the decision makers and bean counters do what they always do and say: "Too difficult, too dangerous, too expensive!" How did any of this catch on?

Before we follow this thread, it is important to appreciate that there are multitudes of structures under roads, enabling the movement of pedestrians, cyclists, domesticated animals, farming equipment, service vehicles, and all sorts of other things that have nothing to do with wildlife. And then there are the millions of pipes, drains, and culverts beneath every road on the planet; ever since they were installed, animals have been using them as a way to move about safely. Such wildlife activities were not planned for or even anticipated by the people who designed and installed roadway drainage systems. But they are now. The basic features of these structures have been reimagined for use as wildlife passages throughout the world.

Historically, however, right up until a few decades ago this adaptation of existing designs has been extremely piecemeal and uncoordinated. Engineering workshops were coming up with solutions to local problems, and experiments and field studies were being undertaken by individuals, companies, agencies, and universities throughout the world—but in general, there was little or no sharing of these potentially important ideas. What was needed was a way of bringing all of this disparate activity together. The integration, in Europe, of global knowledge and practices around ecology and transportation is possibly the most profound achievement of this field so far. If coming up with crossing structures that allow animals to move about safely is the beating heart of this book, then the

Figure 11. Large fauna underpass in Banff National Park, Alberta, Canada.
Photographer Darryl Jones.

story of this extraordinary, cross-cultural, international collaboration is the blood supply.

Integrating

This venture we call "road ecology" is a form of international collaboration that did not just happen suddenly. Enormous amounts of research and experimentation have been underway for decades, in universities, government departments, consultancies, dedicated NGOs, and within the transport authorities themselves. Everyone was doing their own work, often unaware of what was happening elsewhere. It wasn't the lack of information. It was the lack of integration. What was missing was a common goal.

This is the sort of perspective that only comes after decades of constrained impatience and careful observation. Hans Bekker (whose quote this is) and a small international group of dedicated colleagues are responsible for the processes that have enabled the cooperative, complex, and creative enterprise we now call "road ecology" to put down roots, grow, and bear fruit.[9]

I had the privilege of spending several days with Hans at his home in the north of the Netherlands. We searched for signs of otters under bridges, checked badger pipes and amphibian tunnels, and walked over many ecoducts. We shared a lot of cheese and beer, and explored the canals in his small boat, all the time discussing habitat loss and transportation infrastructure, among other things. In Holland it is impossible to limit such a topic to roads alone; the entire country's network of transportation infrastructure includes endless canals, with roads and railways superimposed over the top. Those theoretical exercises in mesh density and habitat fragmentation mentioned earlier take on a far more acute focus when you are walking, driving, or sailing through the landscape to which they relate. It becomes immediately clear why the all-encompassing project of "defragmentation" originated in this part of Europe.

Hans began his career in the sprawling government body responsible for transportation, Rijkswaterstaat, a directorate within the Ministry of Infrastructure and Water Management. Rijkswaterstaat has been operating since 1798, initially as part of the Ministry of Defense. Given the critical importance and complexity of the transportation infrastructure of roads, canals, rivers, and railways in the Netherlands, this is a huge and powerful organization. Thankfully, it takes its environmental responsibilities very seriously, and Hans was pleased to obtain a position in which he could engage in practical management. Although straight out of Wageningen University, his academic training suited this type of work perfectly. His degree was new, nontraditional, and multidisciplinary—eco-engineering," he calls it—a blend of environmental science, ecological theory, and civil engineering. He claims that he wasn't particular good at the science or the engineering but reveled in the mix, enjoying being challenged to think outside the box, to consider alternative perspectives, and to search for solutions in unexpected places. "I think I was one of those students who saw immediately why you need to consider things from many angles, to get other perspectives and seek opinions from elsewhere." This meant trying to bridge the traditional focus on issues within strict disciplines. His most potent skill was neither technical nor scientific; rather, it was the ability to bring people together, to identify who had the relevant information and how to encourage these people to become involved. These were skills Hans learned step by step to employ soon after arriving at his desk at the ministry headquarters in the Hague during the 1970s . . . although I get the impression that he wasn't in the office all that often.

Verging

One of the first issues he was handed was the management of roadside verges. This may seem pretty tame for an ambitious young eco-engineer, but it was a hot topic at the time. The design and maintenance of verges was an important issue in the thoroughly modified landscapes of Holland. What may be regarded as "simple roadside edges" was actually of great significance as habitat and for the conservation of biodiversity. Management of this vast (if narrow) zone throughout the country was mainly a matter of mowing, a massive undertaking, with a large workforce kept busy more or less continuously throughout the warmer months. The standard approach had always been to mow "hard and low," many times a year. But new ecological ideas were starting to be considered. Would mowing less often still work? How best to promote insect diversity in these areas? Should mowing occur when the plants were flowering? What about all the voles and mice living in the verges? How important was the trash thrown from cars? Although these questions may seem almost trivial, at the time they were sometimes seen as dangerously radical. Such notions were emerging directly from the latest ecological studies. Instead of remaining as esoteric debates among university intellectuals, these ideas were being discussed by managers in government departments and in regional offices. This raised a potentially very big problem, something instinctively obvious to Hans: the people carrying out the actual work, the contractors, the men (almost entirely) who drove the mowers, were being left out of the plans. But the radical ideas being discussed by their bosses could completely change the way they did their work.

> These guys, I knew, would not like being told what to do by us "office" people. They assumed that no one would bother to explain to them why things might need to change. That we all thought that they were just laborers, the "shovel and tractor guys." I could see trouble coming so I helped organize meetings all over the country. I knew what had to be done and rang around the maintenance depots, spoke to the local managers and then went, myself, down to the machinery sheds. Over a coffee we tried to explain in simple language what we were trying to do. And you know, the field guys responded really well. They could see exactly what was being proposed and why it might be important. But what they appreciated the most was that someone from HQ had bothered to come and talk to them directly. This way of doing things was an approach I have found to be valuable in all my work: start at the bottom. Respect the people doing the basic work, the mowers, the office helpers, the interns—everyone. People like to be listened to and treated as equals and then they are keen to work cooperatively. It has always worked for me.

This was a philosophy Hans and his colleagues were able to apply across the country. Rijkswaterstaat wanted to roll out new verge–management plans in all the provinces. These changes were best explained in person; sending a letter or simply making a phone call is just not appropriate sometimes. And so began the process of organizing meetings all over the country ("Green people meetings," Hans called them), quietly noting the key individuals in each provincial office so that problems could be solved together. In a relatively short time, Hans found he had a network

Figure 12. Mowing the roadside verge near Itirapina, Sao Paulo State, Brazil.
Photographer Marcel Huijser.

of people from most provinces with whom he could work effectively and share ideas, people he could call whenever he need to discuss an issue. Hans had no idea just how important this network—and his networking skills—would become.

Badgering

Shortly after Hans and his colleagues had established their collaborative network, a project emerged that encapsulated many of the central issues of what would become the field of road ecology. During the 1970s, the concepts of ecological science were still being developed and popularized, leading to radical new ideas about the relationships between humans and nature—including the use of ecological principles to address civil engineering issues. Inevitably, environmental activism also became more prominent in this period.

In the Netherlands during the 1970s and 1980s, an important and symbolic focus of community concern was the badger, a well-loved creature, even though it was actually rarely seen. When researchers discovered that this reclusive animal's numbers were declining dramatically, this became a major priority for the Dutch conservation movement. And as the only badgers most people ever saw were those dead beside roads, the role of vehicle strike, and of roads more generally, quickly became a potent cause for the public. A well-organized NGO, Das en Boom (Badger and Tree), started a public campaign aimed at drawing attention to the badger problem and rapidly attracted support throughout the country. The government body directly responsible for transportation was obviously going to be a target.

At other times and in other places, it would have been normal for any typical enormous, monolithic government agency to simply ignore, deny, or—more likely—pay lip service to a "niche cause" such as badger conservation. Rijkswaterstaat was, for the most part fairly receptive to public concerns, but a positive response was even more likely now that they had a keen young staff member who was both a passionate mammologist and someone with excellent organizational skills. The badger issue was something Hans was prepared to take on. Leveraging the existing network of contacts who had been brought together for the roadside verge work, Hans quickly and efficiently began organizing key people in Rijkswaterstaat's provincial offices to determine what was known about badgers throughout the country and, especially, to identify specific spots where large numbers were being killed on the roads. In a relatively short time, about forty key badger black spots were identified. That type of work was expected of someone from within Rijkswaterstaat. Much less usual was the willingness of a person explicitly "from the government" to engage directly with the community and conservation groups that had formed to campaign on behalf of the badgers. Nonetheless, Hans—and equally as importantly, his boss—were keen to meet the campaigners and to express their willingness to cooperate for a common cause: addressing the role of roads in the decline in badger numbers in the Netherlands. They were unusually open and transparent about these interactions with both the ministry and the conservationists, and it seems to have worked. And in the long run, both sides came to appreciate that much more was possible when they cooperated.

When it became horrifyingly clear how severely badgers were being hammered (at one stage during the 1980s the total number within the entire country was only around 1,200 animals, with 25 to 300 badgers being killed annually on roads), even the national government began to take notice. The Ministry of Nature Protection developed a national badger protection plan, and within Rijkswaterstaat, Hans and numerous dedicated people began to think about what practical measures could be used to address the number one issue: how to stop badgers from being killed by collisions with vehicles on roads. (Substitute "badger" with a species from a very long list of animals killed on roads anywhere in the world and you have a very similar story.)

The most obvious approach was to try and prevent them getting onto the road in the first place by erecting a physical barrier, typically a fence. The next consideration was how to enable them to cross the road safely. As a first step, some sort of tunnel—a familiar and simple engineering solution—was regarded as a suitable crossing structure. And so began countrywide discussions on issues concerning fence design, optimal pipe size, overcoming drainage problems, and many other badgercentric concerns. We don't need to dwell on the details here, but eventually these practical measures were undertaken throughout the Netherlands. There were some spectacular failures and plenty of arguments, as well as a variety of other approaches that were tried—but, eventually, the barriers and crossing structures were installed. More than forty years later, many of those original badger tunnels are still in place. Recovery was slow, but today Dutch badger populations total more than five thousand animals, and the species is no longer classified as threatened.[10]

Among the many things Hans and his colleagues learned from these experiences were the enormous benefits—if not the clear necessity—of collaboration and cooperation. Bringing together a diverse group of people with appropriate backgrounds and expertise to address a common problem, facilitating the process of sharing knowledge, and learning from one another were always going to yield better outcomes than a competitive, individualistic approach. Unusually perhaps, for a huge government department, Rijkswaterstaat had long espoused and supported these values, and Hans was ideally positioned to utilize them. "There are probably entire libraries on business leadership and MBAs specializing on optimal teamwork strategies out there. It was always for me a very simple philosophy: be open, respect everyone, seek out others' knowledge and skills, have patience, and encourage everyone to work toward a common goal."

Poldering

A large, much-used map of the Netherlands has been spread over the dining table where we have just finished our lunch (numerous cheeses and very dark bread I seem to recall as I write this). Hans is smoothing the creases in the paper and closely scrutinizing an area close to his home, near the center of the map. Even from a distance, I can see that much of the land to the west looks quite different from the rest of the map; the road network is more even and rectangular and the spaces between the roads are generally larger. More pragmatically, these parts of the map are in a different color. Hans anticipates my question: "These are the newer Dutch polders; huge areas of reclaimed land, protected by dikes. Until the second half of the twentieth century, this entire area was underwater, yet it is now some of the most productive agricultural land in the world. Truly one of the engineering marvels of the world." That is most certainly not an idle claim. The areas that have been reclaimed from the North Sea are massive and contribute to the remarkable productivity of a small country, about one-third of which is still below sea level.

Although the extraordinary process of constructing dikes, pumping out the water, and gradually rejuvenating the land began in the twelfth century (long before the invention of bulldozers and gigantic pumps—and concrete), the greatest efforts have been much more recent. Following a series of catastrophic inundations (the most serious occurring in 1953, which claimed almost two thousand lives and rendered vast areas of prime farming land unusable), the precarious nature of large portions of this very low-lying country became starkly evident to the entire nation. Living with the prospect of the sea returning at any time seems to be a permanent preoccupation in Dutch thinking. It also compels them to consider, very carefully and critically, solutions to this existential threat that simply must be as sound and trustworthy as possible. And when this threat endangers a large proportion of the country's population and land, the necessity of a collective approach, of working together toward a common goal, becomes paramount.

"We call it 'poldering,'" says Hans, spreading his hands out over the reclaimed parts of the map. "A most suitable word for finding a way through serious difficulties and differences in order to achieve a really large and complicated objective. Our experience with bringing together lots of people to address our badger problem made us think that this could possibly also be applied at a much larger scale." And by that, he meant on a *continental* scale!

Directed

One of the key outcomes of the national collaboration on badger management was the number of great ideas originating in unexpected places and with unlikely people. This is probably the case with almost all large organizations; most of the time there is no method for finding out what is happening in distant and often disparate places. For Hans, an obvious antidote to this all-too-familiar organizational dislocation was to collate these sensible and practical ideas into some sort of publication. But not just another tedious departmental report or dry government document; it had to be something that people within the ministry would actually read and find useful. The resulting book, *Natuur over Wegen* (*Nature across Motorways*), written in both Dutch and English and published by Rijkswaterstaat in 1995, was the complete antithesis of most official government publications.[11] (And although no authors are specified, Hans was project manager and part of the editorial team.) We have become used to colorful, attractive, and nicely designed documents "selling" government policies and promises these days. Back in the 1990s, however, *Natuur over Wegen* was a distinctive achievement, beautifully designed and overflowing with ideas, examples, and suggestions, all of which were illustrated in useful detail.

Even while it was being put together, Hans and his colleagues knew that publishing *Natuur over Wegen* was a significant event. As we sit in his living room, he hands me a well-worn copy with obvious pride. Even from a cursory flick through the pages it is clear that this book project represented a major moment in this story, an opportunity to go well beyond national boundaries and possibly develop something around the world. "When we realized just what had been achieved in one small country, it was obvious that we needed to share these ideas across Europe. This simple book was a remarkable catalyst for some very big things," Hans exclaims. He was not to know it at the time, but publication of *Natuur over Wegen* would be followed by a series of historic events—historic in the sense not just of occurring in the past but, equally, of long-lasting significance"

The colossal specter towering above all the countries of Europe, the unavoidable woolly mammoth standing in the town square, the reality that anyone taking the slightest interest in the environment of this region cannot ignore, is that of fragmentation. This has been the primary environmental issue for decades, and the recent advent of the climate crisis has made this realization even more acute. Species of all types are already on the move as their habitat and the climate change, yet at every turn they face landscape-scale changes resulting from human activities. And of course, transport infrastructure is literally unavoidable. Confronting this dire reality was an important priority even in the early years of the European Union, and it led to a number of important and influential directives issued by the European Council, which obliged member states to take strong action to comply.[12] The first of these was the council directive on the conservation of wild birds—usually referred to as the "Birds Directive"—which was implemented in 1981. This suite of laws sought to ensure the conservation of birds, in particular those migrating through the region, by securing key sites (*Zones de Protection Spéciale*). This legislation promoted considerable research and discussion throughout Europe, in many cases exposing just how poorly some areas were known and how little was actually protected.

Even more significant was the "Habitat Directive" (the council directive on the conservation of natural habitats, and of wild fauna and flora), signed in 1992. This enormously influential instrument required each country to identify sites that would form a network "ensuring continued biological diversity by conserving natural habitats [throughout Europe]." This almost impossibly ambitious project would be based around two rather different elements, one spatial and the other species-specific. Firstly, each country was requested to undertake a comprehensive identification of sites of key conservation significance (to be known as Natura 2000 sites), which in combination with all such places across Europe would provide the best landscape-level framework for biological conservation throughout the entire continent.[13] The second element was the listing of a number of species that were afforded strict legal protection. These included European mink, lynx, stone martin, and blue hare; the presence of such species in an area designated for development required serious attention.

The advent of these directives had a profound influence on the way in which land-use planning and resource development were conducted throughout Europe. For agencies drafting transportation infrastructure, the challenges were enormous. For example, when all of the sites identified by the Natura 2000 exercise were combined for the first time, even the organizers were shocked: more than twenty-three thousand sites had been identified, covering about 17 percent of all EU lands. Today, this vast constellation of places is still arresting. Spend a few minutes online playing with the marvelous Natura 2000 Network Viewer to see the extent of the latest mapping, and then consider the very real challenges facing the transportation agencies. The greatest density of these sites is found in mountainous areas as well as in the eastern areas of Europe, the less-developed countries where new transport routes are integral to progress. If the transportation agencies were to take their obligations to the conservation of Europe's biodiversity seriously, getting this essential infrastructure built is going to need some very careful and creative thought.

Actual Networking

The enormity of this (ongoing) challenge became increasingly obvious to Hans Bekker at quite an early stage in his career. But just as with the achievements for verges and badgers, he knew the solution would not be found in isolation and introspection. There were people with great ideas and proven abilities all over Europe, quietly getting on with their work in their local areas. As early as 1985, the French transportation agency had organized an international symposium in Strasbourg—sponsored by the Council of Europe—which was possibly the first-ever road ecology forum, though no one used that terminology at the time.[14] A young and enthusiastic Hans had been a participant, presenting a poster on the Dutch badger work. What really impressed him about this meeting, however, was the amount of research on the impact of roads on wildlife and the breadth of ideas and practical things being achieved at local levels, all over the region. Almost a decade later, Hans decided it was time to bring all of this knowledge and information together and see what might happen.

The information compiled during the production of *Natuur over Wegen* convinced Hans and his colleagues that Holland had something worth sharing. "In our office we thought: 'See what we have been able to do here in the Netherlands. Let's get together and think about these issues and approaches for the whole of Europe. An international symposium— to bring all these clever but somewhat isolated people to a nice location and see if we could work toward a common though enormous goal: the defragmentation of Europe!' It was crazy but we really did think we could achieve something." His agency was willing to host this cross-Europe conference, presenting the ideas in *Natuur over Wegen* as a logical starting point. Not only did they agree, the ministry provided 200,000 Dutch guilders (about US$56,000 at the time) to support the immediate event as well as a follow-up meeting.[15] Hans was given the enormous task of getting this event organized and immediately began contacting everyone he knew. But would enough people come?

In September 1995, in what would become one of the most significant events in the history of the field of road ecology, 135 participants from twenty-five countries met in Maastricht in the far south of the Netherlands.[16] For those who attended the conference (which was entitled "Habitat Fragmentation, Infrastructure, and the Role of Ecological Engineering"), it quickly became clear that this was not just another bureaucratic meeting, something to be enjoyed at the time but soon forgotten. Many of the participants still recall the sense of urgency and common purpose, the unexpected willingness and desire for genuine cooperation. "It really was remarkable," recalls Hans. "Almost everyone understood what was at stake and the enormity of the challenge. We all saw that serious work was ahead for us. Yet everyone was willing to be involved. I still remember the feeling of energy and determination."

And the challenge was daunting. Despite the apparent unity of the European Union, sharp differences—professional, cultural, technical— abounded. They always do. But sometimes the importance of the task overrides such concerns, and a wholesale plan for the defragmentation of Europe was such a goal; this time, Europe must work as one. Such was the common resolve that the delegates spontaneously developed a communiqué that would starkly acknowledge the clash between transportation infrastructure and ecological systems, and the immediate necessity to work toward workable solutions. This document became *The Infra Eco Declaration* (a nod to both Infrastructure and Ecology) and was addressed to both the European Union and the Council of Europe. Among its other direct statements, this declaration affirmed that "it is important that policy makers become aware of the possibilities to prevent, mitigate, or compensate the negative impacts on ecosystems, caused by infrastructure works. . . . A strategy must be developed for minimizing the impacts of roads on the European ecological network in all countries of Europe by avoiding intervention. If this is not possible, mitigation measures should be considered, such as fauna tunnels, ecoducts, anti-noise barriers and traffic and transport measures."[17]

These were not trivial demands, especially as the entire European continent was being considered. For there to be any hope of achieving these goals, international cooperation was unavoidable. This, too, was part of the declaration. It proposed the formation of an "Infra Eco Network Europe (IENE) consisting of policymakers, planners, implementers and researchers who work in the field of habitat fragmentation and infrastructure [that] can help to coordinate and stimulate cooperation between member states of Europe." This idea was to prove the key. Yes, "key" is an ideal metaphor here, because the birth of IENE was to open a door, allowing a remarkably diverse group of people to enter and join together to achieve things of which no individual country or crack team of specialists could possibly dream. Of all the specific events, moments, or milestones that could be identified as foundational in this field, I will nominate the 1995 Maastricht meeting as the most important, because this was when IENE was conceived. Its delivery as promising infant occurred the following year with a meeting of about twenty key individuals from throughout Europe, who formed the small but determined core of the pioneering organization. The Dutch ministry continued to sponsor the juvenile entity through the crucial first two years. Subsequently, Swedish (1998–2000) and Belgian (2000–3) transportation agencies funded the secretariat in order to keep the organization running.[18]

The network started life with very heavy expectations; there was serious work to be done. The Maastricht declaration was aimed at the European Union in an attempt to solicit interest in facilitating a major international project that would bring together all existing knowledge and develop a framework that could be followed by all countries. The European Commission managed a program known as COST (European Cooperation in the Field of Scientific and Technical Research), and the IENE proposal "Habitat Fragmentation Due to Transportation Infrastructure" eventually became the COST 341 Project. Although the commission provided substantial support and resources, the main cost was borne by each individual country that officially signed up. This massive project, led by Hans Bekker, Bjørn Iuell, and Marguerite Trocmé, ran for five years, from 1998 to 2003, and its main outcomes—the handbooks (see below) and the formation of national groups—were to prove of enormous international significance.[19]

Handy Books

With the overall objective of gathering together the knowledge and practices of countries throughout Europe, COST required each signatory country to provide a detailed overview of their state of fragmentation and what measures, if any, were being undertaken to address this. Obviously, there were going to be very different levels of preparedness and of willingness to be involved (in the early stages, neither Germany nor France were participants, although this changed within a few years). Sweden, Austria, Spain, Norway, Hungary, and the Czech Republic prepared their national overviews, providing a workable template that could be followed by others. Some countries were well advanced in tackling fragmentation, but others had virtually no measures in place. As the chair of the COST 341 Project, Hans recalls spending a lot of time traveling during those years (not to mention endless very strong coffees and long late-night telephone calls). "Plenty of 'poldering,'" he recalls. "I had to keep the wheels turning so that all of the countries would get their National Handbooks completed in time for all the details to be collated. It seemed endless, but I do also remember some wonderful times after a hard day of work. Although, in Spain, they really can work until very late!"

Initially, the project began with just five countries; by its conclusion five years later, eighteen had joined. It would be difficult to overemphasize just how much effort was required of the relatively small number of national representatives to achieve this level of international collaboration. It meant booking endless flights, train trips, and hotel rooms, as well as running ten major international COST workshops, all necessary to achieve the daunting objectives they had set themselves. But somehow, it worked. At what was effectively the first IENE International Conference, held in November 2003 in Brussels, Belgium, 187 people from twenty-seven countries came together to celebrate the successful completion of the COST 341 Project. Pragmatically, the evidence of this achievement came in the form of "just" two publications.[20] The first of these handbooks, *The European Review*, provided a comprehensive overview of the state of habitat fragmentation throughout Europe and the way that each country was (or was not) attempting to address the issue. This was a critical appraisal of the situation current at the time and effectively represented a baseline from which to work. The second volume, *Wildlife and Traffic: A European Handbook for Identifying Conflicts and Designing Solutions*, provided detailed best-practice guidelines and methodologies that could be utilized across the continent.[21]

Again, it is hard to overemphasize the significance of these two handbooks. These volumes provided in condensed form the stark reality of European environmental fragmentation, as well as the rationale for taking

Figure 13. The top of the Ecoduct Kampengrens on the border of the Netherlands and Belgium, visited during the 2018 IENE conference in nearby Eindhoven. This open, sandy habitat was designed especially for the smooth snake. Photographer Darryl Jones.

the action necessary to address it. And this advice was not vague or generalized; it was practical, pragmatic, and project ready. With the release of the handbooks, no transportation agency, government authority, or relevant administration could pretend that they did not understand or have enough instruction. But while the books themselves were major landmarks, far more important was the process that led to their development. As a result of the five years of intense discussion, argument, and cooperation among a relatively small number of people from all over Europe, the sense of common purpose and resolve that was evident at the beginning matured into a strong and enduring set of committed relationships. IENE had moved from a tentative collection of individuals to a thoroughly international, interconnected network of close colleagues. This group had been through a lot together and learned how to get the most out of one another.

IENE describes itself as a nonprofit, nongovernmental, nonpolitical formalized network of experts active in the field of habitat fragmentation due to transport infrastructure. It also epitomizes the contemporary concept of "a community of practice." This sounds like sociological jargon, but it is actually not a bad description of how and why this organization has worked—at least at the beginning. A lot has happened since.

Continental to Global

IENE is not the only organization that attempts to take on these profound environmental challenges, although I would argue it is the most successful and influential. This impact is almost certainly a result of the necessity to find common ground across the whole of Europe. The other groups have rather different roles and histories, but all are vital in bringing people together and facilitating the exchange of practical ideas. In North America, ICOET (the International Conference on Ecology and Transportation) is primarily an event, a biennial meeting, rather than an organization.[22] The planning and running of each conference are usually undertaken by a collective of state transport agencies, universities, and consultancies. So far, each of the ten ICOET conferences has been held in a different state in the United States. From the very first official meeting in 2001, the relationship between IENE and ICOET has been strong, enduring, and highly cooperative; Hans Bekker has been a member of the ICOET Steering Committee since the early 2000s. When IENE decided to host its own biennial conferences (the first was held in Hungary in 2010), they were each scheduled for the year following ICOET, and people from both organizations attend the other meeting regularly. More recently, ANET (Australasian Network for Ecology and Transportation) emerged in Australia to provide a forum for Oceania and Asia, while ACLIE (African Conference for Linear Infrastructure and Ecology) held its first meeting in Kruger National Park, South Africa, in 2019.[23]

So if these are really "communities of practice," what ideas are they sharing these days?[24] Have we moved beyond wooden deer bridges and badger pipes? Let's look at a few very different examples.

Connecting Canopies

I had thought that Mount Kosciuszko's mountain pygmy possums were unassailable as hands-down "cutest" endangered species. But that was before I met the hazel dormouse, a disarmingly attractive creature capable of rendering the toughest red-blooded ecologist tongue-tied with sentimentality. This tiny animal is still found throughout continental Europe, but in the United Kingdom it is in very serious decline. It is not hard to understand why. These mammals are thoroughly arboreal, remaining high above ground as much as possible, traveling along the interconnected branches of tree canopies. This means they are pretty much only found in areas with continuous tree cover. Gaps in the canopy represent a major problem for hazel dormice—they are most reluctant to move along the ground, where they are obviously vulnerable to predators. The widespread clearing of the United Kingdom's forests and the dissection of the landscape—by roads (even narrow country tracks), or by any type of linear infrastructure—have had an enormous impact on these sensitive animals. With its fate in the balance, the hazel dormouse is an important and high-profile species in the United Kingdom.

Given the species' preference, if not obsession, for climbing along tree branches high up in the canopy, road ecologists recognized that dormice needed something rather specialized to assist them across any roads that were preventing them from venturing further afield. Several specially designed overhead structures, made of metal cables loosely suspended over tall poles, were installed in a number of places in southern England. The cables were enclosed by lengths of wire-mesh tubing, presumably to provide a safe passageway for the dormice as they crawled along above the road.

Possibly the most infamous of these installations was the spectacularly ugly structure that temporally spanned a bypass near Pontypridd in Wales. Not only was this structure widely criticized for being very expensive (costing £190,000, or about US$245,000) and derided for achieving a new low in visual pollution—it was a colossal failure.[25] Although some squirrels *did* use the bridge, it appears that no self-respecting dormouse would place even a tentative paw on it.

Now, it's all too easy to be overly critical in hindsight. The local council do need to be acknowledged for actually trying to do something about a serious issue. They worked closely with experts and conservation groups to come up with a structure that would theoretically enable the dormice to climb, in relatively safety, about twenty-seven meters (thirty yards) over a noisy roadway.[26] It's difficult to determine just why the animals did not use the bridge, but it seems likely that the dormice living in the vicinity were simply unable to find the structure's rather small entry points. They almost certainly had no idea that more habitat and distant relatives could be reached if they undertook the long and stressful journey. In any case, this opportunity came to a sudden and ignoble end when the whole structure toppled down in a tangled mess during a violent storm. It was a disappointing and dispiriting outcome for what had been a worthy experiment.

One of the predictable repercussions of this disaster was a strong reluctance to invest time or money on what looked like a lost cause. It seemed that engineering a solution to dormouse isolation was just too difficult, too expensive, too risky—and that this species might simply not be up to learning new tricks. Such a conclusion was not, however, acceptable to some. Ian White, from the People's Trust for Endangered Species, a small but highly effective British conservation charity, was not convinced that the failure of one particular design was the end of the story.[27] Ian found strong support for his concerns at Animex, a modestly sized but extremely innovative company that has been pioneering new fence designs for keeping a wide range of animals away from roads.[28] Ian and a small group from Animex began to discuss whether they should venture into what looked like a highly contentious but important issue.

A couple of independent events offered some concrete grounds for optimism. First, a private group had demonstrated that tame, captive-bred hazel dormice were willing to walk along an enclosed mesh tube suspended on a cable fourteen meters (fifteen yards) in length. Although completely artificial, this observation did show that the animals could travel on materials other than branches, and for a long distance. Even more significant was news from Japan, where Japanese dormice had been recorded using a rather strange triangular tube suspended from a cable within the forest canopy.[29] Although this structure was only ten meters (eleven yards) in length and had been installed over a rarely used road, what was particularly interesting was that many of the animals were traveling significant distances to use the bridge rather than cross the road at ground level. The Animex team were soon brainstorming.

I first became aware of the now famous "dormouse bridge" when videos showing perky little beasts (with disturbingly bright gleaming eyes) running along a triangular structure began turning up all over social media. (Simply Google "dormouse bridge" to find this footage.) A short while later, I chanced on the Animex stand at a road ecology conference and discovered that the young woman in attendance, Sophie Hughes, had been directly involved in the dormouse project from the beginning. When I realized that I would be traveling to the United Kingdom in the near future, diaries were consulted and plans rapidly adjusted. I was determined to see this remarkable construction with my own eyes.

As the ferry surged through the dark, foamy waters of the Solent—the estuary on the Hampshire coast adjacent to Southampton—it was obvious that Animex had an impressive approach to ensuring that foreign visitors received the best possible intelligence.[30] If this required an all-day visit to the gorgeous Isle of Wight (a short voyage from Animex's headquarters), then Sophie, engineer Steve Béga, and even their boss, Dean Swensson, were only too eager to assist. It turned out to be a relaxed, insightful, and informative day. With plenty of time to talk as we traveled, the Animex team were able to describe all the components of a still developing story.

Animex is obviously a commercial enterprise, one that is focused on selling new, innovative products—but only if these things work. The brand is based on both innovation and proven reliability. The company was painfully aware of the history behind designing something suitable for dormice—and of the financial risks involved—but the success of the

Japanese design provided a solid basis for optimism. Animex wanted to come up with a structure that was relatively simple to construct yet both light *and* sturdy, able to withstand all weathers. And, of course, it had to be reasonably priced. After a few iterations, the team believed they had all the components in place. They just needed somewhere suitable to test it, a place that was reasonably accessible (but preferably without offering too much public access), with decent populations of dormice. Did such a place exist in what is, after all, one of the most densely populated places on earth?

The solution to this crucial piece of the puzzle seems almost too impossibly convenient to be believed. Only about thirty kilometers (twenty miles) from Southampton, on the Isle of Wight, there just so happens to be the most plentiful hazel dormouse population in the United Kingdom. Most of these dormice are found in Briddlesford Nature Reserve, in the wooded heart of an island that is both busy tourist destination and ancient rural landscape. The structure of the forest here was dramatically different from almost everywhere else I had been in Britain or Western Europe: the leaf litter was deep and damp, sustaining a complex understory of ferns, shrubs, and small trees. This lower vegetation merged into the lower branches of the trees, more or less forming a continuum of plant material from forest floor to uppermost canopy. "No browsing!" explained Sophie, noticing my expression of surprise. "The native deer were hunted out centuries ago, resulting in an unusually rich habitat. Plenty of seeds, fruits and foliage which the local dormice thrive on."

Another feature I had not expected was a railway line, running directly through the middle of the reserve, another reason this site had been selected for a trial of the dormouse bridge. It would be far too risky to construct an experimental prototype over a real road, but this linear transport corridor was an ideal surrogate. Furthermore, the dormouse crossing structure was suspended directly over an old railway bridge, completely minimizing any risk should anything fall. We clambered onto the top of the railway bridge and I suddenly found myself looking directly into the dormouse structure. It was more exposed than I had anticipated, with the two sides of the triangle of tubular aluminum fitted with long pieces of wood along the bottom and top, leaving a large gap between. The floor was metal mesh and furnished with a number of small boxes, which the animals could use for shelter if required. Throughout, inside and outside, were movement-activated cameras. The structure was about 27 meters (30 yards) in length, made up of separate sections 1.8 meters (6 feet) long and suspended from a thick metal rope, which was attached with considerable tension to two large trees on either side of the railway. Importantly, the ends of the structure extended well into the canopy at either end, with many branches making contact. Although I (and half the world with "cute mammal" social media feeds) knew that at least one dormouse had scampered across, I was not aware of what else had happened. Sophie was very pleased to bring me up to date.

"We were fairly hopeful that something might happen during the first ten-day trial. But not on the first night!" Sophie told me. "Our first dormouse was snapped at nine o'clock that night, and fifty-nine others were recorded during the trial. We also got a red squirrel, another species doing very well in this reserve. You could say we were pretty excited!" And so was I. Standing next to the dormouse bridge and observing the relative simplicity of this modular design, it was easy to see how this could be

Figure 14. Experimental flexible bridge for hazel dormice constructed over a railway on the Isle of Wight, United Kingdom by Animex. Photographer Darryl Jones.

extended to reconnect forest canopies over much greater distances. Sophie and her colleagues are engaged right now in further testing in other, more realistic, situations. Further assessments are inevitable, given the well-publicized and unfortunate outcomes of the previous attempts, but to me this design looked endlessly adaptable.[31]

Staying Alive, Above

Dormice may not be aware of their innate cuteness but they seem acutely conscious of their vulnerability to predation, remaining hidden within their nests and tree hollows during the day and using the cover of dense foliage as much as possible when moving about at night. This is the primary reason for their reluctance to travel in the open, especially along the ground. They are, however, known to venture along the ground if there is sufficiently dense vegetation; indeed, dormice were recently discovered to be breeding—at ground level!—on the top of Britain's first (and still, only) fauna overpass, constructed in 2005 in the Scotney Castle estate in Kent.[32] But this is very much an exception to their usual behavior of staying high and hidden.

This is not the case for many other arboreal, canopy-dwelling species around the world. In Australia, for example, numerous species of marsupial possums and gliders clamber conspicuously along dozens of rope ladders (or canopy bridges) that have been installed over some of the widest and busiest motorways in the country. Unlike dormice, these species show little concern at being exposed for extended periods of time. It can take quite a while to crawl along the entire length of a rope ladder—which is typically between 30 and 50 meters (33 and 55 yards), although the longest ladder is 95 meters (103 yards)—but that seems to be of little concern to these animals.[33] When these connectors were first being considered, concern about the exposure of the animals led to early versions made in a square tube design that allowed them to crawl inside the rope lattice. This design was soon abandoned when it became clear that virtually every animal using the structure simply wandered along the top. Today, the basic—and much cheaper—horizontal rope ladder is the standard type in use, although some now have Perspex tubes as potential hiding places attached at intervals along the structure. Even simpler are single thick ropes, many of which are suspended under large underpasses or broad viaducts.

Some of Australia's arboreal marsupials will not use rope ladders to cross roads. The country has six species of gliders, and although some sugar gliders and squirrel gliders have been detected using these structures, most prefer to "fly" wherever possible and are almost never seen on the ground.[34] It is often impossible for one of these animals to successfully traverse a wide road with a single glide, because of the distance involved. The logical solution would be to provide the equivalent of trees—in the form of "glider poles"—located at shorter distances that would theoretically enable these animals to make the crossing in a series of jumps.[35] This radical idea has actually been tried and will be discussed in some detail in the next chapter.

Other tree-dwelling Aussies animals are, shall we say, not "built" appropriately to manage a floppy rope ladder. Koalas, in particular, are somewhat robust and heavy. They are also reluctant to move along the

Figure 15. Modifications to a sign portal enabling arboreal mammals to cross a motorway. The ropes (on each side of the highway) connect to branches of the surrounding trees. A12 motorway near Maarn, The Netherlands. Photographer Marcel Huijser.

ground although, they have no choice but to do so if they want to change trees. The canopies of most of Australia's eucalyptus trees almost never interconnect, and the necessity of having to climb down, walk along the ground, and climb up again is a laborious inevitability. This time of terrestrial movement is a most dangerous activity for koalas; almost all mortality of adults occurs while they are at ground level. Although predation by dogs (both domestic and feral) is a major cause of death, especially in urban areas, koalas are at much greatest risk when crossing roads. In many locations, vehicle strike is the primary reason for the steady and serious decline in koala populations.

Given the iconic status and popularity of this species, considerable thought has been devoted to koala-appropriate road-crossing structures. The first and only koala-specific overpass was recently built in my home town of Brisbane, located at a tragically well-known black spot on a busy arterial road.[36] It is a large metal gantry about five meters (sixteen feet) above the road, supported by heavy concrete columns. At either end, two large bare logs lean at an angle from the ground to meet the edge of the gantry. In my opinion, the crossing structure is ridiculously overengineered (but apparently it has to be able to withstand a category-seventeen cyclone while being hit by an intercontinental missile during an earthquake); it was, unsurprisingly, very expensive to construct. My team is currently installing cameras to determine whether koalas actually use it; the ubiquitous brushtail possums certainly do.

The excessive cost of this type of overpass is almost certainly going to be the main reason that comparable structures won't be taken up around Australia or in other countries where similarly arboreal species face the same problems. But they do not need to be so expensive. In a mountainous area in Assam, in northern India, the last thousand or so golden langurs—magnificent, long-limbed monkeys, which live high in the rainforest canopy—face the fragmentation of their habitat by roads and illegal logging.[37] Although officially protected and living in part within a conservation reserve, the animals often need to descend to the ground to cross the main road in the area and forage in a nearby tree plantation. Out in the open, the langurs are very susceptible to dog attacks and poaching. This ominous situation changed dramatically in 2010, when a local conservation group joined with the Wildlife Trust of India and some international NGOs to install a series of "ropeways"—made of bamboo and long-lasting marine rope—that connected the canopies of the forest bisected by the road. The rope bridges may look dangerously loose and unstable, but these days the langurs can be seen swinging or even walking casually across them, eighteen meters (sixty feet) above the ground. In the decade since installation, there have been no car-related langur deaths in this area.[38]

Flight Lines

All of the over-the-road crossing structures—overpasses (or ecoducts), bridges, ropes, and rope ladders—are typically physical structures situated above the road. This allows an enormous range of species to walk, run, crawl, slither, or climb safely to the other side. These animals all require direct contact with the structure; even gliders make contact with the poles that enable them to glide in "stages" across the gap. It might seem obvious that flying animals would not require any assistance in simply crossing a road. If you recall an earlier discussion about small forest-dwelling birds, however, you will not be surprised to learn that these species now routinely cross even wide roads using fauna overpasses that have been planted with dense vegetation. There are now many locations around the world where installing an overpass with plenty of cover has enabled long-severed populations of birds (and many other species) to be reconnected. This discovery is one of the most important unplanned-for benefits of this type of connector.

While smaller birds tend to move within the low-level shrubbery, a number of other, typically larger, species have been found to utilize the presence of these structures and preferentially fly low along the vegetation on the overpass when crossing a road. This may be because the plants provide a degree of security, perhaps a place to disappear into should an aerial predator appear.

Bats show similar behavior, especially those species that typically forage just above the canopy of the trees. Among the many unexpected findings made by Mel McGregor, who worked on the Compton Road overpass in Brisbane, was the discovery that the most intense bat activity was directly above the center of the vegetated overpass, effectively directly above the center of the road.[39] She was unable to verify why so many bats were

Figure 16. Recently completed fauna overpass in Queensland, Australia, showing a row of glider poles. Photographer Darryl Jones.

aggregating in such an unusual location, but it seems highly likely that this activity was due to a concentration of the airborne insects on which the bats forage; the insects, too, appear to be using the structure for their movements. Away from the overpass, in contrast, the greatest abundance of bats was located deep within the forest, as far from the road as possible.

Bats are almost always influenced by the presence of vegetation as they traverse their typical commuting routes from roosting place to foraging sites, flying low over the canopy, following forest edges, or hugging whatever cover may exist. Very clearly most species avoid crossing broad, open areas, presumably because of the risks of predation. In rural landscapes where little of their original habitat exists, bats tend to fly along prominent features such as rows of trees or hedges. The main problem—unavoidable and inevitable in many places—is what happens when they eventually need to cross a road. When the vegetation beneath them disappears, many (possibly most) bat species will swoop low over the road—an unfortunate move, because this often brings them directly into the path of traffic. It is virtually impossible to estimate the impact of vehicle strikes on bats, but it is likely to be enormous. Certainly in Europe, the decline of bats associated with road mortality is taken very seriously. In EU countries, any transportation project that may potentially interact with bat populations is obliged to show how it will address the problem. Developers must demonstrate how they will avoid, reduce, or compensate for any possible impacts—the standard bureaucratic requirement. When it comes to the more familiar animal species, compliance involves the usual signage, fencing, tunnels, or other features, most of which have specified designs. For bats, however, there is still very little to play with. Both the engineers and the agencies responsible for approving development plans face a serious lack of reliable information; bats have long been regarded as too difficult and too different to warrant the level of attention paid to most other groups.

Enormous efforts are currently underway to address this paucity of knowledge.[40] All over the world, teams of biologists and engineers are trying to develop structures that might influence the flight paths of bats to keep them above the traffic. This critical work is still in its infancy and has resulted in a variety of unusual—if not fanciful—structures being installed over roads. The general principle they share is to construct something that guides the bats up and over the road, avoiding the vehicles below. Rather than eyesight, bats use sonar to perceive the physical world around them, emitting high-frequency vocalizations that reflect off nearby objects. Using this as a starting point, most bat crossing structures attempt to provide features that can be detected by the bats and then guide them safely over.

The most minimalist design consists of just two parallel tensioned wires spanning the roadway—with one wire about a meter (three feet) above the other—and fastened to trees on either side of the road. Attached to the wires are polystyrene balls covered with a reflective microsurface, ostensibly to "optimize the likelihood of bats receiving sonar echoes while flying."[41] Slightly more elaborate is a simple V-shaped metal-mesh design stretched across the road between pairs of poles. There is then a considerable jump in physical substance—and in expense—to a standard metal gantry normally used for electronic signage; essentially, this is a long open-topped metal box mounted on pillars above the road. Finally, no less substantial but infinitely more pleasing aesthetically, is an open-topped cylinder of organically curved aluminum (a striking structure sometimes referred to as the "Silver Banana Peel"). Most of these devices are single experimental structures erected over roads in France, but there are seven V-mesh structures in Norfolk, England. The effectiveness of each design has now been assessed, and the structure's placement in the landscape appears to be far more important than the shape or even the aesthetics of the design. These installations need to be placed along existing bat commuting routes or they just don't work. In other words, if these elaborate and expensive constructions are not sited on the basis of detailed ecological information, they are simply a "costly waste."[42]

The ongoing development of crossing structures for bats is one of many areas still under dynamic investigation. We can expect plenty of evolutionary developments in the near future, as well as a broadening of ecological focus (insects, especially butterflies, are one group that keeps coming up). But more important is the move away from single sites or specific animals. The major focus now is on roads at the landscape level—how to use all of these structures to make roads much more permeable. In Spain we can see what this might look like.

Parapermeable

I arrived in Barcelona the day after the city had hosted Real Madrid at Camp Nou, another of the famous and passionate "El Clasico" matches between the two football clubs. On this occasion, Barca had prevailed. Such were the celebrations overnight that, as I wandered along Las Ramblas the following morning, I wondered what catastrophe had occurred; this enormous city seemed to be deserted, apart from some Korean tourists being herded toward La Sagrada Família. Locals were hard to find. But then again, "early morning" is not really a concept that is recognized in Spain.

Spain? Careful . . . this is Catalunya, and fiercely so. The maps show this region as a part of Spain, but that is not how it is seen in the streets of Barcelona. You won't find the Spanish flag flying here; instead, banners and bunting featuring vivid red and yellow stripes are literally everywhere. There *may* be more potent sporting rivalries than Barca versus Real, but I doubt it. Here, these ostensibly simple sporting clashes represent so much more than football. This is about Catalunya versus the federal capital of

Spain, about proud regional identity and independence and the perceived threat of homogeneity and subservience. And, of course, at the time of my visit, about Messi versus Ronaldo.

You need to be conscious of such things when visiting this region; it's an important part of understanding cultural sensitivities and national sensibilities. But, while stridently Catalunyan (she did enjoy last night's football, I suspect), my guide is also thoroughly European in perspective. Carme Rosell was directly involved in all of the very first tentative steps of what became IENE and remains one of its most dynamic and influential members.[43] Her environmental consultancy group has also been extremely influential, and she is constantly moving and working all over the country and beyond, providing advice and suggestions on defragmentation. There-fore, I can hardly believe that she has found time, not just to meet me, but to provide a personalized tour of one of the most important road projects in Europe—or anywhere for that matter. It is an excellent example of what is possible when designing brand-new roads.

The C-37 is a relatively new motorway constructed in the early 2000s and running through fairly rugged country to the northwest of Barcelona. This heavily forested country includes some of Spain's most important national parks, extensive wetlands, and a complex tapestry of forestry and farms. It is a landscape where the realities of the European Union's agricultural policies have had a major impact on rural populations. The decline in demand for various commodities has led to many farms being abandoned, their owners moving to the cities in search of employment. As a result, forests are expanding as the farmland changes from managed pastures into dense woods. This spontaneous increase in tree cover follow-ing the removal of cattle—a process occurring in many places throughout Europe—may be celebrated by some as a return to "natural" landscapes and an excellent store of carbon, but for local residents and many ecolo-gists, this revegetation is also a sign of failure and neglect. Almost the entire European landscape can be regarded as anthropogenic: shaped and designed by millennia of human activity such as clearing, grazing, and agriculture. The dense, dark forest of pioneering tree species that rapidly take over as soon as humans stop working the land is not actually "natu-ral" and, unexpectedly, not particularly good for biodiversity.

The C-37 motorway is part of a vast European transportation vision, designed to facilitate the movement of goods, products, and materials throughout the region. This motorway provides an essential connection between Barcelona and the southeastern corner of France. Tourists and lo-cals use it in large numbers, but this is fundamentally a road for big trucks carrying heavy loads. And that meant that one feature of the road's design overrode all others: it had to be flat. Indeed, the extent to which the road rises and falls along its entire length of nineteen kilometers (twelve miles) is almost negligible: it is the flattest new road in all of Europe. And why does this matter? "One of the main costs of transportation is fuel, and consumption is greatest when the trucks have to climb slopes," explains Carme, as we take a late lunch at the town of Sant Esteve d'en Bas. From our open-air table we can see the northernmost end of the C-37 emerg-ing from a tunnel and then sweeping forward on pillars over an extensive wetland as well as farming land. Even from this distance, it is clear that it is an astonishing engineering feat. "This motorway simply does not have inclines or slopes; it continues at the same level across the landscape regardless of the terrain, penetrating mountains through tunnels and then is supported above the valleys as tall viaducts," Carme tells me. "Vehicles travel on a perfectly flat surface for the entire road."

Figure 17. Europe's most permeable road, the C-37 highway in Catalunya, Spain.
Photographer Darryl Jones.

This remarkable (and doubtless expensive) design also means that most of the road does not interact with the land surface at all; much of the road is either within tunnels or above ground. This has dramatically minimized the barrier effect of the road. In fact, if the total length of the ten tunnels and six viaducts is calculated, almost half (48 percent) of the entire road is under or over the land. In other words, wildlife can move unimpeded across about half the route of this major motorway, in most places without even being aware that it is there. So, not only is this the flattest road in Europe, it is also the most permeable.

"So now you are thinking that this is only about engineers building flat roads for trucks?" Carme echoes exactly what I have been thinking. "Sure, this new way of constructing roads saves a lot of fuel costs. That's really good, environmentally speaking. But this amazing design has also been beneficial for biodiversity, leaving so much of the land completely untouched and with minimal disturbance. This has been an excellent benefit of the flat-road approach. But we need to show you what this really means. Come!" We climb into our vehicles and are soon heading southwest along the C-37, enjoying a few moments-worth of superb views from the motorway 80 meters (260 feet) above a broad river (Riera de Riudaura), before disappearing into the tunnels through the mountains.

One of the most important reasons for organizing visits with the people directly engaged in these exciting projects is that they often have access to places the general public don't even know about. After emerging on the other side of the tunnel, we pull onto a narrow service road and park beside a locked gate. A giant wheel of keys is produced and, after about twelve attempts, the padlock clicks open. A thin footpath meanders up a steep hillside covered in a rich sward of grasses and herbs; a thick wall of trees is visible on the other side of the slope. After half an hour of fairly strenuous uphill walking, we reach a low saddle between two hills. Below, the motorway emerges from the land we are standing on before disappearing into another tunnel entrance about half a kilometer (a third of a mile) away. We can see just a small section of the road, but it shows clearly that quite a lot of it is entirely underground.

We settle onto some large, smooth boulders to rest and share some oranges, but I have the feeling that there must be some reason we have stopped at this particular place other than for the view. As far as I can tell, we are resting on a hilltop above one of the tunnels. The "tunnel" we can see directly ahead is actually more of an overpass, where the road has been carved through a hillside and a flat concrete roof constructed above it. This is a well-known road-engineering technique known as "cut and cover" and has been used the world over to construct relatively simple overpasses. Still, Carme informs me, the tunnel is 86 meters (280 feet) in length—much longer than most such structures—and the "roof" has been extensively landscaped and planted with local vegetation. "That one ahead is a nice vegetated bridge now and the wildlife can now cross over the road easily. But the reason we have brought you to this spot is much more special. For you may be surprised to learn that the landform on which we are sitting right now was also constructed in the same way. It too is a 'cut and cover' overpass, though being 475 meters [a third of a mile] in length, it is almost certainly the largest and most ambitious of its type in the world."

"Surprised" would not be an adequate word to describe my reaction. I slowly stand and look carefully around me, taking in the rugged, complex, but entirely natural-looking landscape. It is exactly like any other mountainous hillside. Yet all of these trees, the rows of shrubs, the thick grass cover, the streams and mossy rocks, this boulder . . . "Yes, everything! It all had to be very carefully mapped and surveyed, then removed completely," Carme explains. "And then, of course, everything replaced just as it had been previously. It was not easy and we made many mistakes but we were determined to do something really special. And we did it! Not just Europe's most permeable road but a completely new standard in restoration." As Carme gazes out over this apparently ancient, but in fact re-created, Mediterranean landscape, her pride in this almost impossibly ambitious project is obvious. I feel it is a genuine privilege to be here. That's another reason to spend time with the people who have worked directly on such projects: they love to share their achievements.

Spain's C-37 has certainly raised the benchmark for permeability, and it provides an impressive example of what can be achieved with sufficient funding and resolve. Such a road may even raise the prospect of all new roads being either underground or perched on pillars above the land, a prospect that is simply impossible at large geographical scales. No one has that sort of money. Much more realistic, however, would be the inclusion of whole suites of crossing structures as part of the design of new or upgraded roads. In some parts of the world, this is no longer an optimist's fantasy; the road network of France, one of the densest in the world, already has a crossing structure every eight kilometers (five miles) on average.

More pragmatically, however, the question is not whether these structures are needed, but where to place them—and, indeed, whether they actually work as intended. As we shall see, just because some animals have been detected using a passage does not necessarily mean that connector is effective. It's time to take a serious look at how such things are evaluated.

4

KNOW-HOW

High up in the sharp, clear air of the Irreal Hills of northern Arizona, a small group of people stand silently staring out over the expansive landscape extending toward the horizon.[1] Far below them stretches a dark, almost continuous expanse of pinyon pine forest, which ends abruptly along the long, straight edge marking the boundary between cattle ranches and the vast Nohaylatlugar National Monument (usually abbreviated to "Noha" in conversation).[2] The contrast in color is striking: the bright clay-yellow of the grazing land compared with the rumpled dark green of the pines. The density of the trees is something of a surprise to me, given the aridity of this region—it rarely rains here, and I had expected a much sparser tree cover. But like everything else that lives in these parts (humans included), the pinyon pines are rugged survivors. Running east-west across the view is the jagged zigzag shadow of the Espejismo Canyon, which is located much farther to the south and is much smaller and far less frequently visited than its better-known geographic cousin, the Grand Canyon.[3] In fact, this entire area remains to a remarkable extent unknown; a blessed status almost certainly about to change dramatically, quite soon.

The group seemingly transfixed by the view consists of transportation agency representatives, leaders of local community and environmental organizations, and a diverse collection of road ecologists from all over the world. We have assembled at this location in order to see for ourselves the landscape that is about to be subjected to a major intervention: the construction of a new motorway right through the middle of the Noha National Monument. The reason for our quiet focus was the collective appreciation of the magnitude of the challenge we faced: is it possible to build a road through almost pristine habitat without it having a catastrophic impact?

Nicky McCloud from the Wilderness Arizona Coalition was the first to break the silence.[4] "Most of you are probably asking yourselves the same question that we have been obsessed with ever since we heard of the plans for this road: 'Does it have to be built?'" She was right; there was plenty of nodding in agreement. Nicky continued: "At the beginning, our group was totally opposed to the very idea!"

She explained that this was one of the last largely roadless areas in this part of the United States, and that it was home to many rare animals and unique environmental features. Nicky and the other members of the coalition had long been of the opinion that roads are always destructive and intrusive, bringing unwanted, unplanned issues in their wake. But they had become aware that there was another side to this story, which had led them to revise their approach.

"The Natural Faith Community have been living in the area for almost a century," Nicky explained.[5] "They often get dismissed as a bunch of old hippies and Indians, but they have been trying to live their lives in harmony with nature rather than exploiting it like most people. I realize not everyone is so positive about them, but I got to know some of their naturalists when we were surveying for rare reptiles a while back. Their land was in really great shape and had more significant species than anywhere else around the state. I think they have an important point of view and you all should hear this as well. Joe?" She motioned to Joe Bikéyah, an elder of the Natural Faith Community, who turned and addressed us quietly.

"Our community settled there because we love and honor the land," said Joe. "We believe we have been given the job of being careful stewards of this sacred place. Many of our community are Native Americans—Navajo—and we have learned a great deal about how to care for the land from them. To cause even more harm by building this road would be unforgivable. But we need to be part of the modern world too."

Joe explained that they had lobbied for this road for decades, as a way to connect the people with the towns in the rest of Arizona. Their community at Mesquite Wells had only a single road in and out, and it was in terrible condition. A new road would be a significant improvement, allowing the community to be able to drive to the hospitals, stores, and schools far more quickly and safely than at present. The road, he said, would also make it a lot easier for those who work in the towns.

"We actually believe that this road—connecting us to the economy and services down here—will allow us to persist and prosper without having to forsake the land we dwell on. I hope that you can see our need. But we also want what you want: a good road that is safe for people and wildlife. Is that possible? Brad said that you were the folks who could show us how to do this properly."

Brad Gonarto was a project manager with Transport Arizona, the agency charged with the design and delivery of the new road, officially known as the Mesquite Connector Project.[6] When the state legislature finally approved the road, the task of bringing it to fruition became Brad's main priority. He realized very early on that this project was likely to generate a lot of opposition unless handled properly. His approach was to gather people from all the various groups who were likely to have strong views and have them sit down together around the table.

"There was plenty of hostility and disagreement to start with," Brad explained. "And everyone was lined up against us as The Enemy: the heartless destroyers of all that is good! But once everyone had calmed down, other perspectives began to be appreciated."

The environmentalists began to see just how important the road was for the Faith Community and the region's indigenous people. The local Navajo started to appreciate that the conservationists were trying to protect their totemic species. And everyone agreed that if there was to be a road here, it had to be as low impact as possible.

"And this is where you lot come in—it's why we have brought you all this way," Brad said, looking around at us. "When I went to the last ICOET in Phoenix—where I met some of you good people—that meeting really opened my eyes to what was possible, if things were done properly. I went straight to my boss in TA to see whether we could get the best advice on how to build this sucker, with all the bells and whistles. And to my astonishment, he agreed. 'Let's show them what Arizona can do!' he said. So, here we are and here you are! Now, let's get to work."

Where Should They Go?

A short time later we were all standing around a large table at the Noha National Monument headquarters, trying to take in the features of an enormous map spread out before us, the curling edges weighted down with bowls of candies. Flowing organically down the length of the map was the preferred route for the road, printed in dull blue. Several alternative layouts—shown in pale red—were also evident. These, we were told, had been rejected during the selection process. The road project had made it a priority to avoid the slopes of the region's main hills and to skirt several sensitive wetland areas, which the options in red had failed to do. The preferred route was fairly direct and flat, but did cross watercourses at several points.

"Now, I'm sure you have all read the documentation I sent out," said Brad, as we all self-consciously concentrated on some feature we had just noticed on the map. "But to remind you of our key issues: we have two overriding priorities with the design of this road."

First, the road needed to be as safe as possible for motorists. And second, as it would be cutting through an important conservation park, it needed to cause as little disruption to wildlife as possible. There were two species of particular significance: the javelina and the roadrunner. The javelina, also known as the collared peccary, is a peculiar-looking native pig, perfectly adapted to these arid places. They are quite social and sometimes form large family groups, which makes them a major hazard on roads. "Javelinas are not that big, but they are solid," said Brad. "You don't want to hit one doing a hundred on the open road, I can tell you. We have to keep them off the roads, whatever we do. But in this dry landscape, they need to travel far and wide looking for food. They like to move along the dry arroyos—gullies or gulches—and it is where these features intersect with roads that the javelinas are most likely to cause problems for autos. The roadrunners are a very different species and problem, so I'll hand over to Nicky to talk about these special birds."

"*Very* special," agreed Nicky, who was clearly more than happy to tell us about "her" birds. "The cartoon version is not entirely misleading: they are fast and they are smart. But they just don't seem to understand roads and traffic, and lots are killed by cars, even in the towns." She admitted that she was worried about the impact of a new road in an area where the birds, and the other local wildlife, had never even seen a pickup.

The lower parts of the National Monument offer arguably the best habitat for the species that occurs here, the greater roadrunner. "And this road is going to go smack through the middle," said Nicky. "We have decided to use the 'roady' as the symbol for this project, and it would be just terrible if they were to be affected badly."

Nicky paused and glanced over at Brad, and they briefly exchanged a look of mild anguish. We all noticed. "And that's where we might have a bit of a problem," explained Brad tentatively.

Some of the main people making decisions in the agency, and especially the chief engineer, don't really see the point of these things. Sure, they recognize that the javelinas need to be kept off the road for road safety reasons. But they just don't see the roadrunner, or any type of wildlife, as something they need to be worried about. We would have to prove to them that the road really was a serious threat before they would even consider including any sort of crossing structure in the design. For these guys, most of this 'environmental' stuff is just something that increases costs. They just want to build roads.

Nicky agreed. "I'm afraid Brad's dead right. We will have to have some pretty strong evidence to convince them that the road really could have a serious impact on the roadies. And we will definitely need a way to somehow show that it was worthwhile spending the money on whatever is done to get them safely across the road. But we are at a loss as to how this is possible. That's why we have got you clever people involved. So, 'experts': any ideas?"

How to Spot a Dead Bird

Hearing this, we all swiftly deflected the accusation of expertise by looking over at Éric Guinard. After all, dead birds were Éric's thing, really.[7]
Very few people have spent as much time staring so intently at flattened
clumps of feathers alongside roads. Based near Bordeaux, in France, Éric
has undertaken some of the most important studies on road mortality in
birds, so this topic suited him perfectly. Knowing where, when, and how
often animals are killed on roads is of great importance, but collecting
these kinds of data can be unexpectedly difficult. While most of us had
spent the previous day unpacking and relaxing around the pool after our
arrival at the hotel, Éric had gone out into the field to see for himself what
was happening there. He may have missed the first round of margaritas
last night, but he had already acquired some crucial information.

"Yes, I think I can help you with this," Éric said quietly. "Being quite
certain about patterns of roadkill is very important, but there can be some
big problems in collecting this kind of information."

In his road-mortality studies conducted in France, Éric had found that
two types of information were essential. First, it was important to know
how long a dead animal had remained in place after it had been killed, a
period known as "persistence." Carcasses can sometimes be carried off
by predators or scavengers rather quickly. In addition, it was important
to have a sense of a dead bird's "detectability." The ability to successfully
detect a carcass next to the road depends not only on how quickly the observer is moving (most surveys are undertaken while driving), but also on
the size of the bird's body, its position on the pavement or verge, and how
conspicuous it is. Some of us who had been in the field with Éric could at-
test to his almost supernatural ability to spot a tiny collection of feathers
the same color as dead grass, while we missed several far more obvious
larger species. Éric was now starting to warm to the subject, and he knew
we were all waiting to hear what he had discovered yesterday.

Éric gestured for Nicky to join him beside the map. "I was lucky to have
had the chance to drive out into the reserve with Joe late yesterday afternoon. He took me out along the small service road that leads to the headquarters of the National Monument, here," he said, running his hand along
a thin straight line. It ran more or less parallel to the route of the planned
Mesquite Connector road and cut through much the same type of habitat.

Joe quickly walked across to join Éric and Nicky next to the map.

"Yesterday we were driving along and I was telling Éric that we almost never see dead roadrunners," Joe said. "Suddenly, he told me to stop the car. Ahead, there was a coyote dragging something along the edge of the road. We jumped out, and it ran off when we got close. We found what the coyote was after. Can you believe it? A dead roadrunner! Very fresh, still warm. I've been up and down this road a hundred times and have never seen a dead one before. But even up close, they are pretty well camouflaged and blend in with the ground out there. It made me think that we might not see them when driving—we are usually moving pretty fast."

Éric looked excited. "Exactly!" he exclaimed. "Seeing a flattened roadrunner would definitely be hard while driving. I would classify them as having low detectability, and this chance sighting of the coyote makes me think that they have minimal persistence too."

So, he explained, there were two important problems: dead roadrunners were difficult to spot, and they were probably being moved by scavengers quite quickly. And even though the traffic levels were low, people tended to drive fast on this remote road, meaning that more roadrunners might be being killed than expected. But why were the birds on the road in the first place?

"Probably picking up dead reptiles," said Nicky. "Roadies mainly eat small snakes and lizards, and lots of these get killed while basking on the road in the early mornings. I just thought that they would be too quick for cars, but it now sounds like collecting dead reptiles might be a dangerous thing for them to do."

Éric had already pulled out a large notebook and was making notes (in indecipherable, presumably French, scrawl) while muttering silently to himself. "*Oui*, we have a very sound plan emerging already," he announced. "Okay, these observations on another but similar road suggest that collisions with cars may be a problem for these birds when the new road is constructed."

It cannot be assumed, however, that what happens in one place will also occur in another location. Differences such as the types of plants and microclimates could lead to varying responses from animals. When you are attempting to prove the ecological impact of a new infrastructure project—such as a road—and to prove it convincingly, it is essential to know what conditions were like before the new road was built and to compare them with what happens afterward.

"Of course, before and after," said Brad enthusiastically. "I suppose we would need to find out lots of things that might be relevant to roadrunners—like how many there are, where they live, what they eat, probably information about the numbers of snakes and lizards. Way outside my skill set, but we have some excellent ecologists at the university who are keen to be involved. But you haven't mentioned how we are going to get these birds, and other animals, across the road. How will we know if these crossings—I guess some sort of underpasses—actually work? What if the animals won't use them?"

"Very sensible questions, Brad," said Éric. "There will have to be a lot of discussion with the ecologists and road engineers about the details of any proposed structures, but it seems to me that some sort of underpass—probably a modified culvert with a raised base, so that there is a dry floor—would be suitable."

Fencing would also be necessary to keep animals off the road and to funnel them toward the underpasses. Another issue was where to place the crossing structures to provide the best chance that they would be used.

"From my experience," said Éric, "in fairly flat terrain like this, it is likely that these dry creeks are going to be the only places the underpasses will fit. The rest of the roadbed is going to be level with the land surface. So, I would expect that you might be able to install underpasses where the road crosses these dry depressions." Éric, Nicky, Joe, and Brad all leaned closer, taking in the colored curves of the various arroyos on the map; these usually flowed for less than a month each year, and often not at all.

A key question was whether the installation of these crossing structures would change the movements or behavior of the roadrunners. It was important to know what the birds were doing prior to the road being built, so that this could be compared with what happened after the crossings were constructed. This was the same "before and after" idea used for comparing no road with a new road, but here it would allow the opportunity to compare roads with and without the crossing structures. This was an unusual situation; typically, road ecologists are asked to do things when it is too late, with too few comparisons. Here, however, we really had the chance to prove whether these changes actually *make* a difference.

Nicky looked a little perplexed. "I'm still a bit concerned that the construction company that is going to build the road might be hard to convince. There are some fairly hard-case engineers and bean counters. I know just what they will say, even if we had lots of great information on roadrunner movement and that sort of thing: 'Thanks for the *interesting* stuff on your birdies. But now it's time for the road people to get on with the real work of building this important transportation link. . .'"

"Well, no, it's not as simple as that," interrupted Brad. "I know how you feel about some of these guys, Nicky, but they can't ignore the road-runners this time."

Transport Arizona would need to be shown very convincingly that collisions with cars represented a serious problem for the birds—and that the underpasses being proposed would actually work to allow the road-runners, and other wildlife, safe passage across the road. The contract required TA to demonstrate how they were going to mitigate the impacts of the roads on the roadrunners, so they had to take the issue seriously.

"I agree with you, very much, Brad," said Éric. "It is so important that the people directly involved in the design and building of the road are fully aware of what they are doing, and that the reason for these unusual additions to the normal features that roads have serves a clear purpose. I think it might be a good time for Edgar to say something now. Perhaps it's time to do your study design spiel, Edgar?"

Control Yourself

As Edgar van der Grift—exceptionally tall, even for a Dutchman—stepped over to the table, I realized I'd never known him to be silent for such a long period of time. Edgar has been involved in some of the most important developments in the science of road ecology, and he regards these issues as being of critical importance if the field as a whole is to be taken seriously. I've been privileged to have had Edgar personally guide me around some of the many crossing structures in the Netherlands, and we've shared stories and frustrations—and many beers—following many IENE conferences over the past decade. Australian road ecologists were even able to convince Edgar to be keynote speaker at what was the first road ecology conference in Brisbane back in 2008, where he again pushed the importance of getting the research right.[8]

"I have been listening carefully to Éric, okay! And yes, I can be quiet if necessary!" explained Edgar (apparently because I was not the only one thinking that he had been unnaturally silent). "He has been doing an excellent job of describing how to set up a good experimental study design, one that can gather the strong, reliable evidence that is clearly going to be a critical part of this project."

And he agreed that this was an excellent opportunity to do something that could provide a really strong foundation on which to base suggestions to the people designing the road. Having different locations within the same landscape made it possible to gather strong evidence—something that really mattered, because the people responsible for commissioning, designing, and building any new (or upgraded) road will always have strict budgets and straightforward objectives. Usually, Edgar observed, they tend not to be very impressed with vague arguments about "biodiversity" or "wilderness values" and the like. They want and need strong, clear information that they can include in their decision-making processes.

"In my experience, most of the rigid engineer types relate well to hard data and solid, no-nonsense recommendations—it's the loose, vague stuff they can't cope with. We just have to accept that and give them what they want. In the case of the Noha road, it's interesting to learn that the construction people are obliged to take the impact and mitigation issues seriously."

These days, Edgar explained, if environmental conditions—such as minimizing the risk to wildlife—are an unavoidable part of the brief of the project, they will be looking for reliable information so that they can make sensible decisions. Most road engineers then tend to treat these things as just another component of their project design.

"Being able to visit the actual place, and learning about the people directly involved, makes a big difference to our ability to provide the type of advice you need here," Edgar stated, with uncharacteristic seriousness. "Maybe I should try to illustrate how we could plan a sound way to collect the best information."

He strode over to a large whiteboard and drew two vertical rectangles next to each other. "This first box represents a section of the road *Before* [writing a large *B* above the left-hand box] any work has been done.

The other box is the same part of the road *After* [writing *A* above the righthand box]. In this case, what happens is, of course, the construction of the road: that is, the *Impact* [writing an *I* beside the two boxes]. The parameters being measured can be all sorts of things, but have to be done in the same way and with the same amount of effort in both cases. I expect the university researchers will be interested in things like the number of roadrunners nearby, their movements, and the presence of other species— we mustn't forget those native pigs!"

If we were trying to determine how building the road—the Impact— might affect the birds, we could, for example, compare the number of roadrunners seen at ten places along the route of the future road (before anything had disturbed the area) with numbers recorded at the same ten places after the road was built. That would obviously be useful, but some- thing else could be going on at the site that might influence the birds in some way. If some of the local javelinas were to move into those places because of the dustbathing opportunities, then this—rather than anything to do with the road itself—might serve to scare the roadrunners away. To be really certain of these kinds of things, Edgar explained, you must have a *Control*, somewhere identical to the site where the road is going to be. He added another two boxes below the Before and After boxes and wrote a large *C* next to them.

"You collect the same information as you do for the Before sites, and collect information again when you survey the After sites, even though nothing actually happens at the Control sites. This may sound strange, but it is the only way to be completely certain that it is the road that makes the difference—or not."

The four simple boxes drawn on the whiteboard represent a simple but powerful design that allows a comparison of any changes occurring over time (Before and After) as well as any changes that result from a particu- lar action (Control and Impact). Known as a BACI design, it is the gold standard for obtaining results that can be trusted.

The R-*What?* Agenda

Brad Gonarto had been listening intently throughout Edgar's presenta- tion, jotting furiously in his notebook. I could see the BACI boxes drawn roughly on the pages, surrounded by lots of writing. He looked up, alert and earnest. "Let me know if I'm wrong about this, but it seems that the same study design could be used to assess whether the crossing structures work as well. It would still be the Before, After, Control, Impact idea, but this time all the surveys would be done on roads. The Impact would be the installation of the underpasses and the Control sites would be sections of road without the structures. Have I got this right?"

"Exactly!" said Edgar, slapping Brad on the shoulder. "Understanding these concepts clearly is just the first step, however. The very important next step is to find suitable sites where all of this will take place, and that is something we can start discussing quite soon. But you must also be very clear about what your objectives are. The answers you get will only be as good as the questions you ask."

"Sounds like it might be time for a bit of Rauischholzhausen!" said Éric, conspiratorially.[9] "What do you think, Jochen?"

"R-*what*?" exclaimed Brad, looking at Jochen Jaeger for an explanation. Jochen, originally from Germany, had studied in Switzerland and was now working at Concordia University in Montreal, Canada. Quietly spoken, he is no less passionate than Edgar about getting the science right. "Sorry for that unpronounceable word, Brad," Jochen murmured. "It refers to both a beautiful, romantic place in Germany—a wonderful, grand, old-fashioned-looking (although it was actually built in the nineteenth century) house called the Castle of Rauischholzhausen—and a very important event that I was privileged to attend. It seems so long ago now . . . let me think, yes, 2005."

Jochen explained how he, and other road ecologists, had been looking for a more rigorous and systematic approach to conducting research that would actually be taken up by the people building the roads. Inga Roedenbeck, a doctoral student working with Jochen at the time, was particularly interested in this issue, and he encouraged her to organize a conference that focused on methods of investigating the impact of roads on biodiversity at the landscape scale. When the main conference was over, a smaller group stayed on to look at the fundamental questions facing road ecology and the ways in which they could be studied more rigorously.

Inga had managed to attract some of the main people working in what was still a very young field at the time. She had been particularly hopeful that Lenore Fahrig from Canada would attend. (All of us at Noha National Monument headquarters were aware that Lenore's research on a wide range of topics is among the most significant—and well designed—in the entire field. The big reviews she has led are always essential reading for everyone in road ecology.) The problem being that Lenore is extremely reluctant to fly.

"We had to offer something so special she couldn't resist," Jochen said. "Eventually Inga found the perfect bait: a genuine, old-fashioned castle! And then she was able to make it all happen!"[10]

"For some reason," continued Jochen,

the special atmosphere of the place helped us come up with some important and valuable ideas. These discussions were eventually compiled and published under the title, "The Rauischholzhausen Agenda for Road Ecology."[11] Yes, I know! And possibly made even more unwieldy by having Inga, deservedly, as the lead author. So, the paper that came out was, "Roedenbeck et al. The Rauischholzausen Agenda . . ." Possibly one of those "it seemed like a good idea at the time" decisions, but we all wanted to honor the place where these ideas were formed. Although there was definitely a mischievous desire to have a special title, even if was strange and unpronounceable. At the end of a long discussion, various suggestions had been produced—but none was accepted by everyone. We were kind of stuck, but Jeff Houlahan, a Canadian colleague from New Brunswick, pointed out that many of the really big decisions in human history were named after the place where they had been made. "Think Maastricht Treaty or Rio Convention," he said grandly. "This is at least as important! The . . ." and then he almost broke his tongue trying to pronounce the name. "It's the perfect title," Jeff went on. "Imagine all the scientists attempting to quote this most important of all the important science papers ever published, but when they try to pronounce it—disaster." We wanted it to be memorable but that may have backfired a little.[12]

"It's fairly old now," Jochen added, "but the ideas and methodology we came up with are still completely relevant today. The article is definitely not bedtime reading but has been essential for anyone who is serious about conducting sound road ecology research. Would you all agree?" Every one of us affirmed his statement.

Jochen paused to bite off a piece of the chocolate bar he was holding and shuffle through his leather briefcase. "I brought a hard copy with me just in case," he murmured, as he flipped through the files. "Ah, here it is. I think it is worth reading a bit of the article out verbatim because it reflects exactly what we are dealing with right here and now: the challenge of getting the road designers and builders to take our ecological perspectives seriously. Listen to this. 'Although there is now a growing body of evidence of the negative impacts of roads on wildlife, ecological research has had comparatively little effect on decision making in transportation planning.'"[13] There was plenty of head nodding, and knowing looks were exchanged around the room.

Jochen continued:

"This reflects that, in the face of compelling economic and social arguments for road siting, design, and construction, the effects on ecological values are usually considered of secondary importance. However, this lack of resonance also relates to the nature of road research itself. Maximizing the impact in the decision-making process requires that, first, the questions addressed by road ecologists be directly relevant to the practical issues of road planning and construction, and second, road studies be designed so as to have high evidentiary weight. Much of the road research [often] fails [both] of these conditions . . . with the result that ecological arguments must appeal to general ideas such as the precautionary principle. These are frequently viewed as unscientific apologetics, especially in the face of compelling economic counterarguments."[14]

"That got a bit technical toward the end, didn't it," said Edgar. Jochen concurred:

What it really means is that the road design and construction people we have to convince are used to working with strong logic and clear engineering principles. It is a very quantitative perspective—physics and geology and economics—so when ecologists bring what seem to be far less substantial or solid concepts to the table, when we say things like, "We don't really know all of the effects of your proposed road but you should really be careful just in case" (which is sort of what the precautionary principle can sound like, especially to engineers), they are typically not treated with much respect. And really, that is fair enough from their perspective. They need "proof" or "evidence": sound, solid, and reliable information on which to base their expensive and complex engineering decisions. That's what the bit about "high evidentiary weight" means: we have to offer strong, sound evidence. This was why we still think that the Rauischholzhausen Agenda, although hard to pronounce, is vital. I would say even essential.

Putting BACI Back In

"It might seem that all this discussion of study design issues and science methodology is just esoteric jargon," said Jochen. "But there are plenty of practical examples of how this way of thinking can make a really big difference down where the rubber hits the road. So, enough theory. We need a good example of how BACI works in the real world. I think straight away of your work, Rodney. Your flying possums come to mind."

Rodney van der Ree, despite the obvious Dutch heritage, is thoroughly Australian in demeanor and outlook. Irreverent, informal, and often dangerously funny, he is nonetheless deadly serious when it comes to science. Although somewhat younger than many of the old-hand road ecologists, he has been one of the most active and influential contributors to this field. As I watched, I began to count the extent of his international collaborations—at least those I knew about—and came to the conclusion that with the exception of our hosts, he had published research with virtually everyone in the room, as well as with Lenore Fahrig and Hans Bekker. Most significantly, Rod had undertaken the thankless task of cajoling virtually everyone who had ever conducted any studies even remotely associated with road ecology from around the world to contribute to the new bible of the field: the *Handbook of Road Ecology*, published in 2015.[15] If Forman and colleagues' *Road Ecology* (2003) was the Old Testament, the *Handbook* is the New. The *Handbook* immediately became the very first place to start for everyone interested in this rapidly expanding and maturing field. And if Rod's current plans for establishing an online version come to fruition, it may never be out of date.

Rod strode over to stand next to the whiteboard and took the marker pen from Edgar. "You know how I hate to correct you, Jochen," he said, with a wicked grin, "but they don't fly and they aren't possums."

The species Jochen was referring to is one of Australia's marsupial gliders, the squirrel glider, to be precise (though they are not squirrels, either)—small, hyperactive, and attractive arboreal mammals, which are almost identical to the very well-known sugar glider. They are capable of gliding up to about sixty meters (two hundred feet), but a typical "flight" would be about half that distance, around thirty meters (one hundred feet). Most roads are wider than that, and if you imagine large motor trucks being in the way, the gliders would need to start their jump from very high up to be sure of crossing safely and not colliding with a vehicle. This is why roads are a serious issue for these animals in Australia and around the world—there are about sixty gliding mammal species in all, and they all face similar problems.

Most gliders are very reluctant to move along the ground, so any wide space between the trees will be a major barrier. Some councils in Australia have provided crossing structures such as rope ladders and glider poles, but few have been monitored to see if they work. During the 1990s, Rod had conducted a lot of research on gliders in the state of Victoria. Because of this work, the main transportation agency, VicRoads, approached him to assess the effectiveness of these types of crossing structures. They wanted to know, sensibly enough, whether it was actually worthwhile spending money on installing them. Rod had been talking and writing a lot about the importance of incorporating sound scientific methods into road ecology, so this was an opportunity to put his ideas into practice.

Rod drew two parallel lines close together down the middle of another whiteboard. These represented the Hume Freeway, one of Australia's

Figure 18. Rope ladder erected beneath viaduct bridge near Brisbane, Australia. Photographer Darryl Jones.

major roads, which connects the two largest cities, Melbourne and Sydney. At about the halfway point between these cities, the freeway passes through lightly treed farming country. Within this region, Rod and his research team found an area with plenty of gliders, which looked like a suitable place to install crossing structures. But before that happened, they needed to know as much as possible about the animals, so they spent some time studying the gliders' movements and taking genetic samples. Once they had this information, the road agency was able to install the crossing structures—rope ladders and glider poles.

"The key thing we needed to know was the movement of the gliders in relation to the road," Rod said. "We had plenty of experience in catching these delightful but sharp-toothed marsupials, so we captured several of them, fitted them with tiny transmitters and then followed them around the landscape."

Rod and his team also set up motion-triggered cameras and attached PIT (passive integrated transponder) tags to the animals' collars. These tiny devices, commonly implanted under the skin of pets to enable identification, were "read" by detectors which were attached to the crossing structures when these were installed, recording the gliders' movements over long periods of time. The main question to be answered was: Do the crossing structures allow the gliders to cross the road? The Hume Freeway is one of the oldest roads in Australia, and it had been widened during the 1980s into a multilane divided road with a wide median. This confronted the gliders with a 50 to 80-meter (150 to 250-foot) gap to cross—a serious problem for the animals. Based on his earlier studies, Rod concluded that it was highly unlikely they would even consider a glide of that distance. It therefore seemed probable that the populations living on either side of the road had been completely separated for over three decades.

"You would have to wonder whether it would be possible to bring these forcibly estranged groups back together again. I was slightly hopeful, but also realistic—they might simply have been apart for too long and may not even remember that they had relatives on the far side of the road."

Rod's studies started to become less about the wildlife and more about politics. Although his team were trying to be good scientists and doing the best job they could, the road agencies had their own agendas. Installing these types of road-crossing structures is often necessary for the approval process—something the road designers *have* to do. Some agencies couldn't care less whether the structures work or not.

"I'm happy to say that the road agency we dealt with weren't like that at all," Rod said.

> They were keen to have evidence that might save them a lot of money because it showed the structures didn't work or, conversely, would allow them to announce how wonderful they were at helping our native species to prosper. Maybe that sounds a bit cynical, but there is also the possibility that because these types of crossing structures are so cheap to install, the agencies can claim that all this fuss about permeability can be solved by simply sticking up lots of poles and ropes and, *voilà*, "problem solved!" This made it all the more critical that our research was done very carefully and critically. Whatever we found, it had to be watertight. It is all too easy for others to simplistically claim, "Don't work, so don't bother" or "Works like a dream, stick 'em up everywhere!"

Rod held up a battered sheaf of paper. "This really was a 'Rauischholzhausen' moment for us (and here is my well-used copy): we really wanted a true BACI design if we could manage it. And this is where I need to introduce Kylie Soanes, who was heavily involved in almost every part of this work. Kylie, your turn."

I had been surreptitiously watching Kylie, and it was clear she was keen to have her say. At Rod's invitation, she appeared at the whiteboard almost instantly, swiping the marker pen from him. "Rod was my PhD advisor back then, and he made sure I learned the importance of getting the research design right. We had a long stretch of highway to play with and this set us up well for an experiment."

Their first task, of course, was to get the lay of the land in the "Before" phase. They found a number of places along the freeway that supported gliders on either side and spent quite a while learning about their movements across the road—they even managed to obtain genetic records for later use. Once they had figured out where the gliders lived, close to the highway, they selected some sites that were to be mitigated—the "Impact" sites—and some where they did nothing—the "Controls." Kylie wrote a series of *I*s and *C*s along the road diagram.

> So, three of the B sites didn't have any structures installed, while at five we erected rope ladders or set up glider poles. All were continuously monitored into the "After" phase. This allowed us to compare directly whether

the installation of the crossing structures made a difference to the number of gliders crossing the road. Remember, it could have been thirty years since any had attempted such a journey, and to do so now would require them to find and use a very unnatural artifact. Let's face it: a rope ladder is not a branch, and a glider pole is a pretty poor substitute for a tree!

"Now for the cherry on top!" Kylie continued, drawing what I suppose was a cherry on the whiteboard.

Controls often seem a strange and mysterious part of the BACI design, but they are possibly the most important. These sites are essential if you want to be able to demonstrate conclusively that the crossing structures make a difference. Kylie was lucky to have two types of Control sites. The first type were study sites that had missed out on receiving a structure—these *B*s became *C*s. But the team also had some sites in a eucalyptus forest far from the freeway, in an area with just a small, unpaved farm road—virtually without traffic—where the gliders lived normal lives. These animals had been tagged and could therefore be monitored, enabling the research team to see what they were up to in a place where there was no highway.

"So, what did we find? Did it work?" asked Rod provocatively. "Well, plenty did happen." First, despite the fact that the crossing structures were so different from anything the gliders had ever encountered before, both the rope ladders and the glider poles were used—a lot. Understandably, the gliders were a little slow to begin with, but once the first, more adventurous, animals had discovered the ropes and poles, others began to follow suit. In fact, the rate of their use—the glider traffic levels—increased steadily over the five years of the study. This seemed to show that the local animals were becoming familiar with the structures and probably that other animals—maybe their own offspring—were joining in and crossing the road as Rod and his team had hoped. At the places along the highway without crossing structures, there were no such movements. This was important, because it showed that gliders in the area had not started crossing the highway for some other reason. No, this study design demonstrated powerfully that installing the crossing structures really did enable the gliders to cross what had been an almost complete barrier, and that they were unable to cross without them. Previously severed populations were, indeed, reconnecting.

"This was wonderful news," said Rod. "The road agency were as excited as we were. Especially their accountants. Compared with the big-ticket structures such as overpasses and the like, these poles and ropes were cheap, hardly even 'lunch money.' To get such a positive outcome for so little outlay seemed like an ideal investment."

Rod paused. "But there were also some important 'howevers' to consider. I think these are just as important as the apparently positive findings, and the road people needed to hear this news as well."

Even though the gliders living near the freeway were using the crossing structures, the rate at which they crossed the road was lower than that of the animals who were gliding over the farm road away from the freeway. The team found that these gliders crossed the farm road on about 70 percent of the nights they were tracked. In comparison, the gliders near the freeway only crossed on approximately half of those nights. It is not clear what was behind this lower rate, but one big difference was that the Control sites had no nighttime traffic. And gliders are nocturnal. Of the 2,500 vehicles traveling along the Hume Freeway each day, many were large trucks, which were much more likely to use the freeway during the night. The differences in the levels of noise, fumes, lights, and possibly even vibrations were very obvious.

"When we published this study," added Kylie,

> we wanted to be explicit about the fact that although the gliders were using the structures, a wonderful outcome, we could not pretend that this was the same as if there were no road. We gave the article the title, "Movement Re-Established but Not Restored."[16] That may sound a bit too negative, I know, but we wanted to make it clear that constructing a few crossing structures, no matter how clever the design, does not mean that things have returned to normal; that it is simple to overcome the massive disruption that any large road brings to an area. This study certainly assisted the squirrel gliders, but what about all the ground-dwelling species, the small birds, the reptiles and frogs? Or the koalas? None of these animals is going to use the poles or rope ladders.

And even more important, who makes the crossings? One of the strange things Rod and Kylie discovered during this study was that certain individuals made most of the crossings while some individuals never did. They were not sure why, but again it meant that we have to be wary,

even skeptical, of claims about animals "using" crossing structures meaning that they are "successful." Just because plenty of squirrel gliders were
recorded using the ropes and poles does not necessarily mean everything
is fine. Maybe, just down the road a little way, lots of gliders are still being
killed trying to cross. Of course, every little bit helps—but is it enough?

Is "Use" Useful?

It was time for a break. As we slowly wandered outside onto a broad,
open-air courtyard looking out onto the park, I was surprised to see just
how animated everyone was. We had been taking in a lot of concentrated
ideas and information, yet instead of looking weary, most people appeared to be wide awake and even stimulated. This was probably because the topics being discussed had been presented by people who lived
and breathed this stuff. It was hardly surprising that asking someone to
talk about something they had spent years thinking about worked so well.
It was also illuminating to hear the authors of what was often formidable and dense scientific writing, explaining their ideas passionately in informal and simple language. After all, that was really why we were here:
to provide advice and information that our Arizonian colleagues would
hopefully find helpful.

As I messily consumed a second burrito and watched a cactus wren
flitting back and forth between the top of a saguaro cactus and a sugar
bowl on the coffee table, I began ruminating on Rod's pointed mention of
the word *use* in his talk. This triggered memories and a particular train of
thought. When we returned to the working room, I felt compelled to say
something to the group, rather than just listen.

"This seems like a good time for me to say something," I ventured, a
little sheepishly. "It follows directly from Rod's talk, and I suspect at least
a few of us have been having similar reactions."

My first-ever road ecology study was indeed completely typical of this
approach. We even had "use" in the title: "Temporal Trends in Use of
Fauna-Friendly Underpasses and Overpasses."[17] But that was how we
were thinking at the time: "Do animals actually use these structures?"
I had been invited to provide advice on the design of one of the first fauna-
crossing structure arrays to be constructed in Australia. This included

underpasses, rope ladders, glider poles, and most significantly, a double-span, vegetated overpass. These were early days and no one on the design committee had any experience—or, indeed, understanding—of what we were trying to do, beyond a vague hope that some animals might be able to cross the road safely. As the drawings of concrete culverts and strange loops of rope strung between poles began to appear on the plans, we weren't thinking much beyond, "Are any animals going to use them?" The proposed solutions seemed unnatural and artificial. Why would anything climb up there? With that sort of thinking, all we were after was any sort of evidence of wildlife presence in or on the structures: footprints, droppings, photos from the rather simple (and extremely unreliable) camera traps, or simply observation during spotlighting trips. Anything would do as proof that something was venturing onto the structures. If our goal was as simple as "use," the bar was pretty low.

"So," I continued,

> when we (and by "we," I really mean Amy Blacker, née Bond, who did 90 percent of the work) immediately found lots of numerous species, vast amounts of droppings from kangaroos, wallabies, and hares, hundreds of tiny footprints in the smooth sand layers spread out inside the underpasses, and many out-of-focus photos of furry somethings, we were overjoyed. Vindicated. Case closed: animals did indeed use the structures to cross the road. Like so many others at the time, we rushed our astonishing news into print, announcing breathlessly to the eagerly waiting world: "They work! Wildlife uses them! Isn't that amazing!"

I looked around the room and was relieved to see plenty of knowing nods and smiles; it was the typical reaction of most of us in those days.

"Of course, it didn't take long before we all realized that almost every crossing structure was being 'used' by all sorts of local wildlife," I continued. "So, the fact that 'use' was completely normal and entirely expected soon resulted in far more important questions being asked, just as Rod and Kylie's excellent studies have shown."

This, I explained, led to challenges such as identifying which species were *not* using the structures, and why; gauging how many animals were enough to ensure gene flow; and finding out which *individuals* were making the crossings, rather than just noting the species.

Figure 19. Koala walking through fauna underpass in Moreton Bay area, Queensland, Australia. Photographer Moreton Bay Regional Council.

I was familiar with another example relating to the way researchers were monitoring the use of an overpass in Australia, and I thought this was worth describing to the group. I explained that, as was usual, the researchers set up camera traps to see which species were using the structure. As well as recording a wide range of animal species, the images showed regular crossings by, on average, one koala almost every night. This is a fairly high rate of crossings for this species, which usually doesn't spend much time on the ground, so the researchers were fairly pleased with the results. But when they examined the images more closely, they discovered that nearly all of the koala images collected were, in fact, of a single, territorial male. Instead of the data showing a steady stream of animals, they were actually a record of one belligerent despot ensuring that no other males could cross. That is exactly the opposite of what a successful crossing structure should be.

Rod spoke up. "This is a key point. We all have to be much more critical of what our findings actually mean in terms of the population of animals we are interested in. This koala example is probably fairly unusual, but no one really knows."

And—Rod went on to point out—very few studies of animals moving across roads using crossing structures have attempted to discover anything about the number of different individuals involved. Most of the time researchers have been content to say simply—and simplistically—that "plenty of species X are using the structure," but unless we have some idea of the number of individuals, and the proportion of the local populations they represent, we can't say much with certainty. Just because we detect numerous animals using the structure does not necessarily mean it is making a difference to either the long-term survival of the population or how much interbreeding is going on. One of the fundamental things we hope happens when crossing structures are installed is that enough animals cross the road and breed on the other side. As should now be clear, roads everywhere have isolated populations of many species, and this often eliminates the possibility of movement. If that goes on for too long, there is the real risk of local extinction and inbreeding.

Rod paused and looked around the room. "That makes me think of some of the best and most detailed studies of individuals using crossing structures. I think it's time to hear from Tony Clevenger about Banff, a place where there really are a lot of safe crossing options."

Tony is a research scientist working at the Western Transportation Institute at Montana State University, and one of the most productive and influential road ecologists in the business.[18] Although he is affiliated with a US university, he lives over the Canadian border, just outside of Banff National Park. As we have already discovered, this area is of legendary status among road ecologists for a lot of reasons, one of the most important being the sheer number of crossing structures that have been constructed along a relatively short section of the Trans-Canada Highway. One of the biggest problems for scientists trying to undertake sound scientific studies in road ecology is the lack of replication, the fundamental requirement of being able to compare a lot of sites that are as similar as possible. In most cases, scientists have very little influence on the number of structures included in a road design. Certainly, they are unlikely to get very far by suggesting that the people building a new road should install, say, ten identical overpasses for research purposes so that proper statistical comparisons can be made.

In Alberta, however, the Trans-Canada has been adding crossing structures continually since 1983, when the first wildlife underpass was

Figure 20. One of the fauna overpasses in Banff National Park, Canada.
Photographer Darryl Jones.

constructed. By 2000, there were twenty-three underpasses and two overpasses. At the time of writing (late 2020), forty-five underpasses and seven overpasses had been installed along the same stretch of highway in more or less identical habitat.[19] Bear in mind, this is more fauna overpasses than many entire countries possess, including a fairly large one just to the south. It is little wonder that road ecology researchers view Banff as something like nirvana. Researchers such as Tony Clevenger have made the most of the opportunity, producing an extraordinary amount of important research, most of which is applicable, at least in part, to locations all around the world.

Ecological CSI

"Yep, we're pretty darn lucky, I have to agree," said Tony, in his quiet, deliberate manner. "The number of structures and the collaboration with Parks Canada have been essential to our success. But funding has always been a major issue—most of our work would not have been possible without the support of several private foundations. Thankfully, these folks really believe in ensuring that high-quality research is being done."

Tony explained that the ability to identify individuals could be important for all sorts of reasons. An obvious one was being sure that those animals detected making the crossings are actually different individuals. Sometimes it is possible to distinguish individuals by paying close attention to differences in their natural markings, such as blemishes or a scar. More often, however, turning a generic animal into an individual means catching them so that they can be marked or tagged in some way. He and his team have used ear tags and collars as well as tracking transmitters.

"I appreciate how dangerous it must be for you folks catching otters, gliders, or koalas," Tony stated, with a glint in his eye. "But I invite you to join us next time we need to catch one of our grizzlies or a moose." He knew he had won that round.

These techniques enabling animals to be tracked in detail are routine these days. The latest generation of satellite tags has made it possible to watch animals' daily movements (in real time), whether that involves travel over vast distances or just their local wanderings. Recently at Banff, they have taken a different approach, one that is noninvasive and doesn't require capture and collaring, to assess which individuals are using the many crossing structures, and their sex and age. This has been invaluable in providing detailed information on which animals did what and when. But something that has become increasingly important is knowing how all these crossings relate to breeding and populations. As already discussed, roads can isolate populations.

"Although we have obtained evidence that hundreds of grizzly and black bears have been using the crossing structures," Tony continued, "these were mainly from camera traps, footprints made in strips of sand—track pads—set up in the underpasses, as well as from telemetry."[20]

All of this animal traffic had demonstrated use of the crossing structures, but it was telling him almost nothing about whether these movements were having any influence on the populations on either side of the road. Those animals could be youngsters heading away from home, old males being forced out by younger players, or rogue loners just wandering across the countryside. Were any of these contributing to gene flow, were they simply maintaining a healthy mix of age groups? To answer questions like these, Tony explained, you really have to be able to identify the individuals' species and sex. Today, this can be done by examining samples of their DNA. In the past, it meant literally finding, catching, sedating, taking a blood sample, and waiting until the animal revived and left safely. Every part of that process held enormous risks for everyone, including the animal, so if there were alternatives that worked, the team at Banff was very interested.

"What we needed was a safe way of obtaining a genetic sample that did not involve catching a big, dangerous animal. These days, it is so much easier," said Tony. "We can extract DNA from just about anything: skin, bone, fur, even dung. How we now collect these things is almost laughably easy. We simply set up taut lines of barbed wire across the entrances to the crossing structures."

When the bears—and other large species—brush past these wires, they leave behind a few strands or clumps of hair. It is incredible how much valuable information can be gained from something as insignificant as a strand of hair. The lab work allowed Tony and his team to work out not only how many individuals were involved, but whether they were males or females, and how often they moved through the structures. The exact numbers are not important, but in one study they obtained DNA from about 250 different bears over a three-year study. What was surprising was how many and how often these animals were crossing the structures: most of the grizzlies and about half of the black bears were using them. Interestingly, the grizzlies preferred to cross using the overpasses, while the smaller black bears tended to move under the road.[21]

Nicky—who had been saying very little, although she was clearly paying close attention to all the discussions—modestly put up her hand as if to seek permission to speak. Tony noticed. "Nicky. You look concerned," he observed.

Nicky, somewhat nervously, stepped forward. "Well, yes, this talk about the Banff bears got me thinking about *our* predators and the underpasses we will probably build. This might sound naive but, well, I guess I'm worried whether our much smaller predators—coyotes and gray foxes mainly—might just wait at the end of the tunnels. Could that happen?" The reaction from almost everyone in the room was remarkably spontaneous: there were lots of big grins and several high-fives. "So, I *am* dumb . . ." Nicky said, looking a little confused.

"Absolutely not," reassured Tony. "It's just that that question is asked almost every time any of us, anywhere in the world, gives a talk about crossing structures. We all knew it had to happen, and you are today's

Figure 21. Grizzly bear (*Ursus arctos*) crossing road, Yellowstone National Park, Wyoming. Photographer Marcel Huijser.

winner!" There was a general good-natured murmur around the room, and plenty of supportive gestures toward Nicky.

"Don't feel bad, Nicky. It is a perfectly logical question," said Tony. "If the predators were able to take advantage of these structures, it could have a major impact on the very species we are trying to help. At Banff, we hear this question often from the public—and in fact, even from people who work in the national park. With all those crossing places available to the animals, it seemed like a good place to take a serious look at this issue."[22]

This was possible because the field staff had been recording incidents of prey being killed along the Trans-Canada Highway since 1981. When they looked, they were amazed at just how much data had been collected over the years—including well before the underpasses and overpasses had been installed. This meant they could do some really detailed comparisons of the pattern of predation before these structures were available to the animals, and then afterward.

"One more reason why we are so privileged to be able to work in this place," explained Tony. "There was great data both before and after the structures were built, but we also wanted more detail on the movement of both predators and prey through the structures."

The team at Banff reasoned that if the so-called Prey-Trap Hypothesis was real, the predators—mostly wolves and cougars—would be likely to kill their prey (primarily elk, bighorn sheep, and moose) near the structures—and in greater numbers than they had done before the crossings were present. But that was not what they found. And they had a lot of data to prove it, and from a really long time period: more than 700 kill sites, and recordings of almost 7,000 predators and about 190,000 prey moving through twenty-eight structures. This huge amount of data enabled them to show extremely clearly that there was no evidence that the kills were closer to the structures or were more likely when lots of prey were moving through them. Other studies have not been so clearcut—these mainly investigated smaller species—but these researchers did not have the quantity of data available at Banff.[23] Tony is a modest and rather private guy, but we could all see how pleased he was to be working in Banff; we were left with even more respect for the place and for Tony's remarkable research.

It's a Start

It was getting close to the end of the day by this time, and even the keenest of us were beginning to wane. Spirits revived quickly, though, with the arrival of another type of spirits in the form of five different varieties of tequila. As we gathered to enjoy the gorgeous pastel colors of a cloudless Arizona twilight, a coyote coughed and a nighthawk *"peeet"*-ed plaintively somewhere out among the pines. We reflected on some of what we had learned during a long day of discussion, listening, and thinking. Rod van der Ree called our hosts over, waving a bottle of Patrón Silver. "So, was that useful?" he asked, with genuine concern. "You have invested a lot in flying in this crew from all over the world. We just hope it was worth it."

"Rodney," said Brad, "you cannot be serious! This has been one of the most illuminating and valuable meetings I have been to. Having so much experience and practical knowledge in one room has been brilliant. I feel quite relieved, actually. I thought that the presentations might have been too technical for us non-ecologists to follow, but everyone did an excellent job of explaining their topic." He patted his notebook. "My notes are going to make a huge difference to how we approach the planning of the road and the vital research that is going to have to happen now. I will be calling my contacts at the university as soon as possible."

"Don't forget what we are doing tomorrow, everyone," said Nicky. "You guys have only just begun your work here. Today was the theory. In the morning we will head out to see the land close up. I hope to introduce you to a roadrunner or two while we recon places for wildlife tunnels and BACI sites. Now that I know what needs to be done, and how we should be doing it, I can't wait to get started."

Joe Bikéyah—who had changed into a beautiful shirt embroidered with intricate Native American designs—turned to us and announced, "And after we have finished this important work, it will be my pleasure to welcome you to Mesquite Wells, where our people have been preparing a traditional Navajo celebration for us all. You have come a long way to speak to us and teach us some of your ideas. But please be aware that this road is mainly for us, my community, and we are extremely aware of the risks and threats that might come if we are not careful. Tomorrow, we hope all of you will gain some wisdom to add to your knowledge."

"Thank you, Joe," Brad said. "You have always been so generous, despite having plenty of reasons to be otherwise. And Joe is right—there is much more that we all need to learn about this road. These things are so much more than just a place to drive. All of the ideas we have learned today are great. They will make a huge difference. But they are actually just a start. The real work involves getting all the different people together, around the table, and cooperating. Is that too difficult?"

Part III

Take Alternative Route

5

WORKING TOGETHER WORKS

There is a small, snug place among trees and breeze where I sometimes sit just to watch and listen. The light is filtered through a shimmering canopy of eucalypts, acacias, and melaleucas, all local species, which form a tangle of branches and foliage that reaches all the way from the leaf litter to the spindly treetops. If I'm quiet and still—and lucky—I might see a family of fairy-wrens flittering jaggedly through the lower shrubs or spot a legless lizard stalking skinks among the fallen leaves. When I don't turn up for that Finance and Planning Committee meeting, or the note stuck to my university office door says, vaguely, "In the field," there is a good chance this is where I will be.

"My" spot is in the center of the top of the Compton Road fauna overpass, where the surface dips to form a slight depression. Here the terrain of the overpass follows the curvature of the two concrete arcs below, each one of which has two lanes of traffic passing through it. As Sacred Sites go, it's rather unspectacular: an apparently mundane piece of Australian bush. It could be anywhere. And that is the point. Sixteen years ago, this "hill" and the vegetation growing on it did not exist. A year later, it was a stark, steep-sided mound of soil and mulch, with hundreds of delicate seedlings planted all over the substrate. Now these plantings have grown into towering trees or spread into dense shrubs and understory, or—having reached the end of their natural life—have fallen over, providing refuge for reptiles and amphibians. Just as the structure's designers had hoped, the vegetation growing all the way over the overpass is now contiguous with the eucalyptus-dominated forest on either side of the road. The animals that now pass over every day and night, or live up here permanently, were all born well after this structure was constructed. The row of twelve-meter (forty-foot) glider poles are effectively redundant, as the tallest trees are now much higher than these structures, allowing the gliders to soar deftly from branch to trunk, then scamper up and launch again, moving through the foliage at astonishing speed. They are crossing an endlessly busy four-lane road, but they don't know that. From the edge of the overpass you can see the rope ladders sweeping in taut arcs high above the traffic. It is not at all unusual to see possums or gliders scampering across.

Every time I visit this place, I have to remind myself that all of it— the complex, self-sustaining ecosystem providing continuous habitat for a vast number of animals to live in, breed in, or just pass through—is, or was, entirely artificial. It exists because the overpass—an enormous artifact, an edifice of concrete, steel, soil, and imagination—was designed and built for this purpose. And while there were many, often difficult, steps involved in planning, designing, and constructing this cumbersome structure, these actually represented the easy part of the process. The work done long before the first sod was turned was far more difficult. Calculating weight-bearing vectors, positioning thirty-six massive concrete arches weighing eighteen tonnes (twenty tons) each, and managing thirty thousand vehicles a day passing through a live construction site were nothing compared to dealing with the Karawatha Forest Protection Society.

In 2003, Compton Road was a congested, two-lane arterial road located in the burgeoning southern part of Brisbane. This was one of the fastest-growing areas in the fastest-growing part of Australia, and the pressure on transport infrastructure was mounting. Brisbane City Council had often been accused of neglecting this portion of its huge expanse (the

Figure 22. The recently completed (2018) Illaweena Street fauna overpass near Brisbane, Australia. The first planted tree saplings and glider poles are visible. Photographer Darryl Jones.

city's boundaries encompass 1,343 square kilometers [520 square miles]; by comparison, New York City has a land area of 780 square kilometers [300 square miles]). The Brisbane lord mayor's announcement that the road would be upgraded from two to four lanes was greeted with predictable enthusiasm by local businesses and residents—but with despair by environmental groups.

Although Compton Road connects two densely populated suburbs, the central part of the road traverses a major tract of intact eucalyptus forest, separating two important conservation reserves: to the north, Kuraby Bushlands, and to the south, Karawatha Forest. Both are crucial components of a vast swath of wooded landscape known as the Flinders-Karawatha Corridor, which extends for sixty kilometers (thirty-seven miles) through some densely populated parts of the state. Although the corridor is criss-crossed with numerous roads and is hemmed in on all sides by suburbs and industry, it represents one of the most significant remnants of original forest in the region. And Karawatha Forest, an intact block of 900 hectares (3.5 square miles), is among the largest components of the entire corridor.

For some people, this extensive natural area, surrounded by ever-expanding suburbs, was a priceless wilderness, home to a remarkably diverse community of plants and animals. For others, it was useless, empty land, ideal for residential development. This familiar conflict led in the early 1990s to the formation of the Karawatha Forest Protection Society (KFPS), an energetic and passionate group of local residents committed to protecting this important place. Seemingly endless KFPS deputations to City Hall resulted in Brisbane City Council conferring strong legal protection on the area as well as public acknowledgment of its significance. As a consequence, KFPS gained a well-founded reputation as a strong, effective, yet sensible community group, people who would always play hard for what they regarded as important but who were also willing to moderate their demands—and even compromise a little—when appropriate. This hard-won reputation was largely down to the vigilance and thoroughness of the group's leaders, especially Thomas Creevey and Bernice Volz. "It was bloody hard work at times," Creevey told me recently. "We seemed to be forever at tense meetings at City Hall or in the courts. But all that was worth it: we beat the bastards! When Karawatha was granted conservation reserve status it really looked as though our battles were over."[1]

But then in 2003 came the news that Compton Road was to be doubled in size. This threat had been around for a while, but the announcement, at a time when such battles seemed to be behind them, was felt deeply by the KFPS. Bernice Volz remembers the moment all too well. "I was shattered. I had been recording the roadkill on Compton Road for years and we were seeing a dead wallaby, possum, or reptile almost daily. To think of what a much wider and even busier road would be like was just horrifying."

Roadkill was the central concern. The existing distance between the forest edges across the road was about sixty meters (sixty-six yards).

The upgrade would involve the clearing of vegetation, the construction of new lanes, and the inclusion of a wide central median between the carriageways, increasing the distance between the forest edges from fifty to seventy meters (fifty-five to seventy-seven yards). With the daily traffic projected to increase massively within just a few years, the challenge facing any animal attempting to cross all four lanes would be formidable. "No, it would be bloody impossible," roared Thomas, his ire aroused by the memory. "And that's exactly what I told them. More than double the width! No way. The City Council had in the same year legally protected this forest for its undeniable natural values. Yet now the same people were threatening to wreck the whole thing! Well, I wasn't having it. Not one bit."

Thomas had been at the forefront of the campaign to protect the forest for years and had seen off a variety of challenges. The continuous pressures associated with rapid urban development—housing, transport, recreation, energy infrastructure—as well as acts of vandalism and incursions by feral animals and weeds, had required eternal vigilance. Although most members of the group had jobs and families, these ordinary residents had been extraordinarily successful in seeing "their" forest saved. And yet, suddenly, a potential catastrophe had emerged that threatened to undo all their hard work.

"Some people seemed to think of this priceless area of natural habitat as just empty, worthless bush, somewhere you should be able to do 'important' things like build houses, sports fields or pipelines—or add another bloody great road!" said Thomas. "I was livid when I heard about the plans for Compton Road. Well, this was not going to happen without a fight!" Thomas was already familiar with the corridors of Brisbane's City Hall and was not easily dissuaded from putting his views forcefully to everyone from the lord mayor down. Yes, he was undeniably bombastic and opinionated, but he was always thoroughly informed and well prepared. And the folks in City Hall knew it. Soon after his visit to the mayor's office, an expensively suited delegation paid a visit to Thomas's modest home, located not far from the forest, to try to explain how things stood. They may even have thought he would back down when confronted with "The Facts."

"It was soon obvious that the decision [to go ahead with the upgrade of the road] had already been made," recalled Thomas. "And that there was apparently little we could do about it. But I knew that there was a 'community consultation' process and we were adamant that they had to take that part seriously." The lines in blue printed on the maps laid out on the dining-room table seemed to be the final word. But not to Thomas and the KFPS. "Nothing is really set in stone," he said to me, with quiet defiance.

"We had all the facts and figures: the number of dead wallabies and koalas, how many car accidents there were, the amount of forest that would be lost, the threat to several endangered species. We had come to realize that some version of the road was pretty much inevitable, but we wanted them to be thoroughly aware that if they wanted a serious, well-organized fight, we were ready. Or, instead, they could listen to our concerns as well as our sensible ideas . . . there are always more alternatives than might occur to a flaming road engineer!" Thomas's proven strategy was to always have several viable options ready to offer—and to never be intimidated by authority or Italian suits. At that initial meeting, the city council representatives arrived full of confidence, with a simple plan. They left with a very different perspective and a folder full of notes.

Thomas's strategy worked. The lord mayor announced during the next meeting of the city council that an upgrade of Compton Road would proceed as previously announced. However, according to Thomas—who was present at this meeting—the mayor added that "Although this new road would be much wider and busier, it would have *less* environmental impact than the existing one." Just how this might be achieved was not explained. Thomas recalled that the mayor then turned to his startled transportation planner, who was seated nearby, and said, preemptively: "You're supposed to be a f****** engineer. Engineer it!" The mayor also announced that a committee was to be formed consisting of city council representatives, town planners, and members of community and environmental groups, as well as some "ecologists with relevant experience." Ominously, in the opinion of some, the city council's project manager was to chair this committee. "I knew a few civil engineers and was not expecting much in the way of a sympathetic ear," said Thomas. "To me, having the head logistics guy as boss of the committee just increased the scale of the threat. And the chance of disaster."

I had been observing the escalating tensions between the city council and the local community groups from the "outside," but shared many of the concerns of the KFPS. Colleagues from my university, which is located nearby, had been involved in numerous studies in Karawatha, documenting the many rare and threatened species and assessing the threats. We were all very aware of the terrible roadkill rates and shared the apprehension about what even more traffic could do. My fairly peripheral interest in what was happening changed abruptly when I was invited to join the advisory committee as one of those "ecologists with relevant experience," presumably to bring some ecological science to the table. I could certainly list the endangered species found in the area and explain how best to identify local bat species, but otherwise I was unsure how I might be able to contribute. So, I was far from comfortable when asked to attend the first (and potentially highly contentious) meeting of the committee, to be held in Thomas Creevey's cluttered living room. The implications of that gathering were to have an enormous impact on my life, although I did not appreciate that at the time.

The first shock was that when the City Hall delegation turned up at Thomas's place, his dreaded boss "logistics guy" turned out to be Mary O'Hare, one of Brisbane City Council's most accomplished project managers.[2] As such, she would be making the most important decisions in this project. Mary had an abundance of experience, having been associated with many of the city's biggest transport infrastructure projects, but Compton Road was something else altogether: transport infrastructure, sure, but with the goal of minimizing the impact on the natural environment. That was a genuine challenge.

What was most disconcerting was that Mary had no intention of simply following the "party line." Unexpectedly, and very refreshingly, she made it clear that she viewed the apparent conundrum—designing a fauna-friendly road—not as some fanciful and impossible objective (nor even a tautology), but as a worthwhile and stimulating opportunity. "The lord mayor was correct—this is fundamentally an engineering problem: constructing a bigger yet safer road," she announced at the very start of the meeting. And then she said something no one could have expected. "When I heard about this project, I drove straight out to have a close look for myself. Karawatha is a precious and important place! I wandered through the forest early one morning and said to myself, 'This must not be harmed by this road. We have to come up with something that keeps it safe.' Right then and there I made a commitment. We were going to do this different and do it right!"

No one moved or said anything for a moment. And then the room noticeably relaxed, readjusting to the very new perspective. Many of us had been expecting entrenched views and defensive attitudes. These were, after all, road people. Thomas, Bernice, and comrades had come prepared for battle. Instead, they found themselves somewhat outflanked. We were all rather perplexed, soon realizing that we would have to rethink our strategy. Straightforward, simple-minded opposition is easy; collaboration is fundamentally different. And a lot more fun.

Leading by Listening

There is no need to describe in detail the debates, discussions, disagreements, and discoveries that ensued during the many meetings held by this group of dedicated and passionate people. What is important, however, is that the group worked. Spectacularly. Somehow, decisions were made that eventually led to the installation of what was to be one of the largest arrays of crossing structures all in one location in the world: two large fauna underpasses; a row of glider poles; three rope ladders; and, of course, a large, fully vegetated overpass.

It was an astonishing achievement, particularly when you recall that it had its origins in so much conflict and anger. When Mary O'Hare and her team arrived at Thomas Creevey's place for that original meeting, everyone assumed there would be fireworks. After all, the environmentalists felt that they had been betrayed and misled. By the same token, the engineers and road planners must have been smarting over some of the colorful and damning accusations made about them by Thomas and others. Distrust, fear, and hurt seemed to have gate-crashed the event and threatened to undermine any efforts to make progress. I sat at the back of the room, sensing the tension and wondering how on earth we were going to get anywhere. More recently, I have learned that Mary was several steps ahead of everyone else before she entered the room. "I remember that day like it was yesterday," she told me, when I tracked her down to her new home in Tasmania. "If we had any chance of this actually working, I had to try something no one was expecting."

Mary was an experienced infrastructure project manager and a female. Women don't get very far in that world without serious smarts and acute emotional intelligence. Navigating the terrain of what had forever been an exclusive Boys-Only Club took fortitude and cunning, as well as a razor-sharp analytical mind. When Mary walked through Thomas's door, it was not as the arrogant expert or the colorless bureaucrat. Instead, she immediately made it clear that she was there to learn. "I'm just the facilitator. I've been asked to build a road, but this is not a normal situation," she said. "Karawatha Forest is incredibly special and we have to find a way to make this the safest road in the country. Safe for the wildlife and for the people using the road. I know how to build a four-lane blacktop arterial, but I don't know how to stop the roadkill or get the critters safely to the other side. I need your help with that stuff."

Although the suspicions didn't vanish overnight, it became clear that Mary was being genuine: it was obvious that she really cared about the forest and was interested in our ideas. Her honesty and transparency were refreshing and disarming. A few of her team, taking notes and offering quiet clarifications, often looked shocked at some of Mary's statements. We all remember things like: "Richard, mate. You don't need balls to drive a D9 [bulldozer]—in fact, they might get in the way." Thomas took a bit longer to warm to this new reality; in fact, Mary recalls: "Thomas hated my guts at the start!" But he too came around; once convinced that something remarkable was actually happening, Thomas soon began offering his own ideas. Some were just not possible ("Could we make the entire road underground?"), but it was Thomas who kept coming up with suggestions such as "some sort of rope thing that could stretch all the way over the road gap" or "ledges along the sides of the culverts so little mammals could get through without having to walk on the concrete floor." These ideas, and many others, were fielded and discussed. Although some concepts were ultimately considered too difficult or expensive, often the reaction from the planners and engineers was not dismissal but, rather: "That's really interesting. We'll look into that." And what was truly remarkable? In most cases, they actually did.

The most straightforward crossing structures were the underpasses; culverts and tunnels were universal features and only needed a bit of tweaking to work here. The really big challenge, however, was always going to be getting animals *over* the road. There were a lot of species within the forest that were never going to make use of the tunnels under the road, perceiving them as just too confined, dark, exposed, close to the

Figure 23. Long fully concrete fauna underpass with raised log on wall and ledges above wet zone near Brisbane, Australia. Photographer Darryl Jones.

ground, or strange. This included the largest species, the kangaroos and wallabies, but also the arboreal ones, such as gliders and koalas. These species needed some kind of bridge over the road.

Again, it was Thomas who first came up with a potential solution: building concrete arches to span the road and then covering them with soil. He swears that he had not heard about similar structures that already existed elsewhere overseas. The engineers were similarly unfamiliar with such a structure but started to look into whether it might be a possibility. The suggested overpass would involve a combination of complicated structures capable of bearing extraordinary weight, located in a site with unsuitable foundations—to be designed by people who had never previously attempted anything like it. And the whole thing was being built over a busy road. What could possibly go wrong? Yet, with professional resolve and commitment, the team eventually nailed it. For a while, it looked like topography and load-bearing vectors were going to defeat the team. But perseverance won the day. Mary recalled: "I remember with great fondness the day our designer rang me to say, 'Mare, you won't believe it, but I can make that bridge fit.' That breakthrough led to an important chain of events. I think insightfulness and good management and great communication and great people made Compton Road such a success. It was definitely the highlight of my career."

This was an extraordinarily fortuitous project to be involved in as my first taste of road ecology. Being part of such a cooperative and dedicated group of people, who came to share a vision and, once convinced, worked tirelessly to see it through, was enormously rewarding and encouraging. It also provided a solid foundation in understanding how and why such a process can work. Although I had no idea at the time, I was soon to learn that such a fruitful and collaborative partnership was actually vastly different from what often occurs. Being able to experience how a really successful partnership can work provided some important insights into what might happen when collaborations completely fall apart.

There is a chance this chapter could end up sounding like a cheap "managing your people" book or pop psychology article. I hope not. But I do have to delve into topics that are not the usual territory for an ecologist (and may also be entirely foreign to your average road engineer). This discussion is inescapable because, as in many other parts of life, it turns out that people and the way they interact with one another really are important—even when the issues are to do with transportation, roadkill, and fauna overpasses. Compton Road only happened because all the key people got on. They listened, were willing to consider alternative views, and eventually began to respect each other. When these things happen, the results can be extraordinary. When they don't, progress is so much more difficult and sometimes impossible.

Rather than discuss these interactions theoretically, it would be far more useful to describe some very different examples of real-world projects that eventually worked—despite a difficult beginning, in one particular case—because the people involved saw the value of genuine cooperation.

Respect Can't Be Pretended

Indigenous people have lived for millennia in the northern Rocky Mountains in the United States, occupying parts of what are now the states of

Washington, Idaho, and Montana. Today, the Flathead Indian Reservation is home to the Bitterroot Salish, Kootenai, and Pend d'Oreille peoples.[3] These tribes are now recognized as the Confederated Salish and Kootenai Tribes of the Flathead Nation, with the legal standing of a sovereign nation. The reservation is a (relatively) large area—about 5,200 square kilometers (2,000 square miles)—in northwest Montana. The tribes continue to care for and rely on the natural resources of this remnant of their ancestral land. The landscape and diverse wildlife populations of the area (which includes sixty-six species of mammals) still provide part of the indigenous peoples' subsistence, cultural, and spiritual requirements. Understandably, they are fiercely protective of these essential resources and are fully aware that activities undertaken by the state or federal governments require tribal consent. For the most part, state interest in the reservation has been marginal. But occasionally, decisions made over in Helena, Montana's capital, have led to serious confrontations.

Early in the 1990s, the Montana Department of Transportation and the Federal Highway Administration announced a major upgrade of Highway 93, the main north–south road traversing the Flathead Reservation and a major access route to Glacier National Park. This proposal was long overdue. Highway 93 was in a shocking state and was demonstrably one of the most dangerous roads in Montana: the numbers of both fatal and injurious vehicle accidents were far higher than the state average, and were getting worse. Many local cars carried bumper stickers imploring: "Pray for me. I drive Highway 93." And the people living on the reservation were among those most directly affected by the road conditions. They had been complaining to the transportation authorities for years and seemed to be getting nowhere.

The problem was, of course, that the tribes had not been included in the initial plans for improving the road, even though the entire project had enormous implications for them and their land. "It was as though we were supposed to be grateful that they were finally doing something about the road," recalled a tribal spokesperson. "Of course, we wanted that. But we had many concerns about what they were proposing, concerns about how the road would impact special cultural and historical locations, and the wildlife. They simply did not see the land as we did. It was deeply disrespectful that we were not even consulted. If they had talked to us first, listened, learned, it would have made such a difference. Respect can't be pretended."[4]

This was a difference (or perhaps indifference) that resulted in almost a full decade of bitter negotiation and painfully slow progress. Opposition by the tribes was clearly exacerbated by their early perception of being ignored, a lack of respect that was keenly felt by the community. Perhaps unexpectedly, the engineers and planners similarly felt disrespected. After all, they were the experts and specialists in these complicated matters. When someone actually states the dreaded, "With all due respect . . .," during a meeting, you know things are not proceeding well. The problem—something common if not ubiquitous—in transportation planning is that the process is, almost by definition, the opposite of user friendly. The people who will ultimately benefit from the eventual outcomes (a well-designed road in this case) have traditionally been excluded from any involvement. By the time the shiny "project proposal" document is printed, all of the main decisions have already been made. And everyone knows it. The "public consultation" phase typically comes too late for meaningful dialogue to occur and is often entirely misleading. At best, the community might be granted a token or two (providing advice on the plant species to be used in revegetation is a common example), but the project is usually so advanced within the schedule of the relevant authorities and organizations that little can be done. Apparently. Unless you have the status of a sovereign nation, which means you can simply withdraw your support and the whole project will come to an abrupt stop. And that is what happened in Montana.

New Visions

This drastic moment did not, however, mean the project was abandoned. Although it looked catastrophic at the time, with hindsight it was actually a fortuitous and necessary disruption that led to a fundamental restart. The decision by the Flathead community leaders brought together an initially uneasy collective of what was described as "three governments": the US government (represented by the Federal Highway Administration); the state (the Montana Department of Transportation); and the Confederated Salish and Kootenai Tribes. This was accompanied by a significant reshuffle of those individuals representing each party. As described blandly in an official summary of these important events: "The assemblage of the right people from all three governments was necessary to break the stalemate. Leaders who were able to build personal and working relationships, work together, build trust, and listen and learn from each other so that a greater vision could be achieved."[5]

This new collaborative process did not happen instantly, of course—a lot of bridges had to be built and connections made (if I may), and that took considerable patience, humility, and determination. But, eventually, it worked. Because, ultimately, it had to. Crucially, all sides agreed that the road needed serious attention, but they *also* acknowledged that a lot more consideration was needed regarding cultural and ecological perspectives. As the three parties began working together at last, important discussions on the alignment of the route resulted in the highway moving away from places of cultural significance and in the selection of specific sites for wildlife crossings. Forty-two crossing structures of various types and sizes were included, along with about fourteen kilometers (nine miles) of exclusion fencing on both sides of the road. Significant rehabilitation of wetland areas was also carried out.[6] There were great improvements in human safety, with far fewer large mammals on the road.

On completion of the project, wildlife biologists representing both the Western Transportation Institute in Bozeman and the tribes have continued to undertake extensive long-term monitoring of these sites, providing crucial feedback on local wildlife populations and movements. The tribal wildlife biologists have been included as full partners in all aspects of this research.

From seemingly intractable stalemate and hostility to productive cooperation, the travails and hard-earned insights unfolding in the mountains of Montana (the situation continues to evolve) represent another hopeful story of what can be achieved with mutual respect and common purpose. One of the remarkable revelations to emerge from this prolonged project has been the belated acknowledgment that the apparent intransigence of the Flathead Nation resulted in important lessons of much wider significance. As the official outline of the project concludes: "The insistence of the CS&KT that the highway be designed as a safe, environmentally friendly road instead of other alternatives has set the stage for a new vision for future highway design."[7]

Marcel Huijser, who was involved in much of the ecological research for this project, recently explained to me his understanding of the agreed position ultimately reached by the various parties. The federal, state, and tribal governments' decision to reconstruct the road was based on the idea that "the road is a visitor and that it should respond to and be respectful of the land and the 'Spirit of the Place.'" The "guiding philosophy" for the reconstruction of the highway was to "protect cultural, aesthetic, recreational, and natural resources located along the highway corridor and to communicate the respect and value that is commonly held for these resources pursuant to traditional ways of the Tribes." Clearly, these folks had come a long way down this road together.

Champions

This is an overtly hopeful book. Realistic and critical—but ultimately the message is optimistic. Just as well, because it would be easy to fill a volume many times the size with stories of projects that did not end—or even start—so productively. By far the most common experience is of a local council, government agency, or construction company (often driven by politicians), riding roughshod over the concerns and opposition of community groups. Even if the public is given a hearing, this is often a tokenistic or belittling experience. Too often, the "community consultation" part of the process is something agencies are forced into undertaking and is, therefore, a compliance exercise at best. It is impossible to legislate effective engagement.

For most people operating outside the road agencies, becoming involved in a project of interest can be extremely difficult. Very often, by the time the community hears about a new road or railway that is proposed to run through a favorite reserve or near their back fence, most of the planning decisions have already been made. And even if they do find a way to become involved, the processes of planning and designing a project can be extremely opaque and confusing—sometimes appearing to be deliberately unwelcoming and inaccessible—leaving most nonspecialists with little option other than outright opposition. This situation is changing in some parts of the world, but the overt or unintended exclusion of external views remains one of the major stumbling blocks to improving the relationships between transportation agencies and the public.

Where there have been successful collaborations, one or two key people have almost always made the difference. These individuals may be

from either side of the table, but they usually share some distinct attributes. They are confident, articulate, and well informed, willing to take
a stand and insist on being heard. Okay, that might include any number
of arrogant, self-centered mini-despots whom we have all met, but the
people I am describing also spend a lot of time listening, seeking out those
who are not particularly vocal and considering alternative views. When
you get people like that, almost anything can happen. Such individuals are
sometimes known as "champions," although this is never stated in their
hearing. They are the ones who see what is needed to ensure collaboration
and then work toward it. We were extremely fortunate in having two such
champions involved in the Compton Road project, and their presence,
without doubt, was the reason it succeeded so well: Mary, the project
manager, and Thomas, the community leader. And it was necessary that
both were involved. Without Mary, I think we would have had endless
conflict and no productive outcome. Without Thomas, we would have
had many fewer ideas. Without both, we would now have just another big
road dividing the landscape—and another embittered community.

Top Down

Of course, sometimes *good* big decisions can be made unilaterally. For
some reason, Singapore comes to mind. This tiny island—located almost
on the equator, in steamy Southeast Asia—has a rapidly growing population and few natural resources, but its remarkably resilient people have
somehow developed their tiny state into one of the most technologically
advanced and prosperous nations in the world. And although less than
5 percent of the country's original tropical rainforest remains, the government has determinedly transformed the island into a vibrant "garden city," where parkland, forested water catchments, or conservation
reserves now account for almost all unoccupied land. Despite the early
destruction of the forests and the fact that Singapore is the second most
densely populated country on the planet (about eight thousand people
per square kilometer [twenty thousand people per square mile]), a surprisingly diverse community of wildlife has managed to persist.

The large and almost continuous tract of jungle stretching across the
middle of the island is bisected by the main highway, which connects the

Singapore CBD (central business district) with Malaysia in the north. For more than two decades, the only way for animals to move between the nature reserve on the western side and the catchment area on the east was across the unfenced Bukit Timah Expressway (constructed between 1983 and 1988). As a result, horrifying numbers of macaque, deer, and wild boar were regularly killed on this major highway. Obviously, road safety was a major concern as well. The significance of this small (about 3 kilometers [1.9 miles]) section of road for the wildlife of Singapore was well known to local community groups and demands for action had been building for decades—but without anything substantial forthcoming. And then, suddenly, everything changed. In 2011, the Singapore National Parks Board was instructed to begin planning a structure that could connect the habitat on either side of the highway.[8] Funds became available and the transportation department was instructed to provide all possible assistance.

This monumental development, after years of silence, was startling. "It came out of the blue," recalls Bryan Lim, an ecologist with the National Parks Board. Lim works in Bukit Timah Nature Reserve, which is bordered by the highway. When I visited in 2019, he was willing to explain what had happened, up to a point. "It was a big moment. A lot of money, and announced more or less as a command. It had to have come from the Top." "You don't mean . . ." I asked hesitantly, "LKY?" Bryan looked quizzical, but did not elaborate. I did not persist; in Singapore there are some—well, lots—of things about which it is best not to speculate in public. Lee Kuan Yew was Singapore's legendary and autocratic president, who—after becoming prime minister in 1959—oversaw one of the most extraordinarily rapid political, social, and economic transformations of any country in the world. Although he apparently "retired" in 1990, he continued to influence things quietly from outside the government. Possibly even intervening in a long-standing example of habitat fragmentation? No one was saying, but it has been widely reported that he strongly supported the many progressive environmental decisions that have turned Singapore into one of the greenest urban areas in the world. If so, Lee, who died in 2015, was still making waves until the very end.

The reason for my visit to Singapore was to see what this recent example of reconnection looked like. Although it was 32° C (90° F) and the humidity was about 85 percent (it always is, except when it's raining and then it gets *really* sticky), Bryan insisted that we hike over to see the structure for ourselves. We walked along one of the many paved walking tracks before plunging into the jungle along barely discernible paths known only to people familiar with the place. After about an hour pushing through the dense vegetation we paused, and Bryan announced: "Here we are!" Ahead, the forest was slightly different . . . perhaps. A fraction more light seemed to be penetrating the dense, vivid-green canopy, and there were possibly fewer vines growing among the rainforest trees, but otherwise there was very little change in the habitat that I, at least, could discern.

By now I thought I knew what a vegetated overpass looked like, but this was something else. I had just come from Sweden and the Netherlands, where an ecoduct is usually covered in a broad sward of low grass, with narrow rows of trees and shrubs running along the edges. Here, it was solid rainforest all the way across. What I found really astonishing was that this vegetation had been planted only four years earlier!

Bryan shrugged. "It's the tropics. Things grow fast. In fact, one of our biggest challenges was making sure that some of the rapidly growing weedy vines and shrubs did not smother the other three thousand plantings." Once the canopy had closed over, leading to this deep shading, within just a few years the weeds were much easier to control.

Figure 24. Eco-Link fauna overpass in Bukit Timah Nature Reserve, Singapore. Photographer Darryl Jones.

Of course, what I wanted to hear about was whether animals were using the overpass. Bryan had just completed a detailed and intensive camera-trapping survey and was currently processing the images. So far, the cameras had detected at least twelve species of mammal, including mouse-deer and numerous types of squirrel and civets. The local monkeys—long-tailed macaques—had started using the structure as soon as the first concrete girders were placed across the road. One local species that had not been spotted on the overpass was the Malayan colugo, a strange gliding mammal abundant in the rainforest nearby, but that was probably because the trees simply were not high enough yet. What they had discovered, however, was a species almost everywhere on the brink of extinction, the pangolin, currently the most trafficked type of wildlife in the world. Seeing a pangolin anywhere is wonderful. Bryan's cameras have detected the local species, the Sunda pangolin, regularly crossing the structure. Up until then, no one had any idea that pangolins were to be found here, let alone using the overpass.

We crossed the almost flat structure, the continuous six lanes of traffic below us barely noticeable and descended to the roadside for a different view of the overpass. The sweeping concrete curves were tastefully decorated with silhouettes of various animals—including a pangolin—and the words "ECO-LINK@BKE." If LKY had been involved, he would surely have been delighted to see what his command had yielded. Other interventions of his had been considerably less benign, but this magnificent structure, already a busy thoroughfare for biodiversity, exemplified modern Singapore in its design aesthetics and ecological functionality. Another version of effective decision making by a champion, this particular example incorporates sound knowledge and planning—although with negligible community involvement.

Strange Scenes in Sabah

Elsewhere in the world, there are—unfortunately—numerous examples of dictatorial decisions being made apparently *without* appropriate advice being sought. A few years after the catastrophic expansion of the road through the rainforest in northern Borneo, I was bewildered to discover that both an overpass and underpass had appeared in 2018.[9] These structures were of colossal dimensions, understandable given that the animal most likely to use them was the Borneo pygmy elephant, a subspecies of the Asian elephant. Although the smallest form of any of the world's elephants, they are still very large and very heavy animals. They are also extremely dangerous. By far the most significant risk we face during fieldwork here is being attacked by these animals, so one of our local staff is always on the alert for signs of elephant presence. Should our lookout see fresh dung—which is very conspicuous—or detect any evidence that the animals may be close, whatever it is we are doing must be immediately abandoned. The time we were stalked by a group of elephants moving swiftly and completely silently through the jungle, before being rushed by a belligerent, bellowing male, is one of those experiences I will be able to recall with terrifying clarity forever.

When we stopped to have a close look at the underpass, after very carefully scanning the surroundings, a number of questions came to mind. Why was it positioned here? Seemingly, because it was one of the few

Figure 25. Underpass for Asian elephants in central Sabah, Malaysia, on the island of Borneo. Photographer Darryl Jones.

places where the land dipped steeply below the level of the road and therefore afforded enough space to fit a huge concrete box culvert. But a depression in a place where it rains heavily almost daily leads to some predictable problems, and already we could see where water had started to erode the sides of the underpass and undermine the concrete base. The much more obvious question was, however: Why build it in the first place? This might seem a strange question for me to be asking; surely a structure that enables animals to cross a road safely must be worthwhile? Yes—but only when there are good reasons to build it. Not only are these structures very expensive and challenging to construct, any proposal to build a passage needs to be carefully evaluated in terms of costs and benefits to both animals and people. Although the Singapore Eco-Link, for example, was expensive and challenging to build, the benefits in terms of reduced car accidents and reconnected wildlife communities were obvious. But an elephant-sized underpass along a road with less than one vehicle each hour? Along a road where a dozen elephants could cross safely almost anywhere? And given the roadway was unfenced, why would the animals use the underpass or, indeed, the flat-topped bridgelike overpass that required any animal to climb a steep slope to find it?

When I respectfully asked the manager of the research station—which was located at the end of the road—about these things, the answer was more or less along the lines of: "To allow the wildlife to cross the road and minimize the impact of the new road." It sounded a lot like something he had read in a departmental press release, and with further (equally respectful) querying it became clear that he did not know very much about how the structures had come to be constructed. It will probably never be possible to prove any of this, but it seems plausible that these expensive features were installed as a way of addressing the undeniably catastrophic environmental damage the construction of the new road had wrought on the landscape. The difficulty with this "solution" is that it is completely unsuited to the problem, which is one of fragmentation and nothing to do with safe passage. The only species ever likely to use the structures probably never will because they don't need to; they can wander casually across the almost always traffic-free road whenever they like, while those species fearful of open spaces are now permanently separated from their relatives on the far side of the gap. But these are issues of very little relevance to the people making the decisions far away in Kuala Lumpur.

The crossing structures allowed some nameless official to announce that the "environmental concerns" mentioned in a previous government committee meeting had been resolved . . . next agenda item, please. While that may sound (and is) rather cynical, it is quite possible that at some time in the future someone will ask the obvious question about whether there is any evidence that those expensive features constructed in Borneo actually worked. It is a question that could jeopardize future installations for all the wrong reasons.

Right Begets

When decisions are made for all the *right* reasons, on the other hand, the opposite can happen. Where concerns about permeability are sufficiently acute, and the expertise required to address these issues is present, the inclusion of structures to allow wildlife movement across roads can simply be legislated into existence. Well, perhaps not "simply," but when such measures are required of any linear infrastructure project, much of the conflict is minimized. The stipulations in relation to transportation infrastructure throughout the European Union (while a very long way from being perfect) generally mean that the decisions made are not about whether these structures are needed. More pragmatically, they are usually based on what these structures should be and where they would best be placed.[10]

But sometimes these structures are constructed simply because they *need* to be. Such a ridiculously simple outcome can be achieved not because of a command from on high, following protracted negotiations or even a political deal, but because the people involved realized that something had to be done and they all agreed what that was. And the very best example of this just happens to be the most important road ecology site in the universe. Yes, we are once again talking about the Banff National Park and the extraordinary array of crossing structures along the Trans-Canada Highway.[11]

What is now the busiest transportation corridor in Canada, with twenty-five thousand vehicles and thirty trains each day in summer, is also surrounded by a vast and spectacular landscape supporting large numbers of ungulates and carnivores. Today these animals are able to safely cross the wide highway using the many purpose-built underpasses and overpasses, while continuous exclusion fencing prevents them from accessing the road. This was not the case only a few decades ago. As the outstanding scenery and facilities attracted increasing numbers of tourists to the national park, the number of vehicle collisions with large animals began to raise serious alarms. In the fifteen years between 1964 and 1979, a total 780 collisions with ungulates were reported within Banff National Park, almost half occurring in a thirteen-kilometer (eight-mile) section at the start of the park. In 1978 alone, 110 elk strikes—almost all resulting in serious damage and injury—were recorded along the same part of the highway. Quite clearly, something needed to be done. As a result, the initial fencing was constructed, along with six underpasses. This was the first of a series of three phases of mitigation constructions, leading eventually to the outstanding permeability of the Trans-Canada Highway in the Banff area.

The remarkable thing about this process was that the approach was always based on a balance between road safety and wildlife conservation. The leading agency responsible for the national park, Parks Canada, took their responsibilities seriously: both human safety and biodiversity conservation were crucial. A fence not only protected motorists, it ensured that wildlife was not endangered by the traffic. Equally, the agency recognized explicitly that the highway (as well as the railway) running along the base of the valleys was both an essential means of human transportation and a potential barrier to the natural movement of wildlife throughout the area. Providing the means for safe passage was simply a necessity, though just how best to provide this was often debated.

Initiated at the same time as the first phase of mitigation activities at the eastern end of the national park in the 1970s, intensive field surveys have continued to provide sound information on which species are moving through the area and where they are crossing the highway. The information gathered has been especially detailed since the advent of camera-trapping technology: these movement-activated devices enable continuous surveillance of the crossing structures, providing reliable data on wildlife movements around the clock and in all seasons. Since the commencement of systematic monitoring in 1996, hundreds of thousands of animals have been recorded using the structures; these recordings almost certainly represent the largest collection of crossing data ever assembled. Analyses of the images showed clearly that cougars and black bears preferred to use the smaller underpasses, while the wolves, wolverines, deer, and—in particular—grizzly bears, favored the wider, more open structures. Indeed, it was this type of information that led to the installation of the first of the famous Banff overpasses.

The grizzly bears were always of major interest to the national park officers at Banff. In the early days, it appeared that female grizzlies and cubs were being killed on the roads in disproportionate numbers. The populations of these magnificent animals were in serious decline, and vehicle strike was a significant contributor. Although new underpasses were steadily being added along the highway from the late 1980s, the bears appeared reluctant to use them and would apparently travel considerable distances to cross the roads where the fences stopped, often with tragic consequences. When it became clear that the continued presence of grizzlies in the park might require a new approach, it was inevitable that overpasses would be suggested as a possible solution. Despite all the familiar concerns about expense and construction challenges, Parks Canada did not hesitate, and the first of Banff's overpasses was constructed in 1996. Since then, a further five have been installed. As described earlier, extensive studies have shown the obvious benefits of these structures, with the Banff grizzlies being frequent overpass pedestrians and their populations benefiting from the ability to move freely.

It would be easy to miss the point being made here amid the good news and positive vibes. These justifiably famous and heavily used structures did not require endless debates, public protest, or prolonged campaigns. They were built because they were needed. The problem is that there can be a lot of argument about when things are actually necessary.

Keep Your Enemies Close

We will conclude this discussion with an example of how seemingly insurmountable "people problems" can eventually be overcome, with excellent results for all concerned. It is a many-act drama, which was played out in the snow-covered peaks of the central Cascade Mountains in Washington state, in stuffy community halls and school auditoriums, and in the grandiose buildings of the state legislature in Olympia. A confrontation that appeared destined to be a tragedy of historic proportions became one of the most significant achievements of road ecology in North America. A long-running production, replete with technical problems and misreadings of the script, it was finally salvaged by an outstanding double-act.[12]

The longest road in the United States is Interstate 90 (I-90), a highway that traverses the entire continent from Seattle in Washington to Boston in Massachusetts, 4,860 kilometers (just over 3,000 miles) in length. At its western end, just out of Seattle, the highway crosses through the rugged central section of the Cascade Mountains, which sweep magnificently all the way from southern British Columbia to northern California. This spectacular range retains some of the largest tracts of wilderness in the United States and is home to iconic wildlife species that include bears, cougar, elk, wolf, and wolverine. Many of these animals move large distances through the mountains and have to cross the numerous roads that are found throughout the region. These crossings are always risky for both animals and motorists, but none more so than a section of the I-90 in the middle of the central Cascades known as the Snoqualmie Pass. With about twenty-seven thousand vehicles daily passing through an avalanche-prone zone where you could meet a wall of snow, an ice sheet, or a group of elk around the next bend, this section of road represented a growing problem for many years. In the mid-1990s, the Washington State Department of Transport (WSDOT, pronounced by everyone as "Woshdot") began to develop a major plan to upgrade the highway, which included substantially widening the road and constructing additional lanes. It was time for serious engineering action.

At the same time, but in a parallel universe centered on exactly the same geographical location, a diverse group of environmental, conservation, and recreation organizations had come together over a shared conviction about the importance of this area for wildlife. This group, the Cascades Conservation Partnership (which commonly refers to itself as "the Partnership"), had been steadily acquiring many small parcels of land on either side of the highway in order to provide connectivity across the landscape. Several huge areas of public land already existed in the higher parts of the Cascades—the Alpine Lakes Wilderness, Mount Rainier National Park, and the various parts of the vast but discontinuous Wenatchee National Forest—but historically these had been separated by a strange patchwork of privately owned parcels. By purchasing more than eighteen thousand hectares (forty-five thousand acres) of these "pieces," the Partnership had filled in many of the spaces between the large reserves, providing a far more coherent and connected landscape. The US Forest Service (USFS), one of the key members of the Partnership, had been instrumental in developing a detailed plan for managing the land next to the I-90; after four intensive years of working with the various groups, USFS were feeling they had made a significant contribution to the conservation of local biodiversity. And then WSDOT made their I-90 plans public.

When it became clear that the upgrade involved the removal of a lot of adjacent land currently designated for conservation, and that the road planners had more or less ignored habitat connectivity, it's fair to say "things escalated quickly"! Having been safely ensconced in their engineering bubble, WSDOT was somewhat surprised at the intensity of the reaction to their plans. In particular, they had not been prepared for the scale of the opposition arraigned against them. Unfortunately for WSDOT, the existing Cascades Conservation Partnership—whose members were already used to working effectively together—attracted even more partners, including, perhaps surprisingly, the extremely influential AAA (American Automobile Association), who were particularly concerned about the safety of motorists. Soon, with more than forty organizations signed up, the original Cascades Conservation Partnership was renamed the I-90 Wildlife Bridges Coalition, representing an unusually broad base of interests. USFS were especially vocal. Patty Garvey-Darda, one of the Forest Service's most active biologists, was incensed that "the DOT" thought they could simply carve off a large amount of land running alongside the highway: "Land specifically reserved for conservation," she pointed out, forcefully. What all of the groups in the I-90 Coalition shared was, explicitly, a focus on wildlife-crossing structures. WSDOT were blindsided: "We do highways. We don't do wildlife. We just didn't see this coming," recalled one of their engineers at the time.

The converse was also evident. Patty Garvey-Darda remembers that at the first meeting with all of the stakeholders, when asked about what USFS wanted to see happen, she advocated building a raised roadway (or viaduct) along the entire sixty-five kilometers (forty miles) of highway. "I had no idea how expensive that would be! It was a completely naive idea and just plain embarrassing," she recalled. "The response from the WSDOT folk was deafening silence. The tension only increased after that."[13]

It was a difficult start. "We had all these people in the room, no one trusted anyone, no one knew how we were going to find common ground," said one of WSDOT's people. "DOT knew about roads; we were fixated on engineering. The connectivity issue was simply not part of our mentality at the time."[14] At the conclusion of their first joint meeting, there appeared no clear way forward. It seemed to be yet another example of a long, drawn-out drama where animosities escalate and positions solidify— and the outcomes are typically lose-lose.

What was looking like a serious roadblock turned into slightly better traffic flow when some of the WSDOT participants visited their regional administrator—at that time, Doug MacDonald—to provide a grim briefing on the first meeting. To their considerable surprise, MacDonald saw the importance of fostering a positive relationship with the public, especially when the trend out in the community was now distinctly pro-environment. He directed that WSDOT use the opportunity to engage rather than remain separate: "We need to show that we share the concerns of the community on this. Because it is the right thing to do."[15]

The I-90 Wildlife Bridges Coalition was already actively involved in community outreach and education. "This was not conducted as an anti-highway or DOT-bashing exercise. It was much more focused on explaining the reasons we needed to find a way for our wildlife to be able to pass the highway safely," said a coalition spokesperson. When WSDOT joined this effort in a public way, it was initially seen as a defensive move: "We couldn't let the animals stop the highway, but we realized that we couldn't let the highway stop the animals either," said a Department of Transport participant. Before long, however, any reticence turned into something resembling actual cooperation, perhaps because of the strong support WSDOT received from the public. "We were used to being the bad guys, always wrecking the landscape and ignoring nature. It felt great to be congratulated for working for the environment for a change." Following one particular presentation on plans for making the highway safer for wildlife, WSDOT received thirteen hundred comments, almost all of which were in favor of the proposals to enable better connectivity across the highway. "From that time on, we knew we had to take this stuff seriously and really begin to work together with all the groups."[16]

One outcome of this increased cooperation was the commissioning of a substantial number of research studies, which would be used to inform the many decisions concerning the optimal way to enhance connectivity. This research was thoroughly multidisciplinary: with specialist biologists surveying wolverines and salmon; social scientists interviewing skiers, hikers, and fishers; and engineers investigating water flows and avalanche routes—and everyone coming together to discuss the preferred sites for the structures. The director of the I-90 Wildlife Bridges Coalition, Charlie Raines, was particularly pleased that these collaborations led to mutual respect and appreciation of what people on "the other side" were able to offer. "Everyone started to see things from other perspectives, and there was a much greater appreciation of the complexity of the challenges we all faced."[17]

A crucial moment was a trip north to visit the famous crossing structures at Banff. "This was really important," Charlie explained. "There was still a fair amount of skepticism among the engineers about whether it was possible to build an overpass in this terrain, and whether they actually worked anyway. Being able to see that series of huge overpasses along the Trans-Canada Highway, and to hear firsthand how they had been constructed in a similar landscape; it really changed their thinking. And then to be shown figures on the movement of bears, elk, wolves, wolverines—the same species we were concerned about in the Cascades—brought it home. Some of the most unconvinced guys came away with a realization that we could do something similar."

The most serious obstacle was not, however, overpass location options or bureaucratic inertia; it was money! The expanded crossing-structures proposal—painstakingly developed through an enormous effort by a lot of people—was visionary and exciting, but extremely expensive. The bulk of the cash had to come from the state legislature, an august but hard-nosed collection of elected officials who took their custodianship of the public's taxes very seriously indeed. They would almost certainly be happy to fund an upgraded highway, but the expense associated with all the proposed connectivity features was a very different thing. What the elected officials were not prepared for was a very detailed proposal made jointly by the environmental groups and WSDOT. In an unprecedented and symbolic move, I-90 Coalition director Charlie Raines and WSDOT regional administrator Don Whitehouse presented their case together, with Charlie pointing out the necessity for an upgraded road and Don arguing that environmental connectivity was vital. This show of genuine solidarity made an enormous impact on those members of the legislature who were present. A few years later, Charlie and Don reunited on the I-90 to witness the first concrete spans being lowered into place over the highway. There was plenty of emotion among the assembled crowd of coalition members and supporters. "It really is a dream come true!" announced a beaming Charlie Raines to cheers and tears.

Collaboration Is Uncommon, but So Are Miracles

It would be wonderful to conclude this chapter by stating that these examples of cooperation, mutual appreciation, and governmental support for addressing the road-barrier effect have become commonplace around the world. While there is unquestionably momentum in this direction, the reality is that the problems so often besetting projects at the outset—the lack of genuine community consultation, the disregard for the rights of minorities and adjacent landholders, the mutual lack of trust between environmental advocates and transportation administrators, the extreme difficulties of finding sufficient funds—remain. Around the world, each new motorway or upgrade almost always leads to the same conflicts, with the same predictable dramas being played out as though these difficulties were unique or inevitable. This is the unfortunate but inescapable reality.

What *is* happening, however, is a steady increase in the legislated or codified conditions applying to anyone proposing major linear infrastructure projects, requiring them to show how they will address issues of defragmentation or enhanced permeability. The European Union, again, leads the way in terms of requiring specific conditions to be addressed in the design of these forms of infrastructure, although there are vast differences in the level of compliance and verification across Europe.

Perhaps one of the most promising phenomena currently emerging is the raising of standards from within the transportation construction companies themselves. Rather than taking a "minimal compliance" approach, a number of major firms are applying their own standards and requiring improvements with each new project. This is exactly what happened recently when major upgrades were proposed for a motorway at the southern section of Karawatha Forest, at the other end of the reserve affected by Compton Road (as described at the start of this chapter).[18] Rather than accept the same standard of permeability as provided by the earlier structures, the motorway operator brought together a wide range of conservation and community organizations to form an environmental reference group that would provide advice and opinion from the very beginning of planning for the upgrade. Very sensibly, the Karawatha Forest Protection Society were the first to be invited. I served as the chair of the group.

After a number of intense meetings, the reference group proposed twelve different options that we regarded as a comprehensive "wish list." I was invited to present these options to the construction firms who were tendering for what was a major project. In his introduction to each of these meetings, the spokesperson for the operator announced that his company regarded all of the options as mandatory. "Your designs must include all of these measures," he stated. I was at least as astonished as the assembled road engineers and designers. This project, completed in 2019, about fourteen years after the Compton Road array located only a short distance away, marked an unprecedented new benchmark for Australia. The integrated series of structures—viaducts, rope ladders, glider poles, fauna underpasses, and yet another vegetated overpass—were constructed outside the footprint of the motorway on a busy road (Illaweena Street). The costs of construction were paid for by the company "because it was essential to enable full permeability." It is now the most sophisticated fauna-crossing complex in the country. It is also well and truly in excess of any legal or statutory conditions or requirements—because the operator had become convinced that the structures were necessary to overcome the barrier to biodiversity associated with their road. That actually happened.

6

SIGNS OF CHANGE

An enormous amount of road construction is underway around the world right now. Old roads are being resurfaced and upgraded, additional lanes are being added to existing highways, unauthorized tracks are penetrating into forests in remote regions, and—of course—colossal new roads are marching unchallenged across entire, sometimes undisturbed, landscapes and international boundaries. The scale of all of this work is almost impossible to comprehend or conceive: the areas of land cleared and substrate moved; the amounts of concrete and asphalt being laid; and, eventually, the number of vehicles that will use these vast constructions.[1] The giant continues to grow restlessly and relentlessly.

As the global road network expands, it consumes and modifies the land it encompasses, isolating and fragmenting the places where biodiversity persists. As we have discussed many times already, these impacts and dangers are difficult to perceive. The slow drift toward local extinction is an intangible concept, despite being the reality in almost every patch of forest and grassland now bisected by a road. The invisibility of a phenomenon so profoundly destructive is a big part of why it is so insidious.

What is all too visible, however, is the number of dead animals that result. When it comes to the impact of roads, *roadkill* has always been the part of the story with the biggest influence on people's perceptions. Collisions between wildlife and vehicles are bad for both parties—an obvious statement that brings us to another element of the narrative that we have so far neglected: drivers.

"If only the driver had been more careful . . ." is a universal, if futile, observation made at the scene of every wildlife–vehicle collision the world over. Commonly followed up by the equally ubiquitous and vacuous, "Why can't they drive more slowly or be more alert?" Until very recently, any wistful hopes for drivers devoid of human imperfections were similarly fanciful. But extraordinary new technologies are rapidly making these aspirations a reality.

Inevitably, driverless vehicles will make an appearance sometime soon. But for the moment, let's park these shiny wonders out of sight and deal with the real people behind the steering wheels. Because drivers are central to much of what we have been discussing. Thus far it may have seemed as though vehicles were moving along the roads independently of the humans within, but that would be a fatal mistake to make—because drivers are obviously a critical consideration. How the driver responds to what they see on and around the road is fundamental to the welfare of the people in the vehicle. Yet, compared with the advances that have been made regarding virtually every other element in the transportation and road ecology story, our understanding of drivers remains shockingly inadequate.

In this chapter we will explore some of the innovative methods being used to understand and influence drivers and their behavior. This survey will inevitably take us down various paths featuring all sorts of bewildering technology, before we arrive at a place with vehicles that appear not to need people at all (although that's not the case . . . just yet). Let's start on a quiet road in the dead of night, to confront an all-too-familiar problem.

Aotearoan Anomalies

New Zealanders—residents of those spectacular islands increasingly being referred to as Aotearoa—have the same concerns as everyone else regarding roads and traffic: habitat fragmentation, the isolation of populations, the impact of excessive levels of roadkill. When it comes to solutions, however, their priorities are almost the opposite of those elsewhere in the world. Around the planet, almost all of the thousands of purpose-built fauna underpasses and overpasses, glider poles, canopy bridges, and culvert ledges have been installed for mammals of every shape and size. In general, birds are not among the target species considered in the design of most crossing structures, although they will certainly take advantage of these passageways once they are in place. No, whether it's fair or not, mammals are the raison d'être for most crossing structures. In New Zealand/Aotearoa, things are very different.[2]

For millions of years, Aotearoa was an extraordinary world dominated exclusively by birds. Prior to the arrival of people—the ancestors of the Māori, about eight hundred years ago, followed by the Europeans about six hundred years later—no mammals inhabited these remote islands, apart from two species of microbat. After cleaving off from the southern supercontinent of Gondwana around eighty million years ago, Aotearoa remained completely isolated, and its birds evolved in the total absence of mammalian predators. Although there were dangerous carnivores—including the fast-running moa and the largest eagle ever known to have existed—these, of course, were all birds, sharing the same sensory abilities as their prey. Avian hunters operate primarily by sight; on Aotearoa, the ability to evade detection was based mainly on camouflage and staying still. In such a bird-biased parallel universe, many species became flightless, including numerous small ground-dwelling species.

It's easy to see where this story is heading: utter catastrophe![3] This started with the arrival of the rats and dogs that had accompanied the Polynesian voyagers, but really took off with the stoats, weasels, ferrets, cats, and various rodents that were introduced by the Europeans. All of these mammals were ruthless and effective predators, locating their prey by smell and stealth. The native birds had no answer to the "gray tsunami" that swept over the land, the result being one of the most rapid and appalling rates of extinction ever known. Many unique species vanished within decades, and the toll mounted steadily as the mammals penetrated into the most remote corners of the dense, forested valleys spread across this rugged and mountainous land. And because all of these predators are still there, the threat remains—active and critical—to this day.

This bracing reality has resulted in New Zealanders being some of the most accomplished and innovative conservation biologists on the planet. Facing the extinction of many of your nation's unique and beloved species (most of which are found nowhere else) on a daily basis seems to have that effect. The skills and techniques that have been developed to tackle the situation are now being exported around the world.

So, when an apparently well-meaning Australian (that detail is important as context here) turns up in New Zealand to describe how successful crossing structures have been, all over the world, in enabling mammals to safely cross roads, the reception can be somewhat less than enthusiastic. Actually, the response went something along the lines of: *Why on earth would we want to help mammals to spread even further than they already have?* It didn't take long before I was brought up to speed and confronted with a rather different perspective on the priorities facing the country in terms of the impact of roads. Instead of investing their energies on structures that enable animals to get around—which would almost certainly benefit the predators more than their prey—some ingenious New Zealanders aimed their focus in a completely different direction: toward the person behind the steering wheel. I was invited to see at firsthand an example of this approach.

Kiwi Keepers

We have been standing in the dark for quite a while, deep within the Kaore i Tino Nature Reserve, a conservation park on the Coromandel Peninsula on New Zealand's North Island.[4] All around us, the air is filled with strange sounds and rustlings, the shrill calls of katydids and crickets, the gentle tinkle of a small but rapidly flowing stream. Occasionally a frog squeaks, but most of the noises are unknown to me. Except that one! A piercing, shrill, and surprisingly loud *eek, eek*, repeated several times before stopping suddenly, leaving the forest still and quiet, as though all the other animals had submitted to the silence. The call is from a North Island brown kiwi. Although it is the most abundant of the five species found in New Zealand, this kiwi is still classified as "vulnerable," an accurate assessment: an outbreak of fire or disease, or—as has happened recently— one sustained attack by a dog, and yet another fragmented population can disappear instantly. All kiwi species are now limited to tiny and increasingly isolated patches, although the North Island brown has one of the largest distributions. This spot, a part of the Coromandel Forest Park, is a rare stronghold.

Although we can't see anything (it is completely dark inside this forest, and our headlamps are currently turned off), by remaining completely still we can just make out the busy, shuffling, scuffling sounds the bird makes as it probes hyperactively about in the deep, damp leaf litter. Unlike all other birds, the kiwi has nostrils at the tip of its very long beak, allowing it to sniff out worms and other protein-rich invertebrates.

The quiet abruptly evaporates as the roar of an approaching vehicle fills the world around us. I had completely forgotten how close we were to the main road. The darkness vanishes as the car turns a corner and the shockingly bright lights suddenly blast toward us. And there, backlit by the white glare of the headlights, just for a microsecond, is the silhouette of the kiwi—beak raised, standing alert and defiant on the very edge of the road. Then, just as suddenly, the light is gone. The car rushes past, red tail lights rapidly disappearing in the thick mist.

It is a few moments before we react. My guide, Maia Kaiarahi, a local forest ranger and kiwi devotee, finally speaks, very quietly. "And that demonstrates exactly what our problem is, right there," she says.

> This forest has one of the best populations of kiwi in the North Island. We had a huge problem with stoats and feral dogs, but, with a lot of work, those predators are much less of an issue. Now, it's cars. This spot is crucial because it's where a lot of kiwi try to cross the road. And because it's on a wide sweeping corner, which drivers love to take as fast as they can, it's obviously a very dangerous place for kiwi. Or was. You may not have noticed, but that car was traveling pretty slowly as it came around the bend, presumably because the driver was alert and aware that there may be kiwi about. It's taken a long time and we have been up a lot of dead ends to get to where we are today. It's a long and frustrating but hopeful story. Let's discuss this over a coffee.

A few minutes later we are sitting in Maia's rustic office at the entrance to the nature reserve. A steaming mug of milky coffee is handed to me while Maia shows me a map of the area. She draws her finger slowly along the blue line that marks the road as it sweeps through the reserve, stopping where the road forms a wide curve. "This is where we were just now," Maia indicates.

This location has been the focus of a lot of attention and sadness for decades now. The birds are especially important to the local *iwi* [Māori tribe], who mourn every death. For a while, this was one of the worst black spots for kiwi kills in the whole country. A group of concerned community people, iwi, council staff, and Department of Conservation officers have met around this very table for years, discussing what we could do. We came up with the name "Kiwi Keepers." This species is not only iconic and vulnerable, it's also deeply symbolic of the relationship between the people and the animals that share Aotearoa. We want to keep our kiwis safe. People have made a lot of terrible decisions in the past. We have lost so much that is irreplaceable; it's time to try and repair some of this if we can.

"You might think that it would be simply a matter of fencing. That would surely stop the carnage," Maia says.

Fences are great at preventing creatures from moving onto roads and for directing them toward underpasses, that sort of thing. But here, there are two problems. Firstly, we don't actually want to stop the kiwis from moving. They really need to be able to move up and down the slopes and valleys at different times of the year, visiting different parts of the landscape. The other problem is that the road profile is already very low in what is quite swampy terrain. We have had lots of road engineers examine the road for possible locations for a small kiwi-sized underpass. Unfortunately, any passageway under the road here would simply fill with water. So, underpasses are impossible. We actually started thinking about a small overpass, but it was immediately clear that on this small road, where the forest is close by along its entire length, the disturbance and destruction needed to build anything in what is land dedicated to nature conservation was just unacceptable.

She rocked back in her chair. "That left us with the toughest nut of all to crack: drivers!"

Keep Your Eyes on the Road

Something seems to happen to otherwise normal humans once they climb in behind the wheel of a vehicle. For many of us, it has been a very long time since we endured that terrifying process during our teens when we learned how to drive (with an often impatient or overly anxious parent sitting in the passenger seat), and we have probably forgotten just how fraught that experience was. But driving is an exceptionally complex and challenging activity, requiring a huge amount of effort, intense concentration, and a lot of practice.

My first few driving experiences involved being almost completely overwhelmed by all the separate things I needed to be acutely aware of: other cars ahead, beside, or behind me; as well as pedestrians, cyclists, indicators, traffic lights, road signs. At the beginning, it seemed that simultaneously employing my legs, hands, eyes, and brain in multiple activities, while taking in and responding to all sorts of visual and sensory inputs—while sitting inside a rapidly moving metal box on wheels—was impossibly complicated. How could anyone remember all of those steps, detect approaching objects, assess their distance and speed, all the while interpreting the symbols and words displayed by multiple signals both inside and outside the car? The sheer volume of sights and signs, and the mental capacity required to process them, was often exhausting. I worried that I would miss something vital—how on earth could anyone drive safely when there was so much to take in?

And yet, just a few weeks later, there I was, careening down the road, talking to people in the back seat, changing channels on the radio, surreptitiously glancing at the girls in the convertible in the next lane, almost oblivious to all those vital sensory inputs that had been so important only a little while previously. It is absolutely no mystery why teenage drivers represent the demographic with the highest rate of death and injuries. But there is more to this tragic reality than youthful risk taking and the myth of invincibility. The brain begins to filter out some of those inputs, reclassifying them as (apparently) nonessential, leaving just a few that we perceive as critical. This is an essential process known as "habituation," a well-studied psychological concept whereby certain stimuli are eventually ignored. If this didn't happen, we would be constantly reacting to everything, leading to the kind of bewilderment and stress experienced by those overly stimulated novice drivers. This tuning out is particularly pronounced when the stimuli are repetitive and inconspicuous and entail only a low risk if ignored. There is a good chance that if you stop reading right now and pay attention to the sounds in your vicinity, you will become aware of the traffic noise outside, the leaf-blower next door, or the barking a few houses down, all noises to which you are normally oblivious. That's habituation. If, however, the scream of a siren suddenly penetrates the quiet, you are very likely to forget everything else and pay close attention.

Signs of the Kiwi

This brings us back to the roadside in New Zealand.[5] It is now midmorning on the following day, and Maia, several local council people, and I—all wearing vivid lime-green safety vests—are standing in a small parking lot just off the road that passes through the nature reserve. There has been a fairly steady stream of traffic heading north toward the beach resorts and fishing spots at the top of the famous Coromandel Peninsula. We have been discussing how risky it would be for an animal to cross the road here. The road is only two lanes wide at this point, but the roadkill crew have just returned with a dead blackbird and a stoat, both abundant and introduced species and of little concern—although the stoat does remind us that this small but deadly predator is still present right here in kiwi country. Cars, however, now represent a far greater threat.

On both sides of the road right in front of us are two bright orange signs, the universally familiar diamond shape showing the stylized silhouette of a kiwi. "It's a bit of an irony, really," says Maia. "These signs are supposed to improve road safety, but we have a big issue right here in that these kiwi signs are actually causing car accidents. Lots of tourists stop, often quite suddenly, to take photos of these signs with the view of the mountains in the background." It's easy to see why—the panorama of vast, deep-green forest with mountain peaks in the distance is stunning, picture-postcard stuff. "The drivers see this vista and suddenly decide to stop. Bang! The driver of the car behind, who was probably also looking at the view and not the road, slams into the car in front. The number of times . . ." She sighs.

But the signs themselves? A complete dud. If people actually see them, they think it's a photo op. But most don't notice them at all. There has been a bit of development of the image in an attempt to make them more effective. The earlier version was not very lifelike, more like a cartoon. The current design is much more realistic, I guess—a walking kiwi—but that doesn't seem to make much difference. They don't work because they don't get drivers to think, "Hey, I'd better watch out for kiwis!" I don't think they know what they are supposed to think. These types of standard, static signs just don't work . . . anywhere, as far as I can see.[6]

These static kiwi warning signs—which are, indeed, all over the country—usually display the image alone; although some have an additional component, text below the image baldly stating: CAUTION CROSSING AT NIGHT. (A tourist car-sticker version states, not very helpfully: KIWIS NEXT 1200KM.) Similar wildlife warning signs are found throughout the world, and all have the same laudable aim of reducing the incidence of wildlife–vehicle collisions. The basic design is the same everywhere: either a yellow diamond or green triangle with a silhouette of one of an enormous variety of species: deer, kangaroo, bear, moose, camel, even elephant—usually the types of animals most likely to be involved in a collision. These signs are intended to improve road safety, although some—including those depicting kiwi—are more conservation oriented. The difference between the signs is essentially based on the implications of colliding with the type of animal shown: hitting an elk is likely to have a greater impact on your car; hitting a kiwi is not going to damage the vehicle but will be fatal for the bird.

In every case, the implicit aim of these signs is to reduce the likelihood of a collision. But how? The process is rarely articulated, but it seems to be an attempt to alter the driver's behavior by gaining their attention via the image on the sign. There is an assumption that the driver will react to the sign in two important ways: they will immediately become more alert; and, as a result of being forewarned of a possible collision with the depicted animal, they will quickly reduce the speed of the vehicle (although it is not speed per se that is the problem—even a relatively slow car can still collide with an animal). Ideally, the now-vigilant driver will be much more likely to react appropriately should something appear on the road.

If you think this all seems rather sophisticated for a process that is triggered when someone driving a car happens to notice a picture of an animal on a sign beside the road, you would be right. Although these static warning signs are ubiquitous, there have been remarkably few studies assessing their effectiveness. What we *do* know about the response of drivers to this signage can be nicely summarized in one word: "habituation." Most of the time, drivers just don't notice these signs—or, if they do, they don't react in any discernible way. And crucially, they don't slow down. The use of standard wildlife warning signs offers a textbook example of the elements that lead to habituation. The images are overly familiar and not particularly attention grabbing, and there is no apparent reason for drivers to react. Once these signs are installed, they stay in place more or less forever. Old, faded, rusty signs—often bearing signs of wear, bullet holes, and graffiti—look more like historic relics than vital alerts warning that something potentially hazardous might be about to happen. Road authorities and local councils love to erect these signs as an indication that they are "Doing Something" about road safety or because they want to demonstrate that they really do care about a particular species of interest. And while these may be worthy political aims, the fact remains that static warning signs are, at best, pointless and at worst, misleading.[7]

Introducing the concept of habituation does, however, provide a way of thinking about the fundamental problem: the signs are not being noticed. Can they be made more conspicuous? In what ways can warning signs be enhanced? At the simplest end of the spectrum, more context or

Figure 26. Static wildlife warning sign near Palmer, Alaska.
Photographer Marcel Huijser.

relevant information could be added to the sign. This should never involve a lot of words—drivers are unlikely to try to read more than the very simplest statements (such as TURTLES CROSS HERE or SLOW DOWN FOR DUCKS). In Australia, for example, recent concern about koalas has led to signs that display a KOALA ZONE heading with two columns of text beneath it: "60 7pm—5am AUG—DEC" and "80 OTHER TIMES." All worthy, useful information—but it is extremely doubtful whether any driver, even one sincerely worried about koala conservation, would be able to take in, interpret, and then react appropriately to that much detail in writing.

Enhancements that provide information pictorially rather than as words are increasingly being used. In many places around the world, more explicit messages are being offered to drivers through a variety of pictorial approaches, ranging from wholesome drawings of overtly cute animals (those ubiquitous duck families, for instance), to sketches depicting a car crashing into a large animal, and even horribly graphic photographs of dead animals or smashed cars. Sometimes signs and their messaging are made more noticeable by increasing their size. Unfortunately, if the above examples are simply used as static signs, which will stay in place indefinitely, there is little reason to expect that drivers will not habituate to them as well.

A straightforward way to make static wildlife warning signs more likely to be noticed is to display them only at specific times. One of the best examples of this approach comes in the form of the thousands of temporary signs that are only erected during the mass amphibian migration events that occur all over the Northern Hemisphere. These signs have a lot more "credibility" for drivers, because they relate directly to a well-known phenomenon that occurs at particular times for a limited period and in very specific locations. This sort of signage is quite effective in influencing driver behavior but is obviously much more labor intensive; many of the locations involved are managed by small but enthusiastic community groups or local councils who are able to monitor local conditions carefully and get the timing just right.

Be Dynamic

More overt enhancement of warning signage may involve adding illumination at night, either by directing light at the image or by incorporating a bright neon border. These signs, too, can be activated at key times of the day (dusk and dawn are particularly important, as many nocturnal animals are active then and hard to detect) or during peaks of seasonal movements and dispersal. Both factors were important considerations for the Kiwi Keepers as they continued to improve their attempt to slow down the cars.

"Kiwis are fairly crepuscular in their activities," explains Maia as we walk along a rough track in the forest, a couple of meters in from the road. "Most of the day they are asleep, well hidden beneath a thicket or in an old tree stump, but they get restless as soon as the sun starts to set. This is a risky time because the poor light makes it difficult for drivers to see anything, especially on the edges of dense forests. It is also a busy time on the road, when a lot of people are heading home." It is now late afternoon, and plenty of cars and motorcycles have been going past. I notice a standard static kiwi silhouette warning sign beside the road, but then, some distance ahead, a completely different sign suddenly bursts into illuminated life. Vivid yellow, rectangular, and much bigger and brighter than the earlier kiwi sign, it features a large and different kiwi image, with the message KIWI ZONE clearly visible at the top.

"That's great timing," says Mike, a Department of Conservation technician. "It's getting pretty dark now so I had hoped we would see it switch on." Mike has come with us to undertake a routine check of the power source, which in this case is located in a separate secure box near the forest track and away from the road. "We use solar to power these signs wherever we can, but here inside the thick forest it's just too dark," he explains. "Stuck with old-fashioned electricity for this one, I'm afraid. These signs are only illuminated from just before sunset and stay on for an hour. And it's the reverse for the dawn shift, all activated by a clever combination of sensitive light-detection apparatus and automatic timers. It's one more way to try and make sure drivers don't get used to seeing the signs and hopefully react appropriately."

While Mike is engaged with the technology, Maia points out the messaging on the road, directly adjacent to the sign. A device on the signpost is directing a beam of light toward an enormous green rectangle that has been painted across the entire span of the road. The words KIWI ZONE appear in huge white capital letters across one of the lanes, with the same words painted facing the opposite direction across the other lane. "This is another attempt to grab a driver's attention and make certain that they are thoroughly aware that they are entering a special section of the road. There is an identical display further around the bend, which gives the clear impression that there is a limited zone where drivers need to pay attention, with a distinct start and finish. This seems to be much more effective than the usual undefined and uncertain associate with a traditional sign."

After a couple of minutes, Mike is satisfied with the readouts on his handheld device and we continue along the track. About twenty meters (twenty-two yards) later we see another sign some distance ahead, although indistinctly in the failing light. From here it appears similar to the previous one—rectangular, but with another kiwi image at the top. "This is our latest addition to the collection," says Maia, looking just a little excited. "Things got really interesting when these so-called smart or dynamic signs were installed about a year ago. Let's see what happens when a vehicle passes." I find a clear view through the trees, with the sign directly in front of me, and wait. It's starting to get cool and the air is still. In the quiet I again become aware of the chorus of unseen animals—crickets, katydids, and cicadas—providing a pulsating soundtrack to the early evening.

Yes, a car is approaching from behind us—it seems to be moving rather slowly. When the vehicle is about forty meters (forty-four yards) away from where we are standing, the sign illuminates brightly. It's a vibrant electric-green, the striding kiwi vividly clear. A large square screen immediately below displays the message WATCH FOR KIWIS in large letters. The car passes and disappears around the bend. The sign goes dark.

And then before we can react, another vehicle is heading our way, moving in the same direction. It is immediately obvious that this one is not traveling slowly. As it races toward us, the sign suddenly bursts into light and color. This time the words shout SLOW DOWN KIWIS, while the screen is now bright red, with "83" very prominently displayed in large numerals. And within a clear white strip running across the red screen another display appears: "AB-7658." Just for a moment I am confused, but I quickly realize what it is being shown very publicly (though with only one viewer in mind): the car's speed *and* its registration number plate. The car that generated all this instantaneous electronic information is now passing the sign and has very clearly slowed down. If anything, it moves away even more carefully than the earlier car.

When we get back to the nature reserve's main office, I realize that this remarkable sequence of visual signals provides an unmistakable message for drivers: *Be careful—we are watching YOU!* "We left the traditional static sign in place for historical reasons but also as a demonstration of the evolution of wildlife warning signage, in this country at least," Maia says.

For a driver traveling along this particular road, they may notice the simple kiwi image—but even if they don't, they certainly will see the sign and road marking announcing that they are entering an important area, a Kiwi Zone, suggesting that they should be alert for the possibility of crossing birds. Those first dynamic signs have been in place for about four years and our data showed that they did lead to a small reduction in speed, but only while they were illuminated during the dusk and dawn periods. That was a good outcome, but we still had kiwis being hit late at night when the signs are off. We needed something that really got the attention of the drivers.

The last sign type was actually adapted from some developed for koalas in Australia.[8] These are the latest so-called smart signs, which are able to determine the speed of oncoming vehicles and broadcast that directly to the driver. Even a half-attentive driver should be aware that they have entered a place where kiwis may be present and that they should be alert. If they are conscious of this information, almost all drivers slow down a little as they pay more attention to the road. If they are traveling too fast, however, the sign display broadcasts some important and personal details: exactly how fast they are moving, and—this is the clincher—their car's own number plate. Every driver will think: "Bloody hell! They know how fast I'm going and they will be able to identify me as the driver!" That's the kind of message that seems to make a big difference to driver behavior. In the year since these last signs have been installed, the average speed of vehicles traveling through this section of road has reduced on average by fifteen kilometers [nine miles] an hour.[9] And that has been maintained for almost a year now. It's been one of the best examples of a signage approach—admittedly they are pretty high-tech signs—leading to a significant change in speed.

"Oh, there is one other reason why this exercise might have been particularly successful in getting drivers to reduce their speed," Maia mentions, almost as an aside.

When the last smart sign was installed, we were able to get one of our local policemen involved in monitoring the speed of motorists. The speed limit on this section of the road is only sixty kilometers [about forty miles] per hour—it's a narrow, winding road in a dense forest—so, ensuring that the traffic does not exceed this is an important road safety issue. The fact that he set up speed cameras immediately outside the Kiwi Zone was nothing to do with us, though the 150 speeding tickets issued in the first few months probably made people very conscious of speeding through this area. This copper was extremely helpful and really understood what we were trying to do here. It may have also helped that he was my husband . . .

Walk, Don't Walk

These dynamic, smart signs (which are an integrated combination of detection equipment and electronic display boards) set up along a road in New Zealand are an example of what is certain to be only the first faltering steps in a trajectory toward far greater use of technology to address a variety of road ecology issues. The capacity of these devices to detect vehicles, determine their speed, and respond with appropriate messages directed at drivers in real time may be impressive, but I suspect they will soon be standard at best. One application already in operation in many locations around the world is almost the converse of signs that identify cars traveling along the road. This new form of smart sign is aimed at detecting animals approaching the road—although the signal generated is obviously directed toward drivers. The simplest version is movement sensitive, activating a warning message that alerts the driver that an animal is moving close to the road and is very likely to cross. These devices typically only pick up the movements of larger species close to the road, and so are best deployed in locations with highly predictable and concentrated animal-crossing activity: for example, along traditional animal trails or at the end of a line of fencing. In places where crossings may be less predictable, a series of detection signs are sometimes installed in order to effectively cover the verge for some distance. The vast majority of such signs have been used to warn motorists of deer and macropods—species that often graze along the grassy verges—but there is also a risk that drivers may then come to expect a signal to slow down in every instance, even in locations where no signs have been installed.

One especially clear example of these so-called Animal-Activated Detection Systems has been working for over a decade on State Route 260 in Arizona.[10] The problem in this case was caused by elk, white-tailed deer, and mule deer, with around ten serious accidents occurring annually. Although fences were installed along much of the road, it was important that these animals were able to move across the highway. In several places, fences funneled animals into underpasses, but the flat topography for much of the road necessitated a "crosswalk" for the animals to traverse at grade: essentially, at a gap in the fence on either side. Obviously, this section of the road had the potential to become a very dangerous zone for both animals and vehicles unless the traffic was managed carefully.

The approach taken by the authorities was to give motorists plenty of warning that they were entering a wildlife zone and then alert them if animals were nearby and likely to cross the road. Another innovation was to install electrified mats on the edges of the crosswalk, which produced electric shocks when animals walked on them, thus dissuading them from wandering onto the highway. A static sign announced that vehicles were entering a wildlife-crossing zone: ELK CROSSING 1500 FEET AHEAD (about 460 meters). If an animal was detected near the gap in the fence, a smart sign 280 meters (920 feet) from the crossing displayed CAUTION ELK DETECTED, while a flashing alert next to the crosswalk was activated. This may seem an elaborate and complicated setup, but in its first eight years of operation only a single collision was recorded, a result put down to the fact that vehicles traveled about eleven kilometers (seven miles) per hour slower when the signs were operating.

The next step-up has been smart signs that respond to individual animals marked with some form of electronic tag. Various small transmitters, which produce high-frequency electronic signals, have been used for decades to mark individuals of various species—from bumblebees to blue whales—allowing the tagged animals to be located in space, either by surveys using mobile antennae or through transmission of signals to satellites, a field known as telemetry. Each unit emits a unique frequency, allowing remote identification of an individual (hence the name of this technology: RFID, radio frequency identification). Recently, traditional telemetry hardware has been used to look at the movements of tagged animals on or near crossing structures. While this type of tracking can still be undertaken by people in the field using mobile detectors, and via satellites, stationary receivers can also be set up at either end of a crossing structure to verify crossing rates, as has been done for years at Banff.[11] It's a fairly simple approach, but it can provide important insights into the crossing and territorial behavior of certain individuals. The discovery that one despotic koala was monopolizing an overpass in Australia, as mentioned in an earlier chapter, is a good example of an unexpected outcome.

A major limitation of this form of telemetry has always been the requirement for power to run the transmitter; this is usually provided by a battery or by tiny solar panels. Electronic miniaturization has revolutionized tracking technology, allowing the development of extremely tiny devices, which can be attached to leg bands and ear tags or simply glued onto shells or skin. But no powered device lasts forever, and every tag will eventually stop transmitting when the battery goes flat or the mechanism's casing deteriorates.

This situation changed dramatically in the 1980s with the advent of extremely small PIT tags, initially used for the reliable identification of domestic pets and livestock. The revolutionary feature of these microchips is that they require no power and, once attached or implanted, remain active for the life of the animal. The microchip is either inserted under the animal's skin or worn on an ear tag or collar. Instead of the energy being

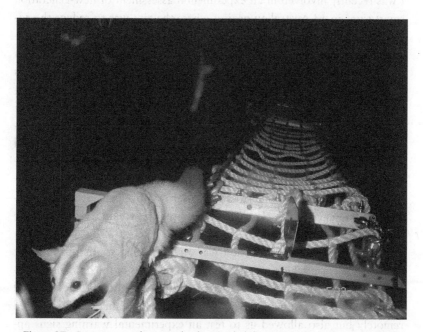

Figure 27. Camera trap photograph of squirrel glider using rope ladder above road on Hume Highway in New South Wales, Australia. Photographer Kylie Soames, University of Melbourne.

supplied to the transmitter, it is the receiver that is powered. The distance from which these chips can be detected is related to the sensitivity of the receiver, the tag "reader." Scanning a tag implanted into a domestic animal involves holding the receiver a dozen or so centimeters (a few inches) from the tag, although the maximum range is probably about thirty centimeters (about one foot). Beefing up the capacity of the receiver, however, can extend the range considerably. Some receivers are able to detect even very small tags at over five meters (sixteen feet), allowing plenty of scope to read a tag moving through an underpass or along a rope ladder. These developments have completely changed the way that wildlife movement can be studied; their application to wildlife warning signs might be revolutionary.[12]

Super-Smart Signs

I was recently involved in an experimental assessment of new-generation smart signs in an Australian project where the aim was to reduce the appalling level of koala–vehicle strikes.[13] The road passed through an important wildlife conservation reserve and was notorious for the speeds reached by many motorists. Although the speed limit was fifty kilometers (thirty miles) per hour in the suburbs at either end of this road and seventy kilometers (forty-three miles) per hour in the section passing through the reserve, the average speed of vehicles driving through was eighty-three kilometers (fifty-one miles) per hour. The carnage was horrific—and it wasn't only koalas that were affected. Although fencing would have stopped this, the reserve had important resources for wildlife on either side of the road; it was vital to allow the free movement of animals, despite the presence of vehicles. This was a situation where trying to change the behavior of drivers was the best option.

The resident koala population was already being studied to monitor disease incidence, which necessitated catching most of the animals for examination. During the process, active RFID transmitters were attached to each koala's ear tag. This enabled specific individuals to be located remotely but also allowed us to test an experimental warning signs approach. These new signs were similar to the kiwi design described above, but instead of detecting cars they detected tagged koalas. A series of these signs were positioned along both sides of the road, with display boards facing both directions. The receivers in the signs were particularly powerful and were able to pick up an approaching animal from a distance of thirty meters (one hundred feet). And there were two other particularly impressive innovations: the signs were able to communicate wirelessly with one another, and the visual signal could be changed depending on the location of the detected koala. If a tagged koala was detected somewhere near the center of the line of signs, a changing sequence of displays would be initiated. The signs positioned at the beginning and end of the series—on both sides of the road—would broadcast SLOW KOALAS NEAR, with an outer neon margin slowly flashing. The sequence formed a visual cascade that traveled from sign to sign, flowing toward the smart sign that had first detected the koala. In the case of the signs that had first detected the transmitter, the words CAREFUL KOALAS CROSSING HERE would appear, with the signs' outer margin flashing rapidly in red. This avalanche of visual information would be impossible for a driver to ignore; the displays were duplicated on both sides of the road and the moving cascade of pulsating lights drew attention to the place where the animal could be crossing.

That may seem almost too visually spectacular; surely all that pulsating neon and electronic light would disturb the surrounding environments. Possibly—although with this system, habituation by drivers was not going to be a problem. For the nonhumans, however, it was a potential issue. After considering this concern, the research team developed several additional design features with the aim of minimizing the level of disturbance. For example, the displays were carefully aligned toward the windscreen height of vehicles traveling along the road; from almost any other angle the display was almost invisible. And because the sign was so tightly oriented, the brightness of the screen could be reduced (which also lowered the amount of power required). It is also worth saying that the colors used in the displays—reds, yellows, and greens—are not distinguishable by most mammals. But most important, this remarkable moving visual display only occurs when a vehicle is detected on the road. For most of the night, when cars are scarce, the road is quiet and dark. These super-smart signs may be fine-tuned to detect moving koalas (well, the tags they carry, anyway), but they haven't lost their original car-spotting abilities.

Messaging the Animals

All of the signage mentioned so far has been aimed at drivers, the supposedly intelligent humans behind the wheel. The aim is to try and alter their behavior by signaling a potential change in risk (the increased chance of hitting an animal on the road ahead), leading to a heightened alertness and a conscious reaction (usually, reducing the speed of the car). Well, would it be worth also trying to change the behavior of the animals? They almost certainly face a far worse risk than the people in the cars do. There have been plenty of attempts, varying from the ridiculously optimistic to the slightly less naive.

Some of the earliest technical approaches to warning animals about oncoming vehicles were signals that were auditory rather than visual.[14] These signals were initially a form of whistle, with the high-pitched noise produced by the movement of air passing over the aperture of a device mounted on the vehicle's front bumper. The thinking seemed to be that the loud, piercing sound would ensure the oncoming vehicle could be heard well in advance of its arrival. More recent versions have gone for high-frequency sound that cannot be detected by humans but is supposedly unmissable when it comes to the target species. Although an awful lot of these devices have been sold all over the world for decades, there is currently precisely no reliable evidence that they work. It is actually very difficult to test the spectacular claims made by the manufacturers. Endorsements on webpages that make statements along the lines of "I've driven thousands of miles with a *Deer Deterrer* [or *Shu Roo* or *Moose Moover*] and never hit anything yet!" don't constitute much of a claim when you consider the vanishingly remote likelihood of any particular vehicle having a collision. Even at the very worst so-called black spots for wildlife–vehicle strikes, most of the hundreds of thousands of vehicles passing through do *not* hit anything.

Whenever these devices have been carefully examined, the assessment has always been either that they simply do not work or that the results are, at best, inconclusive.[15] The studies also point out that these gadgets are unlikely to be effective in the first place, for some obvious technical reasons. For example, the frequency of the ultrasonic sound produced (often claimed to be in the range of sixteen to twenty-five kilohertz) attenuates rapidly, meaning that even if an animal were able to detect the noise, at that point they would be too close to the vehicle to be able to react in time. This low detectability is even worse in areas with dense vegetation or where the road has numerous bends. In addition, when carefully measured in the field, the frequencies emitted are almost always much lower than claimed—leading to interference from engine and wheel noise and resulting in an even lower chance that the sound will be picked up by the animals. This particular approach to messaging wildlife does not sound very promising.

If you read the claims of the companies making devices that produce *visual* messages for animals, the story is apparently a lot brighter. Rather than drawing an animal's attention to oncoming vehicles, these devices attempt to highlight the road itself as a disturbing and risky location—but, crucially, only when traffic is approaching. If the device detects an oncoming vehicle, it produces a sudden and conspicuous visual display along the side of the road, which will potentially drive the animal away. Theoretically, by associating moving vehicles with a specifically located disturbance, the animal could learn to avoid the roadside. If so, the devices would function as a "deterrent" (as they are often described . . . by the manufacturers at least), discouraging animals from moving onto the road and into harm's way. If the result was a more generalized fright response, however, with startled creatures running in unpredictable directions, the outcomes could be a lot less predictable.

These visual deterrents come in two main forms: "passive" low-tech reflectors, and an "active" interactive version.[16] Each type uses the light from the headlights of an oncoming vehicle, either to deflect the light onto the roadside or as a trigger for the device to emit its own beam of bright light. Obviously, this technology only works at night. Both forms of the device are placed in rows flanking the road. A more recent iteration known as a "virtual fence" adds high-frequency noise to the pulsating visual signals that are emitted in a range of colors.

Over the last few years, there has been a significant uptake in the purchase of these devices—particularly by town councils and community groups, all desperate to reduce the carnage on the roads in their communities and conservation reserves. Unfortunately, considerable research, again, is showing that these visual deterrents are expensive, unreliable, and almost completely ineffectual. The extraordinary claims of, for example, "reductions in roadkill rates of 80–90%" have proven to be marketing slogans rather than scientific findings. In summary, the studies that have critically assessed these gadgets have made two crucial, interrelated discoveries: they *don't* work because they *can't* work.

In almost every case, the measure used by the manufacturer to demonstrate effectiveness has been an apparent lowering of the number of collisions with wildlife. This lends itself perfectly to a classic BACI (Before–After–Control–Impact) study design—remember chapter 4?—but that has rarely been applied. A problem with attempting to collect this type of information is that the events being counted are actually very rare and the victims easily missed or moved. Most surveys yield nothing, so shortcuts are often attempted. A common approach is to use a different section of the same road as both the Before and Control sites (really—such things have actually been published in peer-reviewed journals), which leads to all sorts of complications and invalid conclusions.

A much more fundamental problem, however, is the fact that the visual stimuli produced, supposedly as a deterrent, may not be perceived by the

Figure 28. Wildlife detection device beside a road in the Netherlands.
Photographer Marcel Huijser.

animal as anything but a strange light. The range of colors—blue, green, and (of course) red, proudly promoted as key elements of the display—are almost certainly meaningless, given that most of the mammals of interest cannot even detect the wavelengths involved. One study that assessed devices that emitted green and blue lasers reported that the main response of the targeted animals "was curiosity as to the way the lights played on the vegetation while others were startled but somewhat confused."[17] Other studies have found sudden responses, but with little in the way of predicable movements; one investigation of the reaction of wallabies found that although the animals did respond quickly, they fled in almost entirely random directions—including straight onto the road. None of this resembles the confident promises made by the manufacturers or the desperately hoped-for deterrent effect.

For the ecologists conducting these tests, the fundamental problem is that these visual stimuli—clever and sophisticated though they may be—simply lack biological meaning for the animals. They are meant to move them away from the road in a consistent and reliable way, but that is not what happens. The beams and flashes may be scary and possibly alarming, but they have no association with the risk posed by the vehicles moving along the nearby road. The future may, however, bring more meaningful signals into the picture—maybe holographic wolves, accompanied by recorded howls and even wolf smells. Now *that* just might work. Meanwhile, save your money.

Automobile Intelligence?

Sending messages, by whatever means—that is, "communication"—is fraught at the best of times. When the intention is to generate a response such as a driver slowing the speed of the car (or a deer moving away from the road), a lot can go wrong. In both cases, the receiver has to interpret the signal and then act appropriately; and usually very quickly. The main variable in this sequence of events is what happens in the brain of the players: both driver and animal have to think before they can react, which might take a while (this "window" is open for just one to two seconds). And that process may be influenced by previous experiences (or lack thereof), current preoccupations, and all manner of distractions.

Drivers are not only easily distracted; they can also be tired, emotional, angry, drunk, drug-impaired, and inattentive. They may also have slow reflexes, poor eyesight, and little experience. And their vehicle may not be in great shape either. When we consider all these imperfections, it is no mystery that the overwhelming majority of vehicle accidents—and the appallingly enormous numbers of injuries and deaths that result—are due to so-called human error. If only there was a way that those preoccupied, imperfect, mammalian brains could be left out of the equation (or driver's) seat.

This is precisely the impetus behind the current extraordinary levels of interest and investment in designing vehicles that are not reliant on a human driver. The development of so-called driverless, or autonomous, vehicles is advancing exponentially at present.[18] The ubiquity of extremely detailed geographical information already enables cars to navigate and make decisions about routes and speeds while an astonishing array of cameras, lasers, and radar detects and tracks objects all around the vehicle. These features are fast becoming standard in many contemporary models. It is remarkable just how quickly we have become used to inbuilt satellite navigation (complete with verbal directions given with a local accent), beeps, and alarms should the car gets too close to a nearby object—and even autonomous braking when other vehicles are detected approaching too close or too quickly. Humans might be turning the steering wheel and pressing the accelerator, but the message is perfectly clear: imperfect human drivers are quickly becoming redundant. Current predictions are that by 2040, most vehicles on our roads (in more developed places at least) will not have to worry about people making mistakes.

The major concern, of course, is that mistakes are made, even by driverless cars, and these can be fatal. Although such incidents receive a lot of publicity and add to the skepticism about this form of technology, in reality they are extremely rare. It is worth being reminded that every year around 50 million people are injured and 1.5 million people die in car accidents. These are the figures that propel designers working with this new driverless technology to improve the integration between the vehicle's detection systems and its propulsion and braking mechanisms. A defining feature of artificial intelligence (AI) is that every mistake automatically results in learning. Forgetting, ignoring, pretending it didn't happen, regretting, or worrying—these defining features of human drivers are simply not included in the algorithms. Just cold, rational, optimizing decisions based on all the available information. And this information encompasses what other machines have learned as well; sharing is also "natural" in these systems. Far-fetched science fiction? It's already here. *Jump in and relax; let HAL take you home.*

The autonomous Volvo in which I'm traveling looks almost identical to the company's most recent fully electric models, both inside and out, although there is an additional display screen. The "driver," Mats, an AI engineer, is behind the wheel as we glide along a small road in the Scottish countryside, although he doesn't really need to do anything. The destination was typed in on the touch screen and our progress and additional information is being relayed by the friendly voice of Elsa, our unflappable AI communicator. "To the right is Loch Ashie, a scenic reserve well known for its fly fishing. Our destination is seventy-two minutes away. We hope you are enjoying the ride," she says, in a soothing Swedish accent. We are— although, rather perversely, we are also hoping that something unexpected might happen as we travel. Almost instantly, the vehicle slows. "Hazard 73 meters [240 feet] ahead on the right," says Elsa, though she still sounds completely relaxed. "Control steering if necessary," she adds. Mats gently takes the steering wheel and concentrates on the road in front of us. We all look intently along the beam of the headlights and notice something dark and solid on the road ahead. It's a badger, moving, but rather slowly; as we approach, the car slows almost to a stop. The badger seems to notice us at last and shuffles to the other side of the road. The car gathers speed and we resume our journey.

"Excellent!" says Mats. "Just what I wanted to show you. Our most recent innovation in the detection system is for smaller species, none more important around here than badgers. Oh, and I should say that I did none of the steering or braking. That was all Elsa." Mats explains that he is currently based here in Scotland in order to fine-tune the vehicle's systems to local risks and conditions.

Obviously, we are all very aware of the deer problem throughout much of the Northern Hemisphere. But there are plenty of other hazards associated with each location, which need to be accounted for. Here, badgers are a key one. We haven't been able to sort out the really small species yet—squirrel-sized and down—but we are working on them. One of the incredible things about AI is that once it works out how to deal with a particular problem—such as interpreting a badger-shaped object on the road—it can use that learning in other contexts. For example, we have just sent the badger code the system has learned in Europe to Australia, where we think it will work on wombats, which are pretty similar in shape and size. Let's hope it does better than it did for kangaroos.[19] Their strange (to us anyway) hopping gait has proven to be a serious challenge to our systems. Everyone assumed that it would be the same as our very successful deer module, but it proved to be a bigger problem. If AI gets a headache, it's probably going to be because of 'roos.

The rest of the journey is uneventful, until we approach the outskirts of Inverness. Completely unexpectedly, a deer sprints across the road, missing the car by less than a meter. The vehicle reacts almost instantly, slowing down and then stopping abruptly. The hazard lights come on, but the animal has already vanished into the night. It all happens in just a few seconds. "Hazard . . ." starts Elsa, typically unperturbed, but she doesn't finish. Mats, however, looks just a little sheepish. "That was a bit close,

Figure 29. Bull elk (*Cervus canadensis*) on road, Yellowstone National Park, Wyoming. Photographer Marcel Huijser.

you know," he admits. "Sudden, unexpected movements by animals remain an issue, and I'm not sure I can see how we will fix that."

Well, that may be a bit of a problem, because sudden, unexpected movements by large animals can happen at any time, especially among species that are already nervous and easily startled when near roads. Nonetheless, most of the signs are that these super-smart vehicles will learn how to deal with most of the common interactions between wildlife and vehicles, even though surprises will always be possible. Although there are plenty of challenges ahead, the rate of improvement in detection and response systems really does promise safer roads in the not very distant future. Authentic artificial intelligence means learning from every event—something humans have never been able to achieve.

I have discussed this brave new world with road ecologists from all over the globe, and they all tend to agree: autonomous vehicles will mean that we will soon be able to travel with a much lower risk of collisions (with other vehicles as well as animals, it must be said) and, therefore, with far less direct impact on wildlife. Road accidents and roadkill are almost certainly going to become rare events on road networks where most of the vehicles are autonomous. It seems that this technology does mean we can reverse the global impact of vehicles.

There is another point about which we all agree. These advances will have very little influence on the global impact of roads. Unfortunately, even the smartest cars will still need surfaces to drive on.

CONCLUSION

The Giant Is Awake

I visit a lot of roads. This one was particularly difficult to get to. And it is only *just* a road, more a very basic track really, parallel wheel ruts running through soggy leaf litter and sloshing through patches of rich brown loam in the gloom of the rainforest. We are deep within the Western Province of Papua New Guinea, about 125 kilometers (80 miles) from Balimo, the last settlement that could conceivably be called a town. It's not that far away, but it has taken us two full days of driving to reach this forest road. Balimo has paved roads, but these stop at the edge of town, and from that point on, as we journeyed to get here, we had followed a mainly smooth and regularly graded dirt track for about 24 kilometers (15 miles) until the state of the road deteriorated abruptly. The annual rainfall in this tropical region is measured in meters, and it belts down promptly every afternoon. Any ground without vegetation quickly turns into a stream of frothy milkshake, carving deep erosion scars, often right through roads. As we slow to little more than walking pace to negotiate the holes and crevasses, our driver, Awi, explains that this is as far as the council grader drivers will come. Beyond, there is "nothing," he says, just "bush." Still, we insist that we press on, the track becoming increasingly difficult to negotiate, our progress painfully slow. Eventually we stop, mainly because the track ahead disappears into a rapidly flowing stream. We can just make out the faint signs left by other vehicles that had crossed the stream and continued into the forest on the other side, but we aren't willing to risk our vehicle or ourselves any further. Getting bogged or breaking down out here could be fatal.

Although we had driven for a couple of days, we are now still only on the very margin of one of the world's largest "roadless areas": expanses of land apparently without major roads (at least, as can be discerned by satellite cameras).[1] Such "roadless" places are becoming increasingly rare, especially in the tropics. The largest of these areas include our current location on the island of New Guinea (which encompasses both Papua New Guinea and West Papua, a province of Indonesia), as well as most of central Borneo and—by far the greatest in size—what remains of the Amazon Basin. For now, these places represent a large proportion of the earth's remaining (mainly) undisturbed areas of rainforest, a status that is under constant and increasing threat.

Because roads never stop growing. As we gaze into the mysterious, dark, seemingly impenetrable wall of trees and vines across the creek, we talk about the thin, ephemeral vestiges of the track and wonder where it might be going. In this landscape, if it wasn't used regularly, the jungle would quickly swallow all traces. On the other hand, this barely discernible track could be the first stage of something more permanent. Awi, who earlier had stated decisively that "No one goes in there," now confesses that he has often gone hunting down this track with his friends. Encouraged to expand, he reveals he has been trying to convince a council worker to drive one of the bulldozers from Balimo to the site (completely unofficially, of course), to improve the present track so that more vehicles can get through. Awi is only interested in having access to the rainforest to hunt bush meat—cuscus or pigeons—but other people may have different prizes in mind.

Roads never stop growing, because vehicles need them. There are strict limits to where even the most rugged recreational vehicle can travel. The latest-model Toyota we have rented for this trip features all the bells and whistles, but it could still become bogged, break an axle, blow a tire, or get stranded in a flooded river. Vehicles have changed in innumerable ways since Karl Benz's *motorwagen* chugged into a German street in 1885 (Henry Ford's first mass-produced Model Ts arrived just over two decades later in 1908), but they are still basically a horizontal box on four wheels.[2] Modern cars are now extremely fuel-efficient; many are hybrids or even fully electric and have greatly reduced emissions. They also have a remarkable suite of high-tech communication and safety features, including airbags, car-surround detection systems, and onboard navigation. And, of course, autonomous vehicles are just around the corner, bringing the promise of greatly reducing or even completely eliminating car accidents and collisions with wildlife. But they still need roads.

At the start (and heart) of this book is the question: is it realistic to think we can reverse the global impact of roads and vehicles? In relation to the latter, the answer appears to be "yes." Cars are now unquestionably cleaner, quieter, more efficient, and safer than they were only a few years previously. And, although there will probably be around two billion cars driving on the world's roads by 2030, there remains strong evidence that sales of private vehicles peaked in 2018.[3] That year, eighty-six million passenger vehicles were sold around the world, with literally one-third of these (twenty-eight million) being purchased in China. Although the United States—the land of the automobile, we all still assume—did come in second, with just over four million cars being sold there, a similar number was recorded in Japan and Germany, both much smaller countries. Those latter two nations are also home to the largest car manufacturers, Toyota and Volkswagen. America's General Motors now comes a distant fourth. SUVs are still by far the most popular type of car sold, but electric vehicles are the most rapidly growing category, with an incredible annual growth of 40 percent (pre-COVID). Things are definitely changing when it comes to which vehicle are selling.

But at the risk of laboring the point: these cars—clean, smart, and safe though they might be—need roads to get around. And roads, as well as cars, are on the move. At the time of writing, the most recent estimation of the total length of roads globally was thirty-two million kilometers (twenty million miles), with an additional three million to five million kilometers (two million to three million miles) expected to be built in the next thirty years.[4] Most of us are likely to imagine these new roads as smooth, multilane freeways sweeping through rural landscapes, or shiny arterials on the boundaries of big cities in the Northern Hemisphere. Not quite. In stark terms, almost all of these new roads will be built in developing countries and around 65 percent will not even be paved. Most are planned for Central and South America, and Africa; only half of these will be accessible throughout the year. This is because roads in these tropical regions are often impassable or simply too dangerous to use during the normal wet seasons and periodic monsoons.

What these bland statistics don't make explicit is the reality that these unpaved roads—often the main conduit for essential food, services, and communication on which many millions of people are now entirely dependent—stop functioning for significant periods of time because of the weather. It is no mystery, therefore, that struggling countries might be attracted to promises of major new roads, especially when they are funded and constructed by people from somewhere else. Something as simple as a reliable and sensibly connected road system—something most of us never have to even think about—could make a profound difference to the prospects of small communities seeking better mobility or contact with schools, medical facilities, and markets. The traditional connection between road expansion and economic growth has always been attractive to government planners, and when the proposition includes foreign funding, the small print will often be ignored.

In 2017, China launched two initiatives of extraordinary ambition and scale: One Belt, One Road; and the Twenty-First Century Maritime Silk Road. These interlinked projects envision a global transportation infrastructure network stretching across much of the planet, effectively and efficiently linking China with the rest of the world.[5] The size of these schemes—which involve ports, railways, water- and energy-resource development, and especially, a truly colossal amount of roadwork—makes these by far the largest and most expensive infrastructure construction projects ever proposed. The stated economic and social benefits are similarly grandiose and at the time of writing (late 2020) are being discussed in boardrooms, government chambers, and hotel lobbies around the world.

This is not the place to examine the pros and cons of this vast and remarkable plan, although there is plenty of critical debate available for those who are interested.[6] Suffice it to say that the potential economic, social, political, and environmental risks and dangers that have been projected are causing increasing alarm. For the purpose of our current perspective, however, these super-road projects—which are being certified and executed right now—exemplify many of the issues that have been raised and described in this book. These and other massive transportation schemes are being rolled out in many parts of the world, but especially in poor countries in tropical areas, typically, the very places where political decisions—made in the capital cities—have little connection with or regard for the impact of infrastructure projects on the ground. Standards of planning and construction set down on paper often bear little similarity to what actually happens. There are too many examples of shocking neglect and rapid deterioration of newly constructed roads, especially in high rainfall areas, where inadequate design or substandard materials have led to slumping, erosion, the development of potholes, and pavement shearing (uplift). The provision of funds for ongoing maintenance, a critical element in the long-term functioning of these roads, is rarely adequate, or simply disappears. The World Bank has estimated that 30 to 60 percent of the funding provided for roads in developing countries vanishes through corruption and cartel activity.[7]

Even more alarming is the unplanned exploitation of areas adjacent to the roads. From local expansion of bush-meat hunting and opportunistic slash-and-burn farming to sophisticated large-scale illegal timber smuggling, the influence of new incursions can spread into neighboring forests in an almost organic, diseaselike pattern. In Brazil, 95 percent of the rainforest lost over the last decade was within five kilometers (three miles) of a legal road, which initiated the spread of an "expanding spider web of illegal roads," to quote road researcher William Laurance.[8] The neat, contained lines printed on the glossy, professionally produced proposals may be only a small proportion of the area actually impacted.

I want to remind us all of the large-scale impacts of road expansion in remote, poor, tropical regions—the devastation that accompanies a massive, largely unnecessary road in the interior of Borneo, for example, or the future threat implied by a faint forest track in the rainforests of Papua New Guinea—even though they may be far removed from the concerns of most readers of this book. But we can no longer remain oblivious to this truly global phenomenon. The fragmentation that I see occurring almost daily in my own otherwise wealthy and progressive city might be small compared with the denudation of the Amazon, but it is no less significant for me. My reaction to these local losses makes it possible for me to appreciate the many similar events around the world, even if comprehending them is impossible.

It would be all too easy for our understanding and hopes for sensible road development to veer off the road at this point and become mired uselessly in the slough of despond (to use an appropriate *Pilgrim's Progress* metaphor), the magnitude of the problem rendering us helpless and impotent. This is very similar to the ever-present dilemma that confronts those attempting to bring about the urgent action needed to address climate change. Too much reality can lead, understandably, to despondency and inaction—the very opposite of what is so critically needed. The start of the solution is, I think, to focus on what is possible and nearby. Solutions are always most effective when presented and practiced at the local level.

Confronting the global issues associated with massive transportation projects that span vast areas will always be well beyond the capacity of most of us. So, let's leave the international negotiations to the bureaucrats and get on with practical action at the local level.

One of the most influential alterations in perspective to have occurred in road ecology has been the realization that roads and their mitigation need to be considered at the level of the landscape. Too often the focus has been limited to "this black spot for roadkill" or "that new road proposal." Adopting a much wider view—taking in an entire catchment or valley, the flow of the water bodies, and the geography of the forested remnants—has allowed fresh insights into how animals might be able to move through the wider area and how a road might be routed to avoid sensitive locations. This approach has enabled the many practical solutions outlined in this book to be seen as part of an ecological whole, not just as a series of independent structures.

Despite the daunting realities we face as vast transportation networks expand around the world, the key to retaining our optimism is the realization that there are a multitude of proven solutions and that these are likely to work wherever they might be required. The rainfall patterns in Papua New Guinea might be very different from those in Seattle, but engineering suitable drainage structures or designing an appropriate bridge requires the same knowledge and materials. Obviously, the necessary resources might not always be readily available, but relevant information and guidance is becoming increasingly accessible to anyone who needs it. The field of road ecology has been intentionally international in scope

Figure 30. Delegates at the ICOET conference in 2013 Payson, Arizona, visiting a wildlife underpass in Little Green Valley. Photographer Marcel Huijser.

from its inception and has actively sought to include participation from everywhere, throughout the world.

In 2003, such was the apparent lack of urgency and the scale of the challenge before us that Richard Forman envisioned this nascent field as a sleeping giant: a formidable ally, if only it could be roused. Almost two decades later, we can state that this giant is now fully awake—awake, but perhaps uncertain of what it needs to do first.

CODA

Ji-hoon Moon is in a cheerful mood. The air is crisp and cold, but the sun is shining brightly as we sit in a beautiful garden glade overlooking Cheonggye Creek.[1] This stream runs through a very urbanized district not far from the center of the South Korean capital, Seoul. Vibrant purple flowers cascade over the rock walls that edge the garden; further down the terraced slope, lush plantings of vivid green vegetation run parallel to the rapidly flowing stream passing below us. Birds and butterflies abound in the early spring light. On the wide walkways on both sides of the river are joggers, mothers with prams, and elderly couples walking hand in hand, all enjoying their afternoon outing. The sound of birdsong, happy chatter, and the squeals of excited children running around a small playground is embroidered onto the incessant chuckle of the busy stream. The atmosphere could hardly be clearer, cleaner, or more pleasant, yet we are near the center of one of Asia's largest and most densely populated cities. I slowly become aware of the complete absence of traffic noise here. There are no cars to be heard or seen.

"Such days make me so happy," says Moon. "I turn eighty-three this year, and for my whole life I have lived up there." He points a steady hand toward the balcony of his small apartment in a tower overlooking the scene. "All these years I have seen what has happened to this area. I have seen the poverty, the concrete, and the cars, but now light and life is here again. It's alive and . . . it makes me content at last." Large happy tears roll down his smooth cheeks, but he is not embarrassed. "You must hear about the Three Ages of the creek and my life with the Cheonggye."

My childhood was simple and tough. This was a poor and difficult place, but we made the most of it. The creek was dirty and polluted; you would not eat a fish from there even if you caught one. People used it for all their waste and trash. That was what I call the Age of Mist; it was hard to see clearly where we were or where we were going. Everyone worked hard and struggled together.

Then the city decided that cars would lead to development and progress. So, we had to have roads, roads up and down everywhere. It became the Age of Grayness. In 1976, the river was covered by slabs of grey concrete and a raised motorway was built above. I saw it happen; slabs of concrete were lowered over the creek like a coffin lid. I watched the last one being placed and felt that it *was* like a funeral: the death of the creek. Above it, the entire space on either side of the now-buried creek was given over to cars. Cars on either side and then above. A huge raised expressway on giant pillars was built and cars flowed where a stream had once been. We were told that this meant progress and a better life. For us, it was almost 30 years of noise, fumes, and grayness. Everything was gray. Gray skies, gray air, gray lives. Many people moved away. Everyone who lived here was just depressed. If this was development, we didn't see it like that.

Moon pauses, gazing out over the colorful and pleasant scene. His expression—which had turned grim and withdrawn as he told his story— seems to change as he takes in the clean air and clear light. He turns toward me, fixes me with his bright eyes, and beams a vast smile.

And then came the Age of Light. In 2003, Seoul's new mayor listened to the people. She decided that concrete and cars were not what was needed here. She arranged for the roads to be removed. Most importantly, they took away the high expressway that dominated the whole scene. They removed all the concrete and stopped all the cars. All the cars! It took a long time, and it was noisy and dusty while they worked, but eventually it was done. The most astounding thing was the creek. It was suddenly opened up. It was like the discovery of a treasure right where we lived. We realized that back when the stream was covered up, people didn't talk about it. It was like a death in the family. It was like a terrible secret. Many children who lived here didn't even know that the stream was there.

Moon rises to look down toward the swiftly flowing stream. The churning water is clear and full of waving waterweeds. "When they pulled up the slabs of concrete that had hidden the river, all the people gathered to watch. No one said anything. It was scary and strange and everyone was worried about what they would see. At first, the creek looked pale and lifeless. But the light of heaven came in, and slowly it remembered. And now it is alive again! When I was young, there were no fish, no ducks. Now they are everywhere." He pauses to take in the scene, tears again filling his eyes.

"They took away the roads and so the cars disappeared too. But they have left a number of the pillars that once supported the raised expressway. These remind us of the folly of the past. I take my grandchildren to see the ducks and feed the eels and I tell them the story of how people tried to hide the river. But then we changed our minds and life returned. Of course, cars and roads are necessary. But not everywhere, not all the time." He turns and fixes those bright sparkling eyes on mine, his face earnest now. "Please tell them about what happened here. Just as I have told you."

Appendix

SPECIES MENTIONED IN THE TEXT

TABLE 1.

Common name used in geographical context	Scientific name
Invertebrates	
Bogong moth	*Agrotis infusa*
Amphibians	
American green tree frog	*Dryophytes cinerea*
southern brown tree frog	*Litoria ewingii*
Reptiles	
smooth snake	*Coronella austriaca*
Birds	
bald eagle	*Haliaeetus leucocephalus*
blackbird (common)	*Turdus merula*
black-capped chickadee	*Poecile atricappillus*
European nightjar	*Caprimulgus europaeus*

(*Continued*)

TABLE 1. (Continued)

Common name used in geographical context	Scientific name
gray shrike-thrush	*Colluricincla harmonica*
great crested flycatcher	*Myriarchus crinitus*
great tit	*Parus major*
greater roadrunner	*Geococcyx californianus*
house finch	*Haemorhous mexicanus*
lapwing (northern)	*Vanellus vanellus*
nighthawk (common)	*Chordeiles minor*
North Island brown kiwi	*Apteryx mantelli*
red-breasted nuthatch	*Sitta canadensis*
song sparrow	*Melospiza melodia*
woodlark	*Lullula arborea*
Mammals	
African forest elephant	*Loxodonta cyclotis*
American black beer	*Ursus americanus*
antechinus (yellow-footed)	*Antechinus flavipes*
Asian elephant (Borneo pygmy elephant)	*Elephas maximus borneensis*
badger (European)	*Meles meles*
beaver (Eurasian)	*Castor fiber*
bighorn sheep	*Ovis canadensis*
black rat (ship rat)	*Rattus rattus*
bobcat	*Lynx rufus*
Bornean orangutan	*Pongo pygmaeus*
bush rat	*Rattus fuscipes*
camel (dromedary)	*Camelus dromedarius*
cat	*Felis catus*
chimpanzee	*Pan troglodytes*
clouded leopard (Sunda)	*Neofelis diardi*
collared peccary	*Pecari tajacu*
common dunnart	*Sminthopsis murina*
coyote	*Canis latrans*
eastern gray kangaroo	*Macropus giganteus*
eastern quoll	*Dasyurus viverrinus*

Common name used in geographical context	Scientific name
elk	*Cervus canadensis*
fallow deer	*Dama dama*
ferret	*Mustela putorius*
fisher	*Pekania pennanti*
Florida manatee (West Indian or North American manatee)	*Trichechus manatus latirostris*
Florida panther	*Puma concolor coryi*
Geoffroy's bat	*Myotis emarginatus*
golden langur	*Trachypithecus geei*
gorilla (western)	*Gorilla gorilla*
gray fox	*Urocyon cinereoargenteus*
gray wolf	*Canis lupus*
grizzly bear	*Ursus arctos horribilis*
hare (European)	*Lepus europaeus*
hazel dormouse	*Muscardinus avellanarius*
house mouse	*Mus musculus*
key deer	*Odocoileus virginianus clavium*
koala	*Phascolarctos cinereus*
long-tailed macaque	*Macaca fascicularis*
lynx (Eurasian)	*Lynx lynx*
Malayan colugo (Sunda flying lemur)	*Galeopterus variegatus*
moose	*Alces alces*
mountain pygmy possum	*Burramys parvus*
mouse-deer (greater)	*Tragulus napu*
Müller's gibbon	*Hylobates muelleri*
ocelot	*Leopardus pardalis*
otter (Eurasian)	*Lutra lutra*
pangolin (Sunda)	*Manis javanica*
red deer (elk)	*Cervus elaphus*
red-necked wallaby	*Macropus rufogriseus*
roe deer	*Capreolus capreolus*
squirrel glider	*Petaurus norfolcensis*
Stephens's kangaroo rat	*Dipodomys stephensi*

(Continued)

TABLE 1. (Continued)

Common name used in geographical context	Scientific name
stoat	*Mustela erminea*
sugar glider	*Petaurus breviceps*
sun bear	*Helarctos malayanus*
swamp rat	*Rattus lutreolus*
Tasmanian devil	*Sarcophilus harrisii*
weasel	*Mustela nivalis*
white-tailed deer	*Odocoileus virginianus*
wildcat (European)	*Felis silvestris*
wolverine	*Gulo gulo*
wombat (common)	*Vombatus ursinus*

NOTES

Preface

1. This is the Compton Road fauna overpass in Brisbane, Australia, a place we will return to throughout this book. Its history and significance are covered in a fair amount of detail in chapter 5. Some key information on the koala and other research can be found in Dexter et al. 2016 and 2017, Jones et al. 2011, McGregor et al. 2015, Pell and Jones 2015, and Polak et al. 2014.

Introduction

1. This encounter really happened. Since 2012 I have been privileged to travel each year to Sabah, the Malaysian state on the island of Borneo, introducing small groups of young ecology students to the wonders of the tropical rainforest as part of their environmental science degree. The road described here terminates at the Maliau Basin Studies Center.

2. The studies of gap crossing by birds in the Amazon are Develey and Stouffer 2001, Laurance et al. 2009, and Lees and Peres 2009.

3. These catastrophes, past and continuing, have been thoroughly discussed by William Laurance and others (see, for example, Laurance 2009, 2015).

4. These quotations are from Bennett 1991 and Forman et al. 2003.

5. These road statistics are from the World Bank database, http://datacatalog.world bank.org.

6. Road densities are taken from Langevelde and Jaarsma 2009.

7. Roadkill as an evolutionary novel threat was described by Blackwell et al. 2016.

8. The Florida panther situation is nicely summarized by Jansen et al. 2010.

9. The road-barrier effect has been explained well by Bennett 1991, Forman et al. 2003, and van der Ree and Grilo 2015.

10. See Bennett 1991, Forman et al. 2003, and van der Ree et al. 2015.

11. The impact of vehicles in the United States was documented in Forman et al. 2003.

12. Ancient roads in the United Kingdom were described in Forman et al. 2003.

13. The number of relevant Richard Forman references is formidable, but this one is Forman 1998.

14. *Road Ecology: Science and Solutions* (Forman et al. 2003) is the foundational tome (sometimes referred to as the New Testament of road ecology).

15. See Forman et al. 2003.

16. See Forman et al. 2003. Italics added to the quote.

17. This is a surprisingly contentious topic, but I have tried to follow the terminology provided by Smith et al. 2015.

1. Death, Dust, and Din

1. There has been a lot of discussion of roadkill and the associated consequences, including Beebee 2013, Benítez-López et al. 2010, and Coffin 2007. The figures come from Bennett 1991, Blackwell et al. 2016, Coffin 2007, Ehmann and Cogger 1985, Forman et al. 2003, and Forman and Alexander 1998.

2. See Beebee 2013, Benítez-López et al. 2010, and Coffin 2007. For the figures, see Bennett 1991, Blackwell et al. 2016, Coffin 2007, Ehmann and Cogger 1985, Forman et al. 2003, and Forman and Alexander 1998.

3. Roadkill has often been regarded as simply indicating the abundance of local species; for example, see Bennett 1991.

4. Dayton Stoner's pioneering study was published as "The toll of the automobile" (Stoner 1925).

5. See Stoner 1925.

6. The difficulties associated with making reliable estimations of roadkill are discussed by Guinard et al. 2012 and Smith and van der Ree 2015.

7. This appalling toll of amphibians was reported in Glista et al. 2008.

8. This Australian study was published as Hayes and Goldingay 2009.

9. See detailed information in Beebee 2013 and Rytwinski and Fahrig 2012.

10. See Beebee 2013, Benítez-López et al. 2010, and Coffin 2007. For the figures see Bennett 1991, Blackwell et al. 2016, Coffin 2007, Ehmann and Cogger 1985, Forman et al. 2003, and Forman and Alexander 1998.

11. The fascinating history of the Florida panther and other species impacted in this area are described by Jansen et al. 2010.

12. See Jansen et al. 2010.

13. The alarming status of Tasmania in the roadkill ratings is discussed in Hobday and Minstrell 2008.

14. See Hobday and Minstrell 2008.

15. The tragic story of the Tasmanian devils of Cradle Mountain is described by Menna Jones in Jones 2000.

16. See article entitled "Bite club" (Wroe et al. 2005), which very convincingly dethrones hyenas as the animals with the "strongest bite."

17. See Jones 2000.

18. See Jones 2000.

19. See Bond and Jones 2014.

20. These figures come from the Association for Safe International Road Travel, http://www.asirt.org.

21. See the Association for Safe International Road Travel, http://www.asirt.org.

22. This is a main theme in Sperling and Gordon's *Two Billion Cars: Driving Toward Sustainability* (2009).

23. The Gap Creek Road studies were published as Jones et al. 2014, 2015.

24. See Jones et al. 2014, 2015.

25. See Jones et al. 2014, 2015.

26. See Jones et al. 2014, 2015.

27. The impact of noise on wildlife living near roads has been summarized in Parris 2015.

28. This important study of the effect of traffic noise on birdsong is described in Parris 2015.

29. The species that live in the roadside verge are discussed in Ascensao et al. 2015 and Rytwinski and Fahrig 2007.

30. The kangaroo rats were studied by Brock and Kelt 2004 and Shier et al. 2012.

31. See Brock and Kelt 2004 and Shier et al. 2012.

32. See Brock and Kelt 2004 and Shier et al. 2012.

33. The Canadian study was published as Summers et al. 2011.

34. The poorly studied issue of the effect of vehicle fumes on roadside insects is mentioned in Gate et al. 1995.

35. This 2020 review of the global insect crisis makes for bracing reading: Eggleton 2020.

36. See Eggleton 2020.

37. The fundamental concept of the road effect zone, among other key ideas, is discussed in van der Ree et al. 2015.

2. The Land Fragmented

1. Forman's net analogy comes from the very first page of *Road Ecology: Science and Solutions*. Although the preface is attributed to all fourteen coauthors, the essence and poetry of this passage is all Forman. The concepts related to mesh have been extensively reported by Jochen Jaeger (see, for example, Jaeger et al. 2005), but a comprehensive review is provided by the European Environment Agency, *Landscape Fragmentation in Europe* (2011). I am grateful to Jochen for his help in clarifying these somewhat difficult concepts.

2. See Jaeger et al. 2005 and European Environment Agency 2011.

3. See Jaeger et al. 2005 and European Environment Agency 2011.

4. The key references to discoveries about gap crossing in Amazonian birds are Develey and Stouffer 2001, Laurance et al. 2009, and Lees and Peres 2009.

5. See Develey and Stouffer 2001, Laurance et al. 2009, and Lees and Peres 2009.

6. See Develey and Stouffer 2001, Laurance et al. 2009, and Lees and Peres 2009.

7. Chris Johnson's study was published as Johnson et al. 2017.

8. Colleen Cassady St. Clair's Banff study is St. Clair 2003, while the earlier Canadian study mentioned is Desrochers and Hannon 1997.

9. See St. Clair 2003 and Desrochers and Hannon 1997.

10. See St. Clair 2003 and Desrochers and Hannon 1997.

11. The occasionally unexpected benefits of roads for wildlife are discussed by Morelli et al. 2014.

12. William (Bill) Laurance has been critically examining the threads, risks, and implications of major roads fearlessly for many years. His vital contributions are too numerous to

list here, but for a summary see Laurance 2009, 2015. For further details see the website of ALERT (Alliance of Leading Environmental Researchers and Thinkers), http://ALERT-con servation.org.

13. See Laurance 2009, 2015, and the website of ALERT, http://ALERT-conservation.org.

14. See Laurance 2009, 2015, and the website of ALERT, http://ALERT-conservation.org.

15. See Laurance 2009, 2015, and the website of ALERT, http://ALERT-conservation.org.

16. See Laurance 2009, 2015, and the website of ALERT, http://ALERT-conservation.org.

17. These concepts as a crucial context for road ecology are dealt with in *Road Ecology: Science and Solutions* (Forman et al. 2003).

18. These Swedish concepts were published by Trafikverket, in Helldin et al. 2015.

3. Bridging the Gap

1. The mountain pygmy possum story comes directly from Ian Mansergh and his publication; see Mansergh and Scotts 1989.

2. See Mansergh and Scotts 1989.

3. See Mansergh and Scotts 1989.

4. Most of this information on the Florida panther tunnels comes from Jansen et al. 2010.

5. The terminology of wildlife crossing passages has most recently been discussed in the *Handbook of Road Ecology*; see Smith et al. 2015.

6. There is some fascinating discussion of early overpasses in *Road Ecology: Science and Solutions* (Forman et al. 2003). Éric Guinard provided details of the first French overpass.

7. See Smith et al. 2015

8. Paul Wagner is the preeminent authority on fish passages in North America; see Blank 2010 and Wagner 2015.

9. Hans Bekker provided an extraordinary amount of detail and hospitality—as well as plenty of Dutch cheese and beer—during a personal tour through Holland over several days in August 2019. He almost vetoed this section, saying it was too focused on himself. I have retained that focus anyway.

10. The badger situation in the Netherlands was described directly by Hans Bekker and in Dekker and Bekker 2010. For the latest information see the European badger section in http://www.hogeveluwe.nl.

11. This book, *Natuur over Wegen* (*Nature across Motorways*) was published in 1995 by Rijkswaterstaat, a project managed by Hans Dekker and Martin Vastenhout.

12. The extremely influential EU Directives are described in the COST 341 Handbook, Iuell et al. 2003.

13. IENE's history has been concisely summarized in *Joining Ecology and Transportation for 20 Years: History Review of Infra Eco Network Europe* (Georgiadis et al. 2018), a beautiful and informative book. An electronic version is available free of charge from the IENE website, http://www.iene.info.

14. See Georgiadis et al. 2018.

15. See Georgiadis et al. 2018.

16. See Georgiadis et al. 2018.

17. See Georgiadis et al. 2018.

18. See Georgiadis et al. 2018.

19. All of the COST 341 Handbooks are available from the IENE website, http://www. iene.info.

20. See Iuell et al. 2003.

21. For the COST 341 Handbooks see the IENE website, http://www.iene.info.

22. ICEOT information can be found at the ICEOT website, http://icoet.net.

23. The ANET website is http://www.ecologyandtransport.com. The ACLIE website is hosted by Transfrontier Conservation Areas, http://tfcaportal.org.

24. This references the chapter by Paul Wagner and Andreas Seiler, "Case Study: Building a Community of Practice for Road Ecology," in the *Handbook of Road Ecology* (2015).

25. The disastrous Welsh dormouse bridge episode was reported in WalesOnline, August 26, 2010, http://www.walesonline.co.uk.

26. See WalesOnline, August 26, 2010.

27. Ian White is from the People's Trust for Endangered Species in London. For further details see the People's Trust website, http://ptes.org.

28. Animex have provided relevant technical details in *Animex Wildlife Bridge Best Practice Guidelines* (2019), available from http://www.animexbridge.com.

29. The original Japanese dormouse bridge was described in Minato et al. 2012.

30. The visit to the Isle of Wight was organized by the extraordinary people at Animex (Sophie Hughes, Steve Béga, and Dean Swenson), based in Southampton, on August 15, 2018. Details of the construction and results of the bridge were published in White and Hughes 2019.

31. News on dormouse activities in the United Kingdom was found in *The Dormouse Monitor* 1, 2012, which is available from the People's Trust website, http://ptes.org.

32. See *The Dormouse Monitor* 1, 2012.

33. Rope ladders are being rolled out throughout the world, including in Madagascar (Mass et al. 2011), Kenya (Donaldson and Cunneyworth 2015), and Australia (Goosem et al. 2005). See Soanes and van der Ree 2015 for a wider discussion.

34. Glider poles are discussed in Taylor and Goldingay 2012 and Soanes and van der Ree 2015.

35. See Taylor and Goldingay 2012 and Soanes and van der Ree 2015.

36. The koala bridge is described in Jones et al. 2013.

37. The bridges for golden langurs in India are described in Taylor 2012.

38. See Taylor 2012.

39. Mel McGregor's bat studies at Compton Road were published as McGregor et al. 2017.

40. The remarkable crossing structures for bats being trialed in Europe are described in Claireau et al. 2019a, 2019b. Éric Guinard provided additional information.

41. See Claireau et al. 2019a, 2019b. Éric Guinard provided additional information.

42. Information about the United Kingdom's bat structures was obtained from BBC News, http://www.bbc.com/uk-england-norfolk-51193389.

43. Carme Rosell guided me around Catalunya in August 2010.

4. Know-How

1. This "meeting" is entirely fictional, yet completely plausible. If you wanted to get a group of extraordinarily experienced road ecologists together to discuss the importance of science and how to do research properly, these are the people you would invite. All of the road ecologists featured here are real and the topics that they "discuss" are their specialties; the details come from their publications as well as from discussions that I have had with each of them over many years, some specifically for this book. All have reviewed the sections in which they appear and provided permission for me to publish. The places, the organizations mentioned, the project, and the Arizonian people referred to in this story, however, *don't* actually exist (the location names are a hint).

2. No such place, no such group.

3. No such place, no such group.

4. No such place, no such group.

5. No such place, no such group.

6. No such place as Mesquite Wells, and no such group.

7. Éric Guinard is a civil engineer who works for Cerema: Direction Territoriale Sud-Ouest, based in France, and he conducts his research mainly around the Bordeaux area. He has published extensively on the challenges of making reliable counts of roadkill, especially birds. His "presentation" is derived from these publications: Guinard et al. 2012 and Guinard et al. 2015.

8. Edgar van der Grift is a research scientist at Alterra, an independent research organization based at Wageningen University, in the Netherlands. He has published and spoken about these issues extensively; see especially Roedenbeck et al. 2007, van der Grift et al. 2013 and van der Ree et al. 2015. While it took a castle to attract Lenore Fahrig to Rauischholzhausen, we had to promise saltwater crocodiles to get Edgar to attend the 2008 ANET conference in Brisbane.

9. The Rauischholzhausen meeting was an extremely influential event, organized by Inga Roedenbeck as described here. It was published as Roedenbeck et al. 2007 and remains the fundamental statement of how to conduct rigorous road-ecology research. I spoke to Lenore Fahrig in March 2020 and she recalled the event with enormous pleasure. Inga and Jochen Jaeger were extraordinarily generous in providing their detailed recollections as well.

10. "It's true," Lenore explained to me recently. "That castle was just wonderful! After a few days of a typical scientific conference, most people left, so there were just eight of us in the entire place (picture it: big, old stone walls and enormous rooms). I don't know exactly why, but this group gelled amazingly well. I remember especially the excellent meals, while Jochen plied us with a continual supply of excellent chocolate. We had intense debates from early morning to late evening, continuing through meals, but these were all really constructive—and a lot of fun. In fact, I think that was the most fun I've ever had at a scientific meeting. That's probably why we (now informally called the 'Road Castle Group') have carried on getting together for more than a decade."

11. See Roedenbeck et al. 2007.

12. Inga recalled these events. "It was," she wrote, "the absolute highlight of my career. What a team we were! All those experts, and me just hoping for a good paper for my thesis. But that late night when we all sat around talking about what the paper should be called: I will never forget. Jeff, the cowboy with the fantastic sense of humor, struggling to pronounce Rauischholzhausen. We laughed so hard but all knew immediately that this was the right title."

13. See Roedenbeck et al. 2007.

14. See Roedenbeck et al. 2007.

15. The *Handbook of Road Ecology* (van der Ree et al. 2015) is now *the* text for this field. Its sixty-two chapters cover every conceivable topic and the 116 authors who contributed represent a very high proportion of the people working in the field globally. How Rod van der Ree managed to wrangle all of these busy people from all over the world—and get them to deliver their chapters on time (well, almost)—remains one of the greatest mysteries in the history of the world.

16. Rod van der Ree and Kylie Soanes's studies on squirrel gliders were published in Soanes et al. 2013 and Soanes and van der Ree 2015.

17. Yes, a quintessential "use" study, published as Bond and Jones 2008.

18. Tony Clevenger, the key researcher associated with the Banff structures, has published an enormous number of papers, but key publications are Clevenger and Sawaya 2010, Ford et al. 2010, and Sawaya et al. 2012. Tony has provided a lot of additional information.

19. Trevor Kinley from Parks Canada is based at Banff National Park. He provided a guided tour of many crossing structures in August 2019 as well as a lot of detailed information and the history of the famous Banff wildlife work.

20. See Clevenger and Sawaya 2010, Ford et al. 2010, and Sawaya et al. 2012. Tony Clevenger has provided a lot of additional information.

21. See Clevenger and Sawaya 2010, Ford et al. 2010, and Sawaya et al. 2012. Tony Clevenger has provided a lot of additional information.

22. This is indeed an unavoidable topic and is very well discussed by Ford and Clevenger 2010 and Martinig et al. 2020.

23. See Ford and Clevenger 2010 and Martinig et al. 2020.

5. Working Together Works

1. Most of the details presented here are based on interviews with Thomas Creevey and Bernice Volz. Some of the relevant information can be found in the Brisbane City Council's report on Compton Road (Brisbane City Council 2004), and in Mack 2005 and Veage and Jones 2007.

2. Mary O'Hare spoke to me from her home in Tasmania in July 2020.

3. The main details of this story can be found in a chapter by Dale Becker and Patrick Basting in *Safe Passages* (Beckmann et al. 2010) with further information provided directly by Marcel Huijser and Dale Becker. Dale is the Tribal wildlife manager for the Confederated Salish and Kootenai Tribes of the Flathead Indian Reservation.

4. See Dale Becker and Patrick Basting in *Safe Passages* (Beckmann et al. 2010). Further information provided directly by Marcel Huijser and Dale Becker.

5. See Dale Becker and Patrick Basting in *Safe Passages* (Beckmann et al. 2010). Further information provided directly by Marcel Huijser and Dale Becker.

6. See Dale Becker and Patrick Basting in *Safe Passages* (Beckmann et al. 2010). Further information provided directly by Marcel Huijser and Dale Becker.

7. See Dale Becker and Patrick Basting in *Safe Passages* (Beckmann et al. 2010). Further information provided directly by Marcel Huijser and Dale Becker.

8. I was given a personal tour of Singapore's Eco-Link@BKE overpass by Bryan Lim and Teo Sunia from the National Parks Board in August 2019. More information on this vital structure and its history can be found at http://nparks.gov.sg/gardens-parks-and-nature.

9. The construction of this enormous (literally big enough for an elephant!) underpass took me and many others completely by surprise. It is found on the now infamous road leading into the Maliau Basin Conservation Area (see http://maliaubasin.org) in central Sabah, on the island of Borneo.

10. An excellent example of such stipulations from Europe can be found in the COST 341 Handbooks, Iuell et al. 2003, and Trochme et al. 2002.

11. Information on the justifiably famous and thoroughly studied crossing structures of Banff National Park can be found in many publications, but the specific studies mentioned here are from Clevenger and Waltho 2000, Sawaya et al. 2012, and Sawaya et al. 2013.

12. The I-90 project is ongoing, and the latest information can be found on the Washington State Department of Transportation website, http://wsdot.wa.gov/Projects/I90. Excellent information on the troubled beginnings and eventual breakthrough of this wonderful project can be found on the I-90 Wildlife Bridges Coalition website, http://i90wildlifebridges.org, and especially in the remarkable documentary *Cascade Crossroads*, which is also hosted by http://i90wildlifebridges.org. I visited the site in August 2019 when the first span had just been completed.

13. See the Washington State Department of Transportation website, http://wsdot. wa.gov/Projects/I90; the I-90 Wildlife Bridges Coalition website, http://i90wildlifebridges. org; and the documentary *Cascade Crossroads* (also hosted by http://i90wildlifebridges.org).

14. See the Washington State Department of Transportation website, http://wsdot. wa.gov/Projects/I90; the I-90 Wildlife Bridges Coalition website, http://i90wildlifebridges. org; and the documentary *Cascade Crossroads* (also hosted by http://i90wildlifebridges.org).

15. See the Washington State Department of Transportation website, http://wsdot. wa.gov/Projects/I90; the I-90 Wildlife Bridges Coalition website, http://i90wildlifebridges. org; and the documentary *Cascade Crossroads* (also hosted by http://i90wildlifebridges.org).

16. See the Washington State Department of Transportation website, http://wsdot. wa.gov/Projects/I90; the I-90 Wildlife Bridges Coalition website, http://i90wildlifebridges. org; and the documentary *Cascade Crossroads* (also hosted by http://i90wildlifebridges.org).

17. See the Washington State Department of Transportation website, http://wsdot. wa.gov/Projects/I90; the I-90 Wildlife Bridges Coalition website, http://i90wildlifebridges. org; and the documentary *Cascade Crossroads* (also hosted by http://i90wildlifebridges.org).

18. Details of the Logan Enhancement Project can be found on the Transurban website, http://www.transurban.com.

6. Signs of Change

1. The pattern of global road construction, and construction predictions, have been summarized in detail in Meijer et al. 2018. A comprehensive picture of vehicle production and the implications that follow can be found in Sperling and Gordon's *Two Billion Cars: Driving toward Sustainability* (2009).

2. There are plenty of great references to the wonder and tragedy of New Zealand's birds, but two of the best are Tennyson and Martinson's *Extinct Birds of New Zealand* (2006) and Kerry-Jayne Wilson's *Flight of the Huia* (2004).

3. See Tennyson and Martinson 2006 and Wilson 2004.

4. This is a largely fictional account (you can have too much even of koalas, so I have substituted kiwis instead) but is reliably based on our experiences combined with those of our New Zealand colleagues. The people aren't real, however. Technical details can be found in Blacker et al. 2019 and Sullivan et al. 2012. Conservation concerns about the North Island brown kiwi are outlined well in Keast et al. 2010.

5. This is a largely fictional account. For technical details see Blacker et al. 2019 and Sullivan et al. 2012. For conservation concerns about the North Island brown kiwi see Keast et al. 2010.

6. The problems with static signs and the various related issues are discussed by Bond and Jones 2013 and Huijser et al. 2015.

7. See Bond and Jones 2013 and Huijser et al. 2015.

8. This unpublished research was conducted for Brisbane City Council; see Burke 2015.

9. See Burke 2015.

10. This important study was conducted in Arizona; see Gagnon et al. 2018.

11. Much of the enormous amount of research conducted on the famous crossing structures in Banff National Park has been led by Tony Clevenger. The relevant publications for this section are Clevenger and Waltho 2005 and Sawaya et al. 2012.

12. The advances made in animal tracking since the advent of PIT tags are described in Smyth and Nebel 2013.

13. This experimental interactive koala sign design was developed by the wildlife telemetry company Wild Spy, http://www.wildspy.com.au.

14. Auditory deterrent devices are critically examined by Bomford and O'Brien 1990 and Ramp and Croft 2006, and recent developments are discussed by D'Angelo and van der Ree 2015.

15. For an examination of auditory deterrent devices see Bomford and O'Brien 1990 and Ramp and Croft 2006. For a discussion of recent developments see D'Angelo and van der Ree 2015.

16. The more recent proliferation of visual deterrent devices, including so-called virtual fences, has received a lot of attention. See in particular Appleby and Jones 2020, Coulson and Bender 2020, and Rytwinski et al. 2016.

17. See Appleby and Jones 2020, Coulson and Bender 2020, and Rytwinski et al. 2016.

18. There is plenty of discussion about autonomous vehicles, though only a little is associated with the implications for biodiversity. Some useful references are Andrews 2018, Bland 2015, National Centre for Rural Road Safety 2016, and Thompson and Read 2019.

19. Volvo's kangaroo problems were described by Zhou 2017.

Conclusion

1. Pierre Ibisch and colleagues (2017) conducted a recent and comprehensive global estimation of roadless areas, building on an excellent discussion of the importance of these places in the *Handbook of Road Ecology* (see Selva et al. 2015).

2. There are endless articles and websites on the history and development of the automobile industry, but David Gartman's *Auto Opium: A Social History of American Automobile Design* (1994) is still the most entertaining—although, obviously, a little dated.

3. Current and historical information on vehicle sales can be found on http://www.statistica.com and on the International Energy Agency website, http://www.iea.org.

4. A comprehensive review of global patterns of road infrastructure growth is available in Meijer et al. 2018 and in the report, *World Road Statistics* (International Road Federation 2017).

5. China's extraordinary plans for a global transportation system—One Belt, One Road and the Twenty-First Century Maritime Silk Road—have received an enormous amount of attention for obvious reasons. Some of the best critical summaries, some of which include significant contributions from William Laurance, are Laurance et al. 2014, Laurance and Arrea 2017, Owens 2020, Winter 2016, and Yu 2017. The World Bank report is covered in Alamgir et al. 2017.

6. See Laurance et al. 2014, Laurance and Arrea 2017, Owens 2020, Winter 2016, and Yu 2017. The World Bank report is covered in Alamgir et al. 2017.

7. Detailed in Laurance et al. 2014 and Laurance and Arrea 2017.

8. See Laurance et al. 2014 and Laurance and Arrea 2017.

Coda

1. The recovery of the Cheonggye Creek through the removal of roads in the middle of Seoul is an extraordinary story of community demands and a rare example of civil authorities being willing to admit—and reverse—past mistakes. More details can be found on the website of the Congress of the New Urbanism, http://www.cnu.org/highways-boulevards/model-cities/seoul. There are many other such examples of roads being removed around the world, a phenomenon I had no idea about when starting this project.

REFERENCES

Alamgir, M., M. J. Campbell, S. Sloan, M. Goosem, G. R. Clements, M. I. Mahmoud, and W. F. Laurance. 2017. Economic, socio-political and environmental risks of road development in the tropics. *Current Biology* 27:1130–1140.

Andrews, C. G. 2018. Self-driving vehicles could save animal lives. *Good Nature Travel*, November 6, 2018.

Appleby, R., and D. N. Jones. 2020. An experimental trial of "Virtual Fence" devices in an effort to reduce vehicle collisions with wallabies on Heinemann Road, Mount Cotton. Report to City of Redlands.

Ascensao, F., S. Lapoint, and R. van der Ree. 2015. Roads, traffic, and verges: Big problems and big opportunities for small mammals. *In* R. van der Ree, D. J. Smith, and C. Grilo, eds., *Handbook of Road Ecology*, 325–333. Oxford: Wiley Blackwell.

Beckmann, J. P., A. P. Clevenger, M. P. Huijser, and J. A. Hilty, eds. 2010. *Safe Passages: Highways, Wildlife, and Habitat Connectivity*. Washington, DC: Island Press.

Beebee, T. J. C. 2013. Effects of road mortality and litigation measures on amphibian populations. *Conservation Biology* 25:657–668.

Benítez-López, A., R. Alkemade, and P. A. Verweij. 2010. The impacts of roads and other infrastructure on mammals and bird population: A meta-analysis. *Biological Conservation* 143:1307–1316.

Bennett, A. F. 1991. Roads, roadsides and wildlife conservation: A review. *In* D. A. Saunders and R. J. Hobbs, eds., *Nature Conservation 2: The Role of Corridors*, 99–117. Chipping Norton: Surrey Beatty.

Blacker A., K. Aburrow, J. Scott, and D. Jones. 2019. Gold Coast smart signs and smart messages: A driver change behaviour project—final report. Report for City of Gold Coast, Southport.

Blackwell, B. F., T. L. DeVault, E. Fernández-Juricic, E. M. Gese, L. Gilvert-Norton, and S. W. Breck. 2016. No single solution: Application of behavioural principles in mitigating human—wildlife conflict. *Animal Behaviour* 120:245–254.

Bland, A. 2015. Will driverless cars mean less roadkill? *Smithsonian Magazine*, November 2.

Blank, M. D. 2010. Safe passages for fish and other aquatic species. *In* J. P. Beckmann, A. P. Clevenger, M. P. Huijser, and J. A. Hilty, eds., *Safe Passages: Highways, Wildlife, and Habitat Connectivity*, 75–98. Washington, DC: Island Press.

Bomford, M., and P. H. O'Brien. 1990. Sonic deterrents in animal damage control: A review of device tests and effectiveness. *Wildlife Society Bulletin* 18:411–422.

Bond, A. R., and D. N. Jones. 2008. Temporal trends in use of fauna-friendly underpasses and overpasses. *Wildlife Research* 35:103–112.

Bond, A. R. F., and D. N. Jones. 2013. Wildlife warning signs: Public assessment of components, placement, and designs to optimise driver response. *Animals* 3:1142–1162.

Bond, A., and D. N. Jones. 2014. Roads and macropods: Interactions and implications. *Australian Mammalogy* 36:1–14.

Brisbane City Council. 2004. *Compton Road: Principals Project Requirements.* Brisbane: Brisbane City Council.

Brock, R. E., and D. A. Kelt. 2004. Influence of roads on the endangered Stephens' kangaroo rat (*Dipodomys stephensi*): Are dirt and gravel roads different? *Biological Conservation* 118:633–640.

Burke, A. 2015. Effectiveness of portable speed warning signs. *In* Australian Road Safety Association, ed., *Proceedings of the 2015 Australasian Road Safety Conference, October 14–16, Gold Coast, Australia.* Gold Coast: ARSA.

Claireau, F., Y. Bas, J.-F. Julien, N. Machon, B. Allegrini, S. J. Puechmaille, and C. Kerbiriou. 2019a. Bat overpasses as an alternative solution to restore habitat connectivity in the context of road requalification. *Ecological Engineering* 131:34–38.

Claireau, F., Y. Bas, J. Pauwels, K. Barré, N. Machon, B. Allegrini, S. J. Puechmaille, and C. Kerbiriou. 2019b. Major roads have important negative effects on insectivorous bat activity. *Biological Conservation* 235:53–62.

Clevenger, A. P., and M. A. Sawaya. 2010. Piloting a non-invasive genetic sampling method for evaluating population-level benefits of wildlife crossing structures. *Ecology and Society* 15:7.

Clevenger, A. P., and N. Waltho. 2000. Factors influencing the effectiveness of wildlife underpasses in Banff National Park, Alberta, Canada. *Conservation Biology* 14:47–56.

Clevenger, A. P., and N. Waltho. 2005. Performance indices to identify attributes of highway crossing structures facilitating movement of large mammals. *Biological Conservation* 121:453–464.

Coffin, A. W. 2007. From roadkill to road ecology: A review of the ecological effects of roads. *Journal of Transport Geography* 15:396–406.

Coulson, G., and H. Bender. 2020. Roadkill mitigation is paved with good intentions: A critique of Fox et al. (2019). *Australian Mammalogy* 42:122–130.

D'Angelo, G., and R. van der Ree. 2015. Use of reflectors and auditory deterrents to prevent wildlife—vehicle collisions. *In* R. van der Ree, R. D. J. Smith, and C. Grilo, eds., *Handbook of Road Ecology*, 213–218. Oxford: Wiley Blackwell.

Dekker, J. J. A., and G. J. Bekker. 2010. Badger (*Meles meles*) road mortality in the Netherlands: The characteristics of victims and the effects of mitigation measures. *Lutra* 53(2):81–92.

Desrochers, A., and S. J. Hannon. 1997. Gap crossing decisions by forest songbirds during the post-fledging period. *Conservation Biology* 11:1204–1210.

Develey, P. F., and P. C. Stouffer. 2001. Effects of roads on movements by understory birds in mixed-species flocks in central Amazonian Brazil. *Conservation Biology* 15:1416–1422.

Dexter, C., R. Appleby, J. Edgar, J. Scott, and D. N. Jones. 2016. Using complementary remote detection methods for retrofitted eco-passages: A case study of monitoring individual koalas in south-east Queensland. *Wildlife Research* 43:369–379.

Dexter, C., R. Appleby, J. Scott, J. Edgar, and D. N. Jones. 2017. Individuals matter: Predicting koala road crossing behaviour in south-east Queensland. *Australian Mammalogy* 40:67–75.

Donaldson, A., and P. Cunneyworth. 2015. Case study: Canopy bridges for primate conservation. *In* R. van der Ree, R. D. J. Smith, and C. Grilo, eds., *Handbook of Road Ecology*, 341–343. Oxford: Wiley Blackwell.

Eggleton, P. 2020. The state of the world's insects. *Annual Review of Environment and Resources* 45:61–82.

Ehmann, H., and H. G. Cogger. 1985. Australia's endangered herpetofauna: A review of criteria and policies. *In* G. Grigg, R. Shine, and H. Erhmann, eds., *The Biology of Australasian Frogs and Reptiles*, 435–447. Sydney: Surrey Beatty.

European Environment Agency. 2011. *Landscape Fragmentation in Europe*. Luxembourg: Publications Office of European Union.

Ford, A., and A. P. Clevenger. 2010. Validity of prey-trap hypothesis for carnivore—ungulate interactions at wildlife-crossing structures. *Conservation Biology* 24:1679–1685.

Ford, A. T., A. P. Clevenger, and K. Rettie. 2010. The Banff Wildlife Crossings Project: An international public—private partnership. *In* J. P. Beckmann, A. P. Clevenger, M. P. Huijser, and J. A. Hilty, eds., *Safe Passages: Highways, Wildlife, and Habitat Connectivity*, 157–172. Washington, DC: Island Press.

Forman, R. T. T. 1998. Road ecology: A solution for the giant embracing us. *Landscape Ecology* 13(4):iii–v.

Forman, R. T. T., and L. E. Alexander. 1998. Roads and their major ecological effects. *Annual Review of Ecology and Systematics* 29:207–231.

Forman, R. T. T., D. Sperling, J. A. Bissonette, A. P. Clevenger, C. D. Cutshall, V. H. Vale, L. Fahrig, R. France, C. R. Goldman, K. Heanue, J. A. Jones, F. J. Swanson, T. Turrentine, and T. C. Winter. 2003. *Road Ecology: Science and Solutions*. Washington, DC: Island Press.

Gagnon, J. W., N. L. Dodd, S. C. Sprague, K. S. Ogren, C. D. Loberger, and R. E. Schweinsburg. 2018. Animal-activated highway crosswalk: Long-term impact on elk—vehicle collisions, vehicle speeds, and motorist braking response. *Human Dimensions of Wildlife* 24:132–147.

Gartman, D. 1994. *Auto Opium: A Social History of American Automobile Design.* New York: Routledge.

Gate, I. M., S. McNeill, and M. R. Ashmore. 1995. Effects of air pollution on the searching behaviour of an insect parasitoid. *Water Air Soil Pollution* 85:1425–1430.

Georgiadis, L., T. Adelsköld, Y. Autret, H. Bekker, M. Böttcher, E. Hahn, C. Rossel, T. Sangwine, A. Seiler, and A. Sjölund. 2018. *Joining Ecology and Transportation for 20 Years: History Review of Infra Eco Network Europe.* Linköping: IENE.

Glista, D. J., T. L. DeVault, and J. A. DeWoody. 2008. A review of mitigation measures for reducing wildlife mortality on roadways. *Landscape and Urban Planning* 91:1–7.

Goosem, M., N. Weston, and S. Bushnell. 2005. Effectiveness of rope bridge arboreal overpasses and faunal underpasses in providing connectivity for rainforest fauna. *In* C. L. Irwin, P. Garrett, and K. P. McDermott, eds., *Proceedings of the 2005 International Conference on Ecology and Transportation*, 304–316. Raleigh: Center for Transportation and the Environment, North Carolina State University.

Guinard, É., R. Prodon, and C. Barbraud. 2015. Case study: A robust method to obtain defendable data on wildlife mortality. *In* R. van der Ree, R. D. J. Smith, and C. Grilo, eds., *Handbook of Road Ecology*, 96–100. Oxford: Wiley Blackwell.

Guinard, É. J., J. Romain, and C. Barbraud. 2012. Motorways and bird traffic casualties: Carcass surveys and scavenging bias. *Biological Conversation* 147:40–52.

Hayes, I. F., and R. L. Goldingay. 2009. Use of fauna road-crossing structures in northeastern New South Wales. *Australian Mammalogy* 31:89–95.

Helldin, J.-O., T. Lennartsson, A. Seiler, and J. Wissman. 2015. *The Impact of Transport Infrastructure on Biodiversity: A Conceptual Model for Communication and Planning (Trafikverket Papport 210).* Borlänge, Sweden: Trafikverket.

Hobday, A. J., and M. L. Minstrell. 2008. Distribution and abundance of roadkill on Tasmanian highways: Human management options. *Wildlife Research* 35:712–726.

Huijser, M. P., C. Mosler-Berger, M. Olsson, and M. Streen. 2015. Wildlife warning signs and animal detection systems aimed at reducing wildlife—vehicle collisions. *In* R. van der Ree, R. D. J. Smith, and C. Grilo, eds., *Handbook of Road Ecology*, 198–212. Oxford: Wiley Blackwell.

Ibisch, P. L., M. T. Hoffmann, S. Kreft, G. Pe'er, V. Kati, L. Biber-Freudenberger, D. A. DellaSala, M. M. Vale, P. R. Hobson, and N. Selva. 2017. A global map of roadless areas and their conservation status. *Science* 354(6318): 1423–1427.

International Road Federation. 2017. https://www.cia.gov/library/publications/the-world-factbook/rankorder/2085rank.html.

Iuell, B., G. J. Bekker, R. Cuperus, J. Dufek, G. Fry, C. Hicks, V. Hlaváč, V. Keller, B. Rosell, T. Sangwine, N. Tørsløv, and B. I. M. Wandall, eds. 2003. *COST 341: Wildlife and Traffic: A European Handbook for Identifying Conflicts and Designing Solutions.* Brussels: KNNV Publishers.

Jaeger, A. G., J. Bowman, J. Brennan, L. Fahrig, D. Bert, J. Bouchard, N. Charbonneau, K. Frank, B. Gruber, and K. T. von Toschanowitz. 2005. Predicting when animal populations are at risk from roads: An interactive model of road avoidance behaviour. *Ecological Modelling* 185:329–348.

Jansen, D. K., K. Sherwood, and E. Fleming. 2010. The I-75 Project: Lessons from the Florida panther. *In* J. P. Beckmann, A. P. Clevenger, M. P. Huijser, and J. A. Hilty, eds., *Safe Passages: Highways, Wildlife, and Habitat Connectivity*, 205–222. Washington, DC: Island Press.

Johnson, C. D., D. Evans, and D. N. Jones. 2017. Birds and roads: Reduced transit for smaller species over roads within an urban environment. *Frontiers in Ecology and Evolution* 5: 10.3389.

Jones, D. N., M. Bakker, O. Bichet, T. Coutts, and T. Wearing. 2011. Restoring habitat connectivity above ground: Vegetation establishment on a fauna land-bridge in south-east Queensland. *Ecological Restoration and Management* 12:76–79.

Jones, D. N., L. Bernede, A. Bond, C. Dexter, and C. L. Strong. 2015. Dust as a contributor to the road-effect zone: A case study from a minor road in Australia. *Australasian Journal of Environmental Management* 23:67–80.

Jones, D. N., C. Dexter, L. Bernede, and J. Scott. 2013. Koala retrofit works program: Evaluation monitoring for koala-specific overpass structure final report. Report for Department of Transport and Main Roads, Brisbane.

Jones, D. N., M. R. Griffiths, J. R. Griffiths, J. L. F. Hacker, and J. B. Hacker. 2014. Implications of upgrading a minor forest road on traffic and road-kill in southeast Queensland, Australia. *Australasian Journal of Environmental Management* 21:429–440.

Jones, M. E. 2000. Road upgrade, road mortality, and remedial measures: impacts on a population of eastern quolls and Tasmanian devils. *Wildlife Research* 27:289–296.

Keast, J., T. Kelly, H. Moorhouse, J. Tan, and W. Shih-Yun. 2010. Conservation of the North Island brown kiwi (*Apteryx mantelli*): Current approaches, the successes and limitations, and proposals to ensure long-term continuity. Wellington, NZ: Department of Conservation.

Langevelde, F., and C. F. Jaarsma. 2009. Modeling the effect of traffic calming on local animal population persistence. *Ecology and Society* 14(2): 39.

Laurance, W. F. 2009. Roads to ruin. *New Scientist* 26 August 2009: 308–309.

Laurance, W. F. 2015. Bad roads, good roads. *In* R. van der Ree, R. D. J. Smith, and C. Grilo, eds., *Handbook of Road Ecology*, 10–15. Oxford: Wiley Blackwell.

Laurance, W. F., and I. B. Arrea. 2017. Roads to riches or ruin? *Science* 358(6362): 442–444.

Laurance. W. F., G. R. Clements, S. Sloan, C. O'Connell, N. D. Mueller, M. Goosem, O. Venter, D. P. Edwards, B. Phalan, A. Balmford, R. van der Ree, and I. B. Arrea. 2014. A global strategy for road building. *Nature* 403:853–858.

Laurance, W. F., M. Goosem, and S. G. W. Laurance. 2009. Impacts of roads and linear clearings on tropical forests. *Trends in Ecology and Evolution* 24:659–669.

Lees, A. C., and C. A. Peres. 2009. Gap-crossing movements predict species occupancy in Amazonian forest fragments. *Oikos* 118:280–290.

Mack, P. 2005. When fauna corridors and arterial road corridors intersect. Brisbane: City Design, Brisbane City Council.

Mansergh, I., and D. Scotts. 1989. Habitat continuity and social organisation of the mountain pygmy-possum restored by tunnel. *Journal of Wildlife Management* 53:701–707.

Martinig, A. R., M. Riaz, and C. C. St. Clair. 2020. Temporal clustering of prey in wild-life passages provides no evidence of a prey-trap. *Scientific Reports* 10:11489.

Mass, V., B. Rakotomanga, G. Rakotondratsimba, S. Razafindramisa, P. Andriana-ivomahefa, S. Dickinson, P. O. Berner, and A. Cook. 2011. Lemur bridges provide crossing structures over roads within a forested mining concession near Moramanga, Toamasina Province, Madagascar. *Conservation Evidence* 8:11–18.

McGregor, M., K. Matthews, and D. N. Jones. 2017. Vegetated fauna overpass disguises road presence and facilitates permeability for forest microbats in Brisbane, Australia. *Frontiers in Ecology and Evolution* 5: 10.3389.

McGregor, M., S. Wilson, and D. N. Jones. 2015. Vegetated fauna overpass enhances habitat connectivity for forest-dwelling herpetofauna. *Global Ecology and Conservation* 4:221–231.

Meijer, J. R., M. A. Huijbregts, K. C. G. Schotten, and A. M. Schipper. 2018. Global patterns of current and future road infrastructure. *Environmental Research Letters* 13:064006.

Minato, S., K. Ohtake, and P. Morris. 2012. Helping (Japanese) dormice to cross the road. *Oryx* 46:325–332.

Morelli, F., M. Beim, L. Jerzak, D. N. Jones, and P. Tryanowski. 2014. Can roads, railways and related structures have positive effects on birds? A review. *Transportation Research Part D* 30:21–31.

National Centre for Rural Road Safety. 2016. Will technology bring an end to wildlife collisions? http://ruralsafetycenter.org/uncategorized/2016.

Owens, C. 2020. The Belt and Road Initiative's Central Asian contradictions. *Current History* 119:264–269.

Parris, K. M. 2015. Ecological impacts of road noise and option for mitigation. *In* R. van der Ree, R. D. J. Smith, and C. Grilo, eds., *Handbook of Road Ecology*, 151–158. Oxford: Wiley Blackwell.

Pell, S., and D. N. Jones. 2015. Are wildlife overpasses of conservation value for birds? A study in Australian subtropical forest, with wider implications. *Biological Conservation* 184:300–309.

Polak, T., J. Rhodes, D. N. Jones, and H. P. Possingham. 2014. Optimal planning for mitigating the impacts of roads on wildlife. *Journal of Applied Ecology* 51:726–734.

Ramp, D., and D. B. Croft. 2006. Do wildlife warning reflectors elicit aversion in captive macropods? *Wildlife Research* 33:583–590.

Rijkswaterstaat. 1995. *Natuur over Wegen*. Rotterdam: Rijkswaterstaat.

Roedenbeck, I. A., L. Fahrig, C. S. Findlay, J. E. Houlahan, J. A. G. Jaeger, N. Klar, S. Kramer-Schadt, and E. A. van der Grift. 2007. The Rauischholzhausen agenda for road ecology. *Ecology and Society* 12:11.

Rytwinski, T., and L. Fahrig. 2007. Effect of road density on abundance of white-footed mice. *Landscape Ecology* 22:1501–1512.

Rytwinski, T., and L. Fahrig. 2012. Do species life history traits explain population responses to roads? A meta-analysis. *Biological Conservation* 147:87–98.

Rytwinski, T., K. Soames, J. A. G. Jaeger, C. S. Findlay, J. Houlahan, R. van der Ree, and E. A. van der Grift. 2016. How effective is road mitigation at reducing road-kill? A meta-analysis. *PLoS One* 11: e0166941.

Sawaya, M. A., A. P. Clevenger, and S. T. Kalinowski. 2013. Demographic connectivity for ursid populations at wildlife crossing structures in Banff National Park. *Conservation Biology* 27:721–730.

Sawaya, M. A., J. B. Stetz, A. P. Clevenger, M. L. Gibeau, and S. T. Kalinowski. 2012. Estimating grizzly and black bear population abundance using noninvasive genetic sampling. *PLoS ONE* 7: e34777.

Selva, N., A. Switalski, S. Kreft, and P. L. Ibuisch. 2015. Why keep areas road-free? The importance of roadless areas. *In* R. van der Ree, D. J. Smith, and C. Grilo, eds., *Handbook of Road Ecology*, 16–26. Oxford: Wiley Blackwell.

Shier, D. M., A. J. Lea, and M. A. Owen. 2012. Beyond masking: Endangered Stephen's kangaroo rats respond to traffic noise with footdrumming. *Biological Conservation* 150:53–58.

Smith, D. J., and R. van der Ree. 2015. Field methods to evaluate the impact of roads on wildlife. *In* R. van der Ree, R. D. J. Smith, and C. Grilo, eds., *Handbook of Road Ecology*, 82–95. Oxford: Wiley Blackwell.

Smith, D. J., R. van der Ree, and C. Rosel. 2015. Wildlife crossing structures: An effective strategy to restore or maintain wildlife connectivity across roads. *In* R. van der Ree, R. D. J. Smith, and C. Grilo, eds., *Handbook of Road Ecology*, 172–183. Oxford: Wiley Blackwell.

Smyth, B., and S. Nebel. 2013. Passive integrated transponder (PIT) tags in the study of animal movement. *Nature Education Knowledge* 4(3): 3.

Soanes. K., M. C. Lobo, P. A. Vesk, M. A. McCarthy, J. L. Moore, and R. van der Ree. 2013. Movement re-established but not restored: Inferring the effectiveness of road-crossing mitigation for a gliding mammal by monitoring use. *Biological Conservation* 159:434–441.

Soanes, K., and R. van der Ree. 2015. Reducing road impacts on tree-dwelling animals. *In* R. van der Ree, R. D. J. Smith, and C. Grilo, eds., *Handbook of Road Ecology*, 334–340. Oxford: Wiley Blackwell.

Sperling, D., and D. Gordon. 2009. *Two Billion Cars: Driving Toward Sustainability*. New York: Oxford University Press.

St. Clair, C. C. 2003. Comparative permeability of roads, rivers, and meadows to songbirds in Banff National Park. *Conservation Biology* 17:1151–1160.

Stoner, D. 1925. The toll of the automobile. *Science* 61:56–57.

Sullivan, K., R. Appleby, C. Dexter, and D. N. Jones. 2012. Vehicle-activated signage monitoring trial. Report for Department of Transport and Main Roads, Brisbane.

Summers, O., G. M. Cunnington, and L. Fahrig. 2011. Are the negative effects of roads on breeding birds caused by traffic noise? *Journal of Applied Ecology* 48:1527–1534.

Taylor, A. 2012. Bridges for langurs. www.conservationjobs.co.uk/articles/bridges-for-langurs.

Taylor, B. D., and R. L. Goldingay. 2012. Restoring connectivity in landscapes fragmented by major roads: A case study using wooden poles as "stepping stones" for gliding mammals. *Restoration Ecology* 20:671–678.

Tennyson, A., and P. Martinson. 2006. *Extinct Birds of New Zealand*. Wellington, NZ: Te Papa Press.

Thompson, J., and G. Read. 2019. Nothing to fear? How human (and other intelligent animals) might ruin the autonomous vehicle utopia. *The Conversation* 29 (April): 114504.

Trochme, M., S. Cahill, J. G. De Vries, H. Farrall, L. Folkeson, G. Fry, C. Hicks, and J. Reyman, eds. 2002. *COST 341: Habitat Due to Fragmentation Infrastructure: The European Review*. Brussels: KNNV Publishers.

van der Grift, E. A., R. van der Ree, L. Fahrig, S. Findlay, J. Houlahan, J. A. G. Jaeger, N. Klar, L. F. Mandrinan, and L. Olson. 2013. Evaluating the effectiveness of road mitigation measures. *Biodiversity and Conservation* 22:425–448.

van der Ree, R. D. J. Smith, and C. Grilo, eds. 2015. *Handbook of Road Ecology*. Oxford: Wiley Blackwell.

Veage, L-A., and D. N. Jones. 2007. Breaking the barrier: Assessing the value of fauna-friendly crossing structures at Compton Road. Report to Brisbane City Council.

Wagner, P. J. 2015. Form and function: A more natural approach to infrastructure, fish and stream habitats. *In* R. van der Ree, R. D. J. Smith, and C. Grilo, eds., *Handbook of Road Ecology*, 357–363. Oxford: Wiley Blackwell.

Wagner, P. J., and A. Seiler. 2015. Case study: Building a community of practice for road ecology. *In* R. van der Ree, R. D. J. Smith, and C. Grilo, eds., *Handbook of Road Ecology*, 488–491. Oxford: Wiley Blackwell.

White, I. C., and S. A. Hughes. 2019. Trial of a bridge for reconnecting fragmented arboreal habitat for hazel dormouse *Muscardinus avellanarius* at Briddlesford Nature Reserve, Isle of Wight, UK. *Conservation Evidence* 16:6–11.

Wilson, K.-J. 2004. *Flight of the Huia: Ecology and Conservation of New Zealand's Frogs, Reptiles, Birds and Mammals*. Wellington, NZ: Canterbury University Press.

Winter, T. 2016. One belt, one road, one heritage: Cultural diplomacy and the silk road. *The Diplomat* 3:1–5.

Wroe, S., C. McHenry, and J. Thomason. 2005. Bite club: Comparative bite force in big biting mammals and the prediction of predatory behaviour in fossil taxa. *Proceedings of the Royal Society B* 272(1563): 2986.

Yu, H. 2017. Motivation behind China's "One Belt, One Road" initiatives and establishment of the Asian Infrastructure Bank. *Journal of Contemporary China* 26:353–368.

Zhou, N. 2017. Volvo admits its self-driving cars are confused by kangaroos. *The Guardian* July 1, 2017.

INDEX